20 Commedia dell'Arte Scenarios From the 1570s

Translated and Updated with Easily-Staged Scenarios from Abagaro Franscesco Baldi's Personal Manuscripts, Including his Prologues, Monologues, and One-liners

JOHN A. CROSS

WITH CHIARA DURAZZINI

TRUTH AND BEAUTY
MEDIA

TRUTH AND BEAUTY MEDIA, LLC
BERLIN, MA
2024

TRUTH AND BEAUTY MEDIA, LLC.

Published in the United States of America

By Truth and Beauty Media, LLC.

http://www.truthandbeautymedia.com

53 Village Court, Berlin, MA, 01503, USA

Cover: "Magnifico 20" by Carl West

Relationship Diagrams by Jess Rudolph

"A Dedication" by Dr. Olly Crick

Typefaces: Georgia & Calibri

ISBN: 979-8-9864884-2-4 (Paperback)

ISBN: 979-8-9864884-3-1 (Hardback)

ISBN: 979-8-9864884-4-8 (eBook)

Library of Congress Control Number: 2024902142

Thanks to all the amateurs and academics working together,

on so many projects, to bring the past alive.

Prologue

(Prologomeno for the academically inclined)[1]

Here we have both literal translations and playable texts drawn from the surviving papers of Abagaro Francesco Baldi a.k.a. Abagaro Frescobaldi, stage name Stefanello Bottarga, travelling player and keeper of notebooks. Hopefully, both actors and academics will gain something from this book. The troupe Frescobaldi performed in was successful in Spain and arrived there fifteen years before the start of what is canonically considered to be The Golden Age of Spanish Theatre. Were they pioneers of a 'new' form of comic theatre or opportunistic bandwagon jumpers? History draws its curtain, and we will never know, but what we do know is that fifteen years after their arrival, theatre was one of the most popular forms of entertainment in Spain. You make your own mind up.

What was the importance of Spanish drama in the Renaissance and the Baroque eras, and how significant is this translation in relation to Spanish theatre as a whole? The Spanish Golden Age of Theatre existed roughly between 1590 and 1681, and during this period theatre in Spain flourished, not only in quality but in vast quantity. Spain produced dramatic works for all levels of society, and the numbers of plays produced were staggering. Spain produced more drama than Elizabethan England by a factor of four. Like Elizabethan England, not all the plays survived, but enough did, and in such numbers, as to make inclusive analysis extremely problematical even now.

The first professional public theatre, the Corral de la Cruz, was built in Madrid in 1579. It had similarities to an Elizabethan playhouse in that it was an enclosed area, though square rather than round, with a platform stage at one end of a central area and surrounded by tiered galleries on three sides. Unlike Elizabethan playhouses, however, gender segregation was enforced upon the audience. Only in the top tier, where the aristocrats sat in boxes, was there no gender segregation. Below them in the second tier, was the *tertulia*, where the clergy sat, carefully separated from the women. On the bottom tier and in the central area in front of the stage, it was, once again only men allowed.

---

[1] Thanks to John Rudlin for this suggestion.

> Women entered through a separate door [from the men] and sat in enclosures at the back of the corral, opposite the stage, expressively called the *cazuelas* or stewpots. These were at ground and first floor levels. (Wilson, 1: 1969)

It was, like the early modern playhouses, a safe and lucrative place to perform, and entrance fees could be charged: the risks of alfresco performance funded by taking the hat round was removed forever. Once acting troupes, actors, and actor managers had seized the means of production, theatre could develop and flourish.

Spanish Theatre was generically diverse, and there seemed to be no official or clerical condemnation of secular dramas in favour of the religious, as happened in Italy. As the amount of theatre produced increased, through public pressure, central control by the government increased but the system managed both to regulate, police and encourage the art form. Actors could perform in both secular and religious dramas without official censure or punishment. Both flourished and both were sponsored by the court and wealthy patrons. More popular genres such as rude or bawdy comedies, early opera, mixed media verse and sung shows, as well as 'honour' shows, and tragedies ,were performed by companies and individuals aiming to make money by ticket sales.

One of the most popular genres was the 'cloak and sword' play, involving complicated plots involving the uniquely Spanish notion of aristocratic honour, whose plot lines would be mimicked, copied, commented on and generally messed about with by the servants. After many duels, misunderstandings, renunciations and declared love, these cloak and sword plays usually ended with happy endings and multiple marriages. Women were allowed on Spanish stages, unlike pre-restoration England, as long as the actress was married to another member of the company.

Fifteen years prior to the Spanish Golden Age of Theatre, a troupe of Italians, already experienced in the politics of performing, learned in Mantua and Paris, arrived in Spain around 1573 to, as they say, seek their fortune. They were led by Alberto Naselli, known by his stage name of Zan Ganassa and the troupe included, among others, his wife Barbara Flaminia [2], and Abagaro Frescobaldi. In 1574 they collectively contributed hard cash to help renovate a religious brotherhood's hospital courtyard, to make it very similar to a permanent theatre, this securing both a safe venue to perform in and clerical approval. This was, perhaps, a business masterstroke, given the continuous sniping and harassment from the church the comedians received in Italy. It was called the *Corral de la Pachecha*. This seemed to be a model that was copied by Spanish theatres, in that actors were allowed to perform in their courtyards in return for 'generous donations' to the hospitals.

> The same year, 1574, there was a company of Italian comedians in Madrid, whose head and author was Alberto Ganassa. They represented Italian comedies, mimes and buffoons, on trivial and popular subjects. They also performed puppets and

---

[2] She was somewhat of a prodigy: "Above all, Barbara Flaminia's parable of artistic maturation appears exemplary in this respect. Acrobat and street artist, this Roman woman of obscure origins managed, in the space of a few years, to acquire singing skills and reciting techniques such as to make her celebrated as 'wonderful' by important exponents of the high culture of her era. Recent studies, which have documented her frequent contacts with Bernardo Tasso, the poet Torquato Tasso's father and esteemed author, have led us to suppose that the actress was able to make this surprising leap in quality by conducting, with the man of letters, a silent and willing apprenticeship which allowed her to transform from an anonymous street performer into a celebrated interpreter of a cultured and complex dramaturgy (Simoncini, 2018).

sleights of hand, and "maybe they turned over a monkey".(*Casiano Pellicer: Historical treatise on the origin and progress of comedy and histrionics in Spain with theological censorship, royal resolutions and providences of the Supreme Council on Comedies. Madrid, 1804. Barcelona: Labor, 1975)*

By 1575 they were attracting such crowds to it that there were petitions raised against them, as apprentices were sneaking off from work to watch the shows. Perhaps this was the true reason, or perhaps the educated and erudite elite did not like the common people coming to their shows. Performances ...

> ... had originally been given only on Sundays and holidays, then permission was granted to hold them on two week-day afternoons, then on three, and finally all limitation was abandoned. With a performance most days, and a relatively small population, plays naturally had a much shorter run ... but the habitues of the Madrid corrales probably demanded a new play at least once a week. (Wilson, 3: 1969)

The ability of the Italians to perform from a scenario rather than just a full text, must have allowed them to carry a large number of 'plays' in repertory, and to have new ones 'ready' much quicker than these acting companies requiring full written texts. Perhaps it was this ability that contributed to their success in Spain.

The higher incidence of mortal and near-mortal fights in the scenarios printed here may indicate that Ganassa and Co. quickly learned to tailor their shows to the local audiences. Compared to Scala's scenarios, these storylines and are certainly more bloody, at least in my opinion. After their initial impact, Ganassa's company remained in Spain and managed to maintain their successful run of performances. The success, and the wealth that it brought, allowed Ganassa to retire and settle in Spain and his spouse, Barbara Flaminia, allegedly became the richest woman in Spain. Was it significant that fifteen years before the Golden Age of Spanish theatre, albeit retrospectively, was announced, a troupe of experienced Italian theatre professionals came to Madrid and got their feet very firmly under the table? I suspect it was significant, but sadly the lack of records and historical distance will keep the exact answers from us. What is important is that we have records of a lot of people seeing them, and artists whose work is validated by large swathes of the public parting with hard cash to see them play, do tend to have some kind of influence. With more duels and a far more unyielding notion of honour than exists in Flaminio Scala's Italian commedia scenarios, what Ganassa, Flaminia, and Frescobaldi produced was certainly not the same as the mercantile bourgeois comedies of Northern Italy. They performed from scenarios rather than a fixed text, and so could, and in fact did, adapt their subject matter and not their acting style, to the audience in front of them.

If, as is claimed, that Commedia dell'Arte was one of many strands that contributed to the Golden Age of Spanish Theatre, it is not just their performances that helped build the foundations, but their business acumen. They got the local authorities onside by donating money to a local religious hospital, which then doubled up as their secure performance venue, and kept the quantity and quality of their shows high: one of the plays listed in accounts is 'The Intronati play', which may have been 'the Deceived' (1531) [3] as written by 'The Intronati' , a

---

[3] Though first performed in 1532, It was internationally successful and translated into many languages, including French, Spanish and even Latin. The Intronati were a literary academy based in Siena, and writing comedies collectively was only one string to their bow.

Sienese literary collective, and many of Frescobaldi's speeches are copied from Andrea Calmo's letters (1510-1571), who was a Venetian theatrical entrepreneur and comic playwright [4]. The members of Ganassa's troupe, though they could certainly play 'low' when it was required, were also in touch with the best of printed drama available at the time, and if you are going to steal your material, then steal it from the best.

The scenarios, speeches and fragments presented here are all we have left of their performances, and results of this very small Italian invasion were perhaps, as these things cannot be proved, quite likely one of the building blocks upon which Spanish theatre was constructed. Perhaps future Spanish playwrights saw this troupe perform and thought they could do the same, if not better, if they wrote their own words rather than perform from a scenario. I commend these ragged fragments to you, in this version, adapted by "the greatest Commedia dell'Arte troupe in the entire world", i Sebastiani.

-Dr. Olly Crick, Commedia enthusiast and proselytizer – January 2024

References

Simoncini, Francesca (2018). Le Pioniere dell'Arte: Barbara Flaminia e Vicenza Armani,(research in progress) *Drammaturgia*.Firenze University Press.

Wilson, Margaret (1969). The Golden Age of Spanish Theatre. London & Oxford: Pergamon Press

---

[4] The plays he wrote were as follows: *Las Spagnolas* (1549), *Il Saltuzza* (1551), *La Fiorina* (1552), *La Pozione* (1552), *La Rodiana* (1553), and *il Travaglio* (1556). He also wrote volumes of letters and a volume of eclogues.

Contents

Preface & Acknowledgements

Preface

How were Commedia dell'Arte plays performed in the Sixteenth Century? This is a question that we'd wondered about for decades. Our troupe, i Sebastiani, has focused on performing in a context that suggested the Sixteenth Century, and tried to be increasingly true to that period (with exceptions for things that are simply too offensive today). For a long time, it seemed like secondary contemporary sources, such as travelogues of people who had seen the plays, and receipts and contracts, would be the best we could do. Then one day we heard about an actor's notebook (*zibaldone*) written and kept by Sixteenth Century actor Abagaro Francesco Baldi AKA Frescobaldi, (whose stage name was Stefanelo Botarga, or Magnifico in Zan Ganassa's troupe) that was now a manuscript in the **Real Madrid Biblioteca**. We were unaware of the work that would be required to transcribe this document.

Fortunately, in 2007, Professor Maria del Valle Ojeda Calvo (Now at the University of Venice) had taken on the task of transcribing this collection of folios, and published the results. If you read Italian and Spanish and are interested in knowledge and informed speculation about the sources that the Sixteenth Century actors used for their plays, prologues, poetry, monologue suggestions, and witty and thoughtful one-liners, her book is worth acquiring. It is named **"Stefanelo Botarga e Zan Ganassa – Scenari e Zibaldone di Comici Italiani nella Spagna del Cinquecento"** and was published in 2007 by Bulzoni Editore (Rome), which we refer to as 'Calvo-2007'. For intellectual property reasons, we could not simply translate Professor Calvo's excellent transcriptions, but her book was a great resource for verifying difficult bits of penmanship, and her footnotes added clarity to doubtful texts. It is important to note that while both her book and ours cover the same manuscript, our goals are substantially different. If you have an academic interest in the history of Commedia dell'Arte, and the sources that seem to have been used by Ganassa's troupe to create plays and monologues, our book will be a mere shadow of Calvo-2007. You should get access to a copy of that book, too.

Our version is actor-friendly: it is designed to be comprehensible to performers, and to aid in the planning of performances. The focus of our book, and the value it gives, is in the analysis for modern performance of the plays, prologues, short notes, and scene fragments that are in Calvo-2007 (plus one play that is in part of the manuscript that Professor Calvo did not transcribe). We translate each of the nineteen plays in Calvo-2007, plus one more play "Emperor Maumet" into English. As far as we can tell, only three of these plays have been previously translated to English (Costola-2022). We then took these translations and built Commedia scenarios that are similar in form to the ones we published in 2022 in "40 Brilliant Comedies", the comic scenarios from Flaminio Scala. This form has explicit entrances and exits for all characters and resolves some of the mysteries of why certain actions are taken, while staying faithful to the story in the original.

To our delight, beyond our original goals, Abagaro Francesco Baldi's manuscript provides more content than mere plays (performed from the 1560s to early 1580s). It provides several play-independent prologues, dozens of partial monologues, and scores of single sentences that can be used either on stage, or as something to think about before a performance. Calvo-2007 also includes a number of poems and other verse content which we have not translated for this book for two main reasons: 1. One of the prologues discusses how to perform Commedia dell'Arte, and very explicitly avoids verse, and 2. Doing justice to translating poems requires poets.

Acknowledgements

As noted above, this book would not have been possible without the work of Professor Maria del Valle Ojeda Calvo and her team. Thanks to her for taking time to talk to us and guide us on some difficult phrases. Thanks to her also for pointing out the other collection of folios written by Abagaro Francesco Baldi, which includes one additional play (included here), one and a half additional prologues, and many monologues and one-line notes, none of which we felt we were able to include here for reasons of space and, to us at least in some cases, comprehensibility.

Professor Calvo published a paper in 2004 listing the contents of the other manuscript but didn't transcribe it.

Thanks to **Real Madrid Biblioteca** for digitizing these manuscripts and putting them on-line. The ones we have used are bound together with numerous other manuscripts. Most of the content of this book comes from Codex-II-1586 Madrid, Real Biblioteca, and the play "Emperor Maumet" comes from Codex-II-1391 Madrid, Real Biblioteca. BTW, if you are new to this, 1586 is just a document number, not a date, and is not related to when the volume was acquired or written.

Sergio Costola, with Olly Crick, published a book in early 2022 called "Commedia dell'Arte Scenarios". This book first alerted us to the existence of Professor Calvo's book, and Professor Costola spent a lot of time with me discussing how to get a copy, and other details about the scenarios, and their history. At the same time, we acknowledge Olly Crick, who has become a good friend, frequent contact, and constant source of inspiration and cleverness on all things Commedia dell'Arte. He provided the dedication in the front of this book, suggesting that the actors, and these plays from Zan Ganassa's troupe may have triggered the Golden Age of Spanish Theater.

The translations for this book were done by several people: First is my collaborator, wonderful friend, and fellow Commedia dell'Arte performer Chiara Durazzini, who translated all of the Italian. She also translated some of the Spanish short bits when they were mixed with Italian, or had Venetian spellings. Most of the Spanish was translated by another amazing Commedia dell'Arte performer, Aranzazú Becerra Michel, and about a third of the Spanish was translated by Alex Sucheck, with some additional Spanish translated by Elena de la Palma. Some of the difficult Spanish penmanship was transcribed by Cecilia Salazar. The Latin was translated by

Steven Mesnick. It is important to note that, aside from the plays, which are translated carefully and literally, all of the translations were done with me interacting with the translators in real time with an ear toward making a sentence that had the same meaning but would also be something a performer would be comfortable reciting on stage. That said, in minor ways, some of the translations are not word-for-word accurate, and that is my responsibility. The translators are great. Most of the excursions from word-for-word translations have been foot-noted. Our aim, outside of the plays, was not an academic translation, but a document that would be useful to today's actors and re-enactors. Where there was a choice, we looked for a comprehensible *equivalent* word or phrase.

The play "Emperor Maumet" was a challenge. You can see the original as images 206 & 207 of Codex II-1391 in the **Real Madrid Biblioteca** on-line resources. A fair amount of the play is lost due to the lower left corner of the page being torn out. Some little bit is lost because the binding covers a few letters at the start or end of the line. There are inkblots. But, also, Abagaro Francesco Baldi was a sloppy penman, an inconsistent speller, and used some unfamiliar idioms, ligatures, and abbreviations. The eyes of many friends looked at this, and thanks especially to Tricia Postle for working out many difficult words and ideas and realizing that a lot of the second page was a play within a play. Additionally, John Joseph Cash (friend and collaborator on other projects), Chiara Durazzini, and Michael Bergman solved a few puzzles on this. Once we had the translation, creating the play that it represented involved another team including TC Clare, Gary Dryfoos, and Michael Bergman. We had a great respect for Professor Calvo's team and the safety-net they'd provided with the other content prior to this exercise, but this experience amplified that respect.

Our process of working out each play to make it ready to perform is: to perform it several times, making modifications as we spot the need (missing exits, required motivation, same character-different name, etc). This is done by a team of performers that have been working together performing Commedia dell'Arte in some cases for over 30 years. Jennifer Kobayashi stands out as an intuitive genius for spotting issues with the plays and having excellent suggestions for how to fix them. Additionally, Catherine C. H. Crow, Carl West, Michael Bergman, Jess Rudolph, Bethany Rowling, Ben Coffee, Gary Dryfoos, TC Claire, Amanda Catherine Mulder, Aaron Santos, Dina Ternullo, Andrew Clough, Andy Kobayashi, Mike McAfee, Naomi Hinchen, Rozi Galea, Rose Carmichael, Tamasin Evans Milner-Wohlers, Summer Joy Harris, Anthony Cagle, Chris Shannon, Leslie Ann Cardwell, Jim Letchworth, Larry Littany Litt, Thomas Cusack, and Anne & Elizabeth Rookey were all part of this process.

Thanks also for the support of my wife Denise Cross, whose library skills got me a copy of Professor Calvo's book, and to Anne Rookey, who also managed to acquire some books from a library we didn't have personal access to.

The proofreading and improvement suggestions came from: Olly Crick, Jim Letchworth, Ben Coffee, Catherine C. H. Crow, Michael Bergman, and Vicki Wyan.

Introduction

It is astoundingly fortunate that you have started reading this book. It was written for you. Well, quite likely written for you. Do you have a strong interest in Commedia dell'Arte? Do you want to read, and perhaps perform some authentic scenarios from the 1560s through 1580s that have never previously been available in English? Do you wonder what material Sixteenth century performers may have had in their heads, or notebooks, to use in performance when required? Are you curious about the prologues that were spoken before such plays? At this writing, for these and other topics, this book, and only this book, is for that portion of your essence just described. You should read this tome cover to cover.

It is also possible that you are only dimly aware of Commedia dell'Arte, but you are interested in learning drama. This is the next book in a series, aimed at making it possible to learn drama, or build a theater troupe based on the same ideas that were used by Sixteenth Century troupes that used: masks, improvised spoken word, eye-catching props, music, dance, acrobatics and other tricks to put on a spectacle that tells a story. As you will see from the plays in this book, not all of the plays were comedies. This method was used to also tell histories, tales of the gods of Olympus, tragedies, melodrama, and magical pastorals. To perform in this style, it is often best to form an ensemble in which everyone contributes, and there is an expectation that every day new things will be done, previous successful bits will be put aside to try new ideas, old gags will be reworked, new insights into the human condition will be made public, and new glories achieved.

A third fraction of humanity that might find this book fascinating are people with an interest in seeing a snapshot of the minds and culture of people in mid to late Sixteenth Century Italy and Spain. What was polite? How did romance proceed? What did men imagine women liked, and vice versa? How did the rich treat the poor? Did the poor respect the rich? How did people deceive kings, and how did they pay for their treachery once discovered? ... and so much more. The contents of this book let you see the world from the eyes of one man who made a living entertaining, appealing to the imaginations, and supplying some sense of verisimilitude to people from the stage. Seeing that view may add more than you'd guess to your view of that time and place.

Commedia dell'Arte in the Sixteenth Century

Many people drawn to this book already know about Commedia dell'Arte, and this short section is for those who don't. The term 'Commedia dell'Arte' is used to describe a genre of theater that developed and changed over a roughly two century period from perhaps the 1540s to the late 1700s (and arguably beyond) with a modern reawakening in 1949 to present. The start and end dates are fuzzy, in part for lack of extant information, and in part for the fact that it is difficult to define something that itself is constant innovation. In the early years, you might think of it as simply a way for a troupe of performers to perform a play, improvising to please a particular audience, and being boldly expressive. While Commedia dell'Arte eventually came to be almost exclusively comedies with characters in contemporary environments, in the first several decades, this style was used to perform all types of plays, including tragedies, fantasies, histories, and others. That period is where the manuscript described in this book comes from.

Please note that we refer to these plays as '**the Botarga plays**', '**Botarga scenaros**', or '**the Botarga collection**' in this book, and usually use '**Botarga**' (stage name) to indicate Abagaro Francesco Baldi (the actor). We refer to him as [Abagaro] Francesco Baldi when discussing the act of writing, or his off-stage personal business.

What is obvious when you look at the 20 plays that Botarga passed down through his actor's notebook (*zibaldone*) is that the plays they performed took on several different styles. Some of these scenarios are two parallel plays, typically one a tragic bit of history or mythology, and the other a comedy or pastoral that parallels the first in some way. Others are stand-alone plays, of various sorts. Twelve of the twenty are comedies. When you read about Commedia dell'Arte, you will see a lot said about stock characters. Some of those stock characters appear in most of these plays, including Magnifico, who is quite similar to the more familiar Pantalone. Both are heads of family, proud, and tend toward the avaricious. Many of these plays include a soldier called the Capitano. In these early plays he is less the butt of jokes about presumed manliness, but he is here. There are also servants, and young lovers in the comedies, again very similar to those we see in later scenarios. However, these plays are closer to the time of invention of all this and are less tied to the traditions that define how characters must be played in the later periods of Commedia dell'Arte. We love these plays because of that freedom. If you perform these plays, you must do a lot of inventing.

Note that our previous book "40 Brilliant Comedies" includes a few chapters about how to perform Commedia dell'Arte, and some pages devoted to the history of this form, and this book does not. This is not an oversight. There are many schools of thought on how to perform, with many rightfully proud teachers of the topic. Pick one or invent it yourself. That is one of the beauties of this form of drama: It is intentionally flexible to your time, place, skills, and interests.

Commedia dell'Arte is a spectacularly well documented topic in history. If you want to learn more, we suggest that you buy books that our friends have written, or, if you are on the same kind of budget that most actors are on, start with Wikipedia, and look at the bibliography. Download what is available on-line and go to a library for the rest. There are some very good English-language books summarizing the history of this topic, but for explicit details, most of the best books, articles, and papers on the topic are in Italian. Translation software can get you partway there, but if you become obsessed with learning all there is to know, it may help to cultivate a friendship with an Italian-speaking person.

The Context for the Manuscript

Abagaro Francesco Baldi (stage names: Stefanello Botarga, Magnifico) was an established comedian. He joined forces with Alberto Naseli (stage name: Zan Ganassa, Zani) and joined Ganassa's troupe in the 1570s. In the early years that they were together they started in Mantua with the support of the Gonzagas, and then went off to perform all over Southern Europe, including Austria, Paris, and Spain. They liked Spain, and Spain liked them, making it easy for them to get licenses to perform, so they stayed until they split up in 1581. Francesco Baldi continued in Spain until about 1584. During this time Francesco Baldi was writing notes that he kept. These are the manuscripts that we used to prepare this book. We don't know if this is the complete collection, or if some additional folios are out there somewhere else waiting to be found. We do know that Ganassa's troupe had many more plays in their repertoire that are not listed here, including some named in the accounting sheets at the end of the manuscript, and some named in the records of the Dukes of Mantua and elsewhere. Francesco Baldi also included ideas for things to say, and topics to bring up in scenes. That's the short version. For more details about the history of the manuscripts, or of Ganassa's troupe, or the life of their ingénue Barbara Flaminia (later, Ganassa's wife), there is plenty already published.

About the Text

Abagaro Francesco Baldi, was part of Zan Ganassa's troupe for a decade in the second half of the 1500s. So far as we know, he is the only actor from that period whose notes and notebook (*zibaldone*) is still extant. It is possible that there are lost folios from his notes, but the material currently known contains:

- The outlines (scenarios) of twenty plays, including comedies, tragedies, pastorals, and operas[5].
- Nine or ten[6] Prologues varying in length from six to fifteen minutes to perform.
- Numerous scene fragments, which are mostly eloquent monologues, but also include some lengthy bits clearly spoken to another character.
- Hundreds of single sentences, containing wit, insults, inspiration, advice, and prurient bits.
- Poetry and verse, which we have not included or translated as mentioned below.
- Several pieces of accounting paperwork, of which we've translated all available.

As in our previous work "40 Brilliant Comedies", the comic Commedia dell'Arte scenarios published by Flaminio Scala in 1611, we have taken the plays as they appear, and also expanded them with details making them playable by a modern troupe, including:

- adding missing entrances or exits,
- clarifying pronouns,
- explaining why various actions were done,
- adding scenes that appear to be missing,

---

[5] Some plays are referred to as operas, though that is a misleading name as today we think of operas as big productions whose stories are mostly expressed through singing. The operas here are plays about the gods, or perhaps stories about ancient monarchs, which probably did have some of that spectacle quality, but no written libretto.

[6] There is a fractional prologue in the untranscribed manuscript.

- footnoting where we are guessing at an intended meaning.

Unlike the previous work, in this case there are no previous English translations for most of these plays, the three published recently by Sergio Costola in his 2022 book "Commedia dell'Arte Scenarios" are the exception ("Three Cuckolds", "Two Crazy People", and "Perseus"). For that reason, we have included both the literal, terse translation, as well as our playable version of each of the twenty plays. All of these translations are original to us, which we have taken from our own transcription of the original manuscript images. There are two pieces in this book for which Professor Calvo has not published a transcription, and for the play, "The Emperor Maumet", we have included ours, the other is a short scene fragment that is a statement of condolence to a character whose father has just died.

There are a number of pieces in the manuscripts that we have not included in this book. They fall into two categories:

1. Poetry. There are ten works that are either poems, song lyrics, or fragments of whole plays written in verse, which we have not translated because they are not really part of the purpose of this book, which is to inform about the improvised Commedia dell'Arte plays from that period.

2. Most items in the second manuscript. We did include the only play from that collection, the above mentioned "Emperor Maumet", but mostly the other collection of folios was composed of notes for monologues and other inspirations. Many of these seem to be borrowed from the four volumes of Letters of Andrea Calmo (arguably the original Commedia dell'Arte actor)[7], which themselves are amusing and worthy of being a future project for an inspired person who can read old Venetian. Our ambition to make these plays available promptly led us to choose not to include these bits.

A note about the translations: For the twenty plays we have been careful to make the translations accurate reflections of the epoch which produced them. Following these accurate translations, we include for troupes and actors the elaborated plays, in which we have taken a few liberties by clarifying pronouns, making complete sentences, and in some cases even adding scenes, changing names, naming the unnamed, and such. We have treated the non-play texts differently; with the prologues, monologues, and single sentences, we have been a little looser with the translation to create English text with the same meaning, but that reads more smoothly on stage. In no case are we far from a direct translation, but sometimes we didn't always maintain a word-for-word product. In some cases, there is doubt about the meaning, and in those cases, we have footnoted what our choices were.

Many thanks to **Real Biblioteca del Palacio de Madrid – Patrimonio Nacional** and everyone in the chain of possession preceding them from the 1560s to today for the existence of the folios that led to this book, and thanks all the more to the library's RBDigital for beautifully digitizing this manuscript and making it available for all to see. You can find this yourself by going to: [**https://rbdigital.realbiblioteca.es**/] from which page you can search for manuscripts and look for "italiana de comediantes" under **Title**. The top two choices IBIS – II/1586 & IBIS -II/1391(2) are the focus of our book here.

---

[7] Calmo and Ruzzante were contemporaries in the 1530s and 1540s, each developed plays with local characters, dialects, dances, and Calmo especially developed the lazzo.

One issue with the manuscript is that, many years ago, during the process of binding the folios into a book, the pages were trimmed, and on many of the pages, some or all of the final line of Francesco Baldi's writing is lost. In these cases we have inserted **[…]** into the text, and usually included a footnote discussing how much text is missing. We've done the same for most inkblots and other lost text where context didn't supply an obvious choice.

Note that Professor Calvo numbered the items in the order in which they appear in the manuscript[8], and this number is convenient if you have her book and want to go find her footnotes about a particular item. You won't need to look it up if you are simply performing a piece, but if you want more analysis, or ideas about what previous sources the actors may have been referencing, this will prove valuable. For each item we also include which image of a manuscript page this item appears on. For example, the play "**Leone**" which is essentially the Pyramus and Thisbe play performed by the mechanicals[9] in Shakespeare's "A Midsummer Night's Dream" twenty to thirty years later, begins on image **II_1586_0100.jpg** and is Professor Calvo's item 31 which we've marked as **C-31**. In Calvo-2007, all the items are in the order they appear in the manuscript. Here, we have categorized them, so supplying Professor Calvo's numbers will be valuable to some of our readers.

---

[8] There are two items that are actually split into different areas of the manuscript, and Calvo's numbering refers to the first part that appears.
[9] The mechanicals were amateurs, not Commedia actors – The traveling acting troupe portrayed in Hamlet may have represented a Commedia dell'Arte troupe.

The Characters

Each collection of plays has some differences in the characters. Here we will describe the characters that appear in the Botarga comedies, including a few that cross-over into the pastorals and operas. We ignore the one-off characters that that only appear in one play as well as any of the Roman gods, such as Jove, Juno, and Diana, who appear in multiple plays.

Magnifico

Magnifico[10], also called Stefanelo Botarga (various spellings), is essentially the character that later actors called Pantalone. He appears in seventeen of the Botarga plays including three of the pastorals or operas. The actor who played him, Abagaro Franscesco Baldi (sometimes called Frescobaldi), was the author of the manuscript from which these plays are recovered. Compared to Pantalone in the Scala scenarios, Magnifico in the Botarga plays gets less direction about the avarice of the character. The parallel is largely that he has money, strong opinions, a fragile influence, and sometimes an unsatisfied wife who is too young for him, or children whose lives he wants to run. Some of the humor in these plays comes from tricking him into doing embarrassing actions.

In our performances we treat him exactly as Pantalone, and our audiences enjoy that.

Zani

Zani (or Zan or Zanni), also called Ganassa, is what Commedia dell'Arte scholars refer to as the first zanni, not because Ganassa was the inventor of the Zani character (he wasn't), but because he plays an intelligent trickster rather than a foolish impulsive character (second zanni). He appears in eighteen of the Botarga plays including four of the pastorals or operas. In the world of Scala scenarios, he'd be Pedrolino. Historically, Alberto Naselli, who played Ganassa was the leader of the troupe, and so we imagine that his comedy both physical and spoken, were a driving part of every play. In the Botarga plays he does some mean or self-serving things to people but is mostly driven by trying to get a good outcome for all but the villains.

---

[10] In later years, this character was called 'il Magnifico', or 'The Magnifico' (Queen's "Bohemian Rhapsody" being an exception to this rule simply mentions 'Magnifico'. In this early period manuscript there was never an 'il' before Magnifico, and so we do not include it here.

In our performances, we treat him as a little older and more self-directed than Pedrolino, and unlike Pedrolino, the historic record shows that he wears a mask. If there is someone in your troupe that through quick wit, big gestures, or personality tends to dominate the stage, this is the role for that person.

Ortenzia/Silvia

Ortenzia (in one play Silvia) was played by Ganassa's wife Barbara Flaminia. She was ingenue and prima donna, appeared in twelve of the comedies, and played the lead nymph (usually Flori) in the pastorals. In the Botarga plays, this character is the sweet, innocent, loyal, and intelligent young woman sought by a worthy younger man. She is often pursued by some other man who is obviously wrong for her. In most Commedia dell'Arte scenarios, the romantic story is about the ingenue's (inamorata's - Inamorata and inamorato are words used to identify characters as young lovers) path to true love. In the historic troupe this role is mostly the only one played by a woman because of the legal restrictions of that time and place.

In Commedia dell'Arte, there isn't much that distinguishes one prima donna from the others in the scenarios themselves. When you practice toward a performance, simply do what Ganassa's troupe did and play to the strengths of your actor and keep her sincere.

Curzio

Curzio was the leading man, or first inamorato in twelve of the plays. The same actor usually played a romantic shepherd in the pastorals. There is a wide variation on his character within the Botarga plays. Sometimes he's a jealous villain, sometimes he's the sweet genuine well-meaning fellow. Either way, love is almost always his primary or secondary motivation, with honor (perhaps poorly interpreted) being another top motivation.

Because Curzio is all over the map in terms of character and motivation, in our performances we take a close look at how the play resolves and try to play him in a way that will make the audience hunger for, or at least accept his outcome. Sometimes that requires inventing some nuance that is not obvious in the original scenario.

Orazio

Orazio is usually the second inamorato, though in a few plays he's the first. Orazio appears in eight of the comedies, and the same actor plays a romantic shepherd in the pastorals. There isn't much in the plays to make universal statements about what distinguishes him from Curzio, though play-by-play they are certainly different men. Orazio is likely younger looking than Curzio.

Trastulo

Trastulo is a servant (or innkeeper) who appears in ten of these plays but is not listed as a character in any other early historic scenarios that we've seen as of this writing[11]. The name means 'childish toy or plaything', and he does sometimes get played with and manipulated. In

---

[11] A Trastulo does appear in the Basilio Locatelli collection 30 to 50 years later, and then even later there is a well known character with this name who has much better luck romantically than the unfortunate Trastulo in these plays.

the Botarga plays, he is naively obsessed with following all the rules, while hoping to be recognized for his loyalty. He is emotionally disrupted when other people obviously break rules, but it is even worse when rules he wants to follow are contradictory and there is not one true path to follow. He is sometimes drawn to reward or romance, but mostly because it represents approval from someone above him in the chain of command.

In our performances, we love this character. There are so many people in life that he represents, and this easily manipulated rule-following servant is not found anywhere but these comedies.

Franceschina/Francese

Franceschina is a servant woman, or inn keeper's wife. Francese is a man who appears as a guard and may or may not have a French accent. He is, in one scene, lured away from guard duty by an offer of some wine. In either case, historically this role was played by a man. Collectively, they appear in nine plays. The character Franceschina is usually portrayed as being very aware, in a practical sense, of the nuts and bolts of how men and women interact. She is sometimes driven by poverty or business opportunities to work with those parts.

Capitano

An otherwise unnamed Capitano appears in seven of these plays. In Commedia dell'Arte as we know it from later, the Capitano is usually a boastful braggart who wants the world to think highly of him, often representing an occupying power. In this set of plays there is nothing to indicate that he is more than a hired man to be present to assert some physical authority. In one of the Botarga plays he has a wife, and he wants to recruit Zani into marching off to war with him. It is possible that playing him with excess pride and panache would add considerably to the reception from your performance, but for these early scenarios, it is not a built-in feature of the character. In the Scala scenarios, he was a Spanish Capitano, and so his mere presence created some amusing irritation for the Italian characters and viewers. These Botarga plays were mostly performed in Spain, so that issue was not front-of-mind to their audiences.

In our version of these plays we have given him the name Capitano Gamberro, because as actors we like to name the other characters and prefer not to have to invent names on the spot. If you want to stay true to the original, feel free to name him anything or simply call him 'Capitano'.

Isabella

In these plays Isabella was the second amorosa, and when she did appear was typically needier and trickier than Ortenzia. She appears in six comedies and all of the pastorals. In the Pastorals the actor playing Isabella played a nymph (various names), but in those plays there is not much to distinguish the characters of the two nymphs.

As we said of Ortenzia, organize the play to let the actor play to their strengths. Isabella frequently gets fewer scenes, so, make the most of them in terms of establishing the character.

Tofano/Dottore/Philosopher

Tofano is often Magnifico's brother or good friend. Counting the Dottore and the Philosopher (Play #19, "The Deadly Sword"), this character appears in five of the plays. In Scala's plays and later there are Dottore characters who have a highly refined kind of malapropism humor among other things. In Scala's plays there is a Tofano character who is essentially a second Pantalone. In the Botarga plays, he is a second respectable, perhaps more kindly, older adult. The scenarios are sparse in their details, so feel free to play him any way that fits your style.

Cassandro

Cassandro is a businessman. He appears in three of the plays. He seems to be a little better at bookkeeping than Magnifico is. This makes him worthy of getting tricked, and his fury in being tricked all the greater.

Laura/Coralina

Laura and Coralina might be the same character as each other. Collectively they appear in four plays, and are either an established wife, a widow, or a single mother with an adult child. The characters aren't well defined but are often sympathetic, long-suffering characters that deserve a break. The exception to this is "Three Cuckolds" in which Coralina might be sympathetic or not as she plays some tricks to facilitate a younger man coming to visit while her husband pursues a different woman.

Prince/Signore

Unlike the Scala plays, which never (except in "Isabella the Astrologer") have anyone of higher rank than Pantalone, in these plays a prince or other nobleman, 'the Signore', appears in three plays, and is used as an off-stage entity in a few others. Not much is given in the scenarios to describe him, but since such people and their minions often saw these plays, it is unlikely that they'd have been portrayed as having less than the utmost dignity. They'd be similar in impact on the other characters to the Duke in Shakespeare's "The Comedy of Errors".

Lazzi

The manuscript does not contain the word 'lazzo'[12] or 'lazzi'. This is a somewhat more modern term used to describe a preplanned action or exchange. That said, it is very common in Commedia dell'Arte scenarios for some specific action to be called for. These actions are often at the ends of acts one or two, so that the acts end with a bang. In this collection, as in Scala's, they are called 'baie', 'burle', 'cosa' (thing), or 'prova', often with some one-word or other very short identifier as to which trick it is. Sometimes it is simply 'fa' or 'fanno' as in 'they do …'. In our translations we have converted all these terms in the right context to 'lazzo' to be consistent with the more thoroughly studied and documented later period scenarios.

Another recurring expression that isn't quite a lazzo, and so we don't list it here is '*li dà l'ordine da …*'.(She gives the order of …). In these cases, a woman is making a requirement for how a would-be lover must disguise himself. Usually this is 'the order of a woman' so that he must cross-dress to enter the house. Other options in these plays are that he dress as a porter or a beggar.

The names for the lazzi were shorthand that the troupe members knew, but which we readers centuries later can only guess at. In some cases, knowing stage comedy and the story, it is possible to construct some aspects of what each lazzo is, but as with many aspects of these plays, they also offer your troupe an opportunity to be creative.

There are a number of times in the play that call for a special effect, such as ghosts telling a story, Pan and Cupid fighting, Zani turning into a frog, gods ascending to or descending from the sky, a character reciting poetry, stage combat, fires, explosions, or numerous other such displays. We have not included them in this list, though in many ways they must be prepared and rehearsed in ways similar to how a troupe would prepare lazzi.

In this collection there are 29 lazzi specified. Some are mysterious, and some are obvious. In the performance versions of these plays we have declared several of our own lazzi. In such cases they are described well enough to know their intent. Concerning the original lazzi, in the

---

[12] Note that most scholars, including John Rudlin, prefer to use the word 'lazzi' as both the singular and plural of these actions. Here we are using the term 'lazzo' to mean one instance of a prepared bit in a scenario. How we take this term and use it in English doesn't appear universal, and 'lazzo' is in popular (if not scholarly) use. Respect your local teacher and use their sense of it.

performance versions of the plays we have included footnotes telling what we know about each lazzo as it appears. Here we provide a list of these lazzi and provide context for each.

Silvia's Trick w/ int: Sesto Tarquino

La burla del tabarino, Lazzo of the large tabard

A tabarino is a long two-sided (front and back) cloak. In this scene at the end of Act 2, a sad Trastulo, whose promised bride has been taken from him, is going off to try and find a wife. Franceschina appears and does this lazzo. In the original play, this pair never appears on stage again. It is likely that the tabarino for this lazzo is one of the 'beautiful clothes' put on the bride and groom a few scenes earlier, and probably removed from Orazio before he is taken away. Franceschina uses this to turn Trastulo into a happy bridegroom.

The Wheat w/ int: Epaminondas

Fano la figura, They make the figure

A young male lover reveals his love to his love, and then they make the figure. This is some sort of expression of affection. It could be an embrace, or a dance, or something else. In any case, after this, in the play, they are committed to each other.

La prova de i legni, The trial of the wood

This lazzo is performed by some tough teenaged boys on an old man. They try to beat him with sticks or wooden bats. It's not clear what ends this, but the boys see some young children go by, and they exit to beat them too. Brutal as it is, it could be an opportunity for some rehearsed synchronized baton work.

The King Artaxerse

Fano baie, They do a lazzo

In this case Zani, Trastulo, and Franceschina appear and Franceschina can't speak; perhaps she never could. This is their first appearance, and the lazzo could be something related to Franceschina desperately trying to communicate something that the men can't figure out. The net result must be that Zani wants her to be able to speak. In the next scene Zani gets a doctor to try and heal her.

Fano baie del molto parlare, The lazzo of much talking

Formerly mute Franceschina is now talking up a storm. This must be fun at first, but either in this scene or before his next appearance, Zani must have had too much of not being able to get a word in edgewise.

La burla del fuoco e scopa, The lazzo of fire and kindling

In this situation at the end of Act 2, Franceschina has taken a dive pretending to be unconscious, and Zani and Trastulo try to rouse her with water, but that failing they pretend to get ready to set her on fire. That seems to work, since they all leave the stage with end-of-act energy without actually creating a fire.

Constant Love

La burla di fortarelo, The lazzo of weak defense

At the end of Act 2, Magnifico and a disguised young man appear, and to satisfy a promise to a woman, the man prepares to beat Magnifico. The name of the lazzo suggests that Magnifico's fighting style is laughably weak and awkward. The bit ends when Trastulo joins in and beats one of them.

In Between

Fanno baie, They do a lazzo

In the middle of Act 1, two young shepherds are arguing about whether love is better than eating. Zani enters and judges in favor of eating. They do a lazzo. In the end they bond and agree to help each other. The lazzo might be about Zani eating all the food while judging, or perhaps there is some preplanned word-play comparing love and food; or maybe both! They can all work.

Burlano, They do a lazzo

At the end of Act 1, one of the shepherds has food, and Zani arrives. This lazzo must be about energetic eating.

The Three Cuckolds

Fano baie, They do a lazzo

At the end of Act 1, Zani needs help getting a large crate of lemons into a house. Trying to get into his lover's house without her husband noticing, Curzio has dressed as a thug, but he pretends to be mute, and won't help Zani. The lazzo is about Zani trying to get him to help. Zani gives up, hauls the crate inside, and then comes out, beats Curzio, and makes him talk.

La burla del muto, The lazzo of being mute

Once again, Curzio is pretending to be a mute thug, Coralina (his lover) presents him as such to her suspicious husband. It must work because the husband gives Curzio a donation.

La Burla de la quarta, The lazzo of the fourth

It isn't clear what this one is. Zani comes home while Magnifico is having a liaison with Zani's wife Franceschina. Somehow Magnifico exits Zani's house. Franceschina comes out and does this lazzo of the fourth. Zani isn't alarmed by Magnifico, and perhaps doesn't even notice him. Zani cheerfully goes into the house with his wife. Magnifico then goes to his house to see his wife. Could the lazzo be that Franceschina blocks the view while Magnifico climbs out of the window, or goes out the door? Is it instead some excuse that Magnifico was in for laundry or advice? Later in the Act Zani is told about the trick and is quite upset.

La prova (del occhio), The test of the eye

Ortenzia needs to distract Magnifico while Cassandro escapes unseen, so she pretends to have something in her eye, and needs Magnifico to look for the irritating speck. This is later referred to by Cassandro as 'the trick' as opposed to 'test'. In this case the the phrase 'prova del occhio' doesn't appear directly in the text, but mention of the eyes is close by so we identify it with that name. The trick was successful until Magnifico hears about it later.

Thefts

Quella cosa del torsi girato, The turned bosoms thing

In this situation, Ortenzia successfully distracts her mother Laura, while her new lover Curzio sneaks out the door. This could be as simple as Ortenzia standing in a place that forces Laura to look away from the door, or it could be daughter-mother dialog about their bodies, appearance, underwear, lacing, or anything else that might rivet the mother's attention to a small field of view.

The Most Inane Lady

La burla delli confetti, The lazzo of confetti

At the end of Act 1, Franceschina is part of a new catering service helping to prepare for a wedding that just got called off. She sees her two partners crying and does the lazzo of confetti to them. Confetti in this case are colorfully decorated almonds. Does she throw them? Does she feed them to the sobbing men and cheer them up? It must be something along those lines.

La simula, The imitation

A young lover does something to mimic the movements or speech of a bitter woman.

The Inn

Fano l'ombre, The lazzo of the shadows

A young man pretends to be Zani with Zani. This is likely a mirror-movement exercise.

Burlano un pezzo, the lazzo of a piece

Magnifico and Zani, drunk, and dressed as women do this lazzo, and then get beaten up. Perhaps they are trying to wiggle like available women.

The Tunnel

La prova de la persona, The test of the person

Curzio wants Ortenzia. He knocks at her door or window, and she comes out. He explains what he wants. She gives him a test of some kind, and he fails. She shoos him away. What kind of test? Such information seems to have been lost over time, but how different could it be from modern methods? For the stage, it would be best if it were lively and involved a lot of movement.

Fighting for Love w/ int: Adonis

La burla de la fonte, The lazzo of the fountain

Flori the nymph arrives and sees two older men, Magnifico and Zani, who are in love with her. The old men sing, and she does the lazzo of the fountain. Then she leaves. This doesn't tell us much, but shortly after she leaves the next lazzo happens that seems to require that the old men get wet before the next scene.

La burla con la farina, The lazzo with flour

As the first act ends, a nameless shepherdess arrives and does the lazzo with flour with or to the old men, Magnifico and Zani, who moments ago were part of the lazzo of the fountain. It seems likely that the lazzo involves caking the flower on the the wet parts of the old men. When performing this, keep in mind that cleaning flour off the stage can take a few minutes.

La burla di strapar gl'ochi, The lazzo of tearing the eyes out

Zani shows up when Flori the nymph is quite agitated. She does the lazzo of tearing his eyes out, and then she leaves. After this Zani can't see, but there are indications that by the end of Act 3 or perhaps before, his vision is restored. This could be a horrifying lazzo. It is happening in a magical world, so Zani getting his sight back is not impossible, especially after a round trip to the underworld.

La burla de lo scorpione, The lazzo of the scorpion

In a big fight with spirits at the end of Act 2, the last thing that happens is that Zani does the lazzo of the scorpion. While most people were captured by a spirit or the wizard, this lazzo seems to help Zani escape, because he is free at the beginning of Act 3. Is this lazzo a martial art move? Is it flinging an alleged scorpion at someone and running away while they panic about it? Whatever you do with this, it should be visually interesting to the audience, because it ends the act.

Two Crazy People

Fano baie, They do a lazzo

The two old men, Magnifico and Tofano, have just agreed that Tofano should marry Magnifico's beautiful young daughter, Isabella. They do a lazzo and then call Isabella. The lazzo is probably the idiosyncratic way that these two old men seal a deal: special handshake, recited oath, special dance. Alternatively, it could be Tofano's fantastic ideas about his wedding night, or other such things to strongly emphasize why he should be unappealing to Isabella.

Fano baie, They do a lazzo

Zani and Magnifico interact with a crazy man for the first time. The lazzo may have to do with trying to understand each other.

Fano baie, They do a lazzo

Zani and Magnifico interact with a crazy woman for the first time. This lazzo most likely parallels the one just before it, but with a possible added bit of doubt having now seen two crazy people in short order.

Jewels of Chastity w/ int: Perseus and Medusa

Burla de la Burbe, The lazzo of the gruffness

Two nymphs, Flori and Delia, each holding a jewel that makes them want to stay chaste, and having just shood away two handsome young shepherds, are approached by two older men, Magnifico and Zani, who are utterly smitten with them. The nymphs do this lazzo of the gruffness. After the lazzo, the nymphs are not on stage, and a wizard arrives and interacts with Magnifico and Zani. One option for this lazzo is that the nymphs are very rude to the old men in a way that you don't imagine sweet little nymphs being. They could really lay into the qualities these men have that repulse them. Alternatively, it could be defensive angry shouting as they run away.

The Deadly Sword

Loro la burlano, They do a trick to her

Zani's wife has just come out of Zani's shop and appears to have made an arrangement to provide intimate entertainment to Magnifico, but Zani thought Magnifico's deal was with Franceschina. The trick is probably some kind of joke about either her honor, or Zani's

Li la fa burla, She does a lazzo to him

There is a box with an important one-of-a-kind jewel in it. It has gone through many hands already in this scenario, and Magnifico makes Ortenzia give it to him, while Zani watches. Magnifico leaves. To end the Act, Ortenzia does a lazzo to Zani. What is the lazzo? It should be eye-catching. Perhaps it is about the box that Trastulo gave her, and she's now lost. Perhaps it is an opportunity to show that she has feelings for poor abused Curzio, whom Zani has victimized. The specifics not being clear provide any troupe performing this play an opportunity to invent something wild.

The Plays

There are twenty plays in these manuscripts. As noted in the introduction, this will be the first English translation of seventeen of them, and the first effort to make playable stories for all twenty.

For each of these plays we are supplying both a literal translation of what is written in the manuscript, and a more elaborated version of the scenario to be convenient for people that would perform it. This second version has been play-tested by the modern Commedia troupe i Sebastiani with friends from other troupes to catch all of the entrances and exits that Botarga assumed everyone would figure out, as well as other issues that needed some clarification.

Literal Translations

In the literal translations, there are a few conscious choices we made that are a slight difference from the original.

- Abagaro Francesco Baldi was inconsistent about the spelling of names, and we have mostly unified them (e.g. Oracio & Orazio). There are times when he used different names for the same character (e.g. Ganassa & Zani are the same person, but both names get used in a single play). In those cases, we have mostly used both names as the manuscript gives them.
- There is sparse punctuation in the manuscript. We have freely added commas, colons, semicolons, periods, and quotation marks, et cetera, as seems appropriate to the context.
- Some of the plays are not named in the manuscript. For those plays we have supplied a name, and a footnote mentioning the omission and insertion.
- Some acts end with an explicit 'End of the act' message, and some have either one built into the final action, or no mention of the end at all. Because of the structure and format of how we are representing the translations, it should be clear to the reader where acts begin and end, and we have omitted most of the 'End of the act' messages. Similarly, we have used a unified way of saying Act 1 etc. Our main focus of these translations is to accurately supply the text of the play as written.
- There are a few recurring phrases or idioms that have specific meanings in this stage context, such as 'in questo' which literally means 'in this' but is usually translated as 'at that' meaning, as soon as this action happens, the next scene begins; or 'batte' which

literally means 'he beats', but in these plays, it means 'he knocks' at someone's door or window. For these and similar phrases we have used the practical meaning rather than the direct translation.

- In some situations, it is important to know if a pronoun is masculine, feminine, neutral, or plural. In cases where it resolves an ambiguity, we have footnoted it. Similarly in cases where there is a verb with no subject, if the verb indicates a plural subject, we have inserted 'they' before the verb.

It will be the case when you read the translated plays that it will sometimes be confusing as to who is on stage, and who isn't, or among the people on stage, who is doing some specific action, and to whom they are doing it. There will also be confusion as to why any stated action is taken. That is the nature of the original. This is why we have also supplied our more elaborate 'Performer' version of each play.

The Performer Version

Similar to what we supplied for the forty comedies from Flaminio Scala's collection of scenarios in our 2022 book "40 Brilliant Comedies", we have taken each of these plays and given information that will be helpful to anyone who might perform these plays, including Dramatis Personae, Props, Backstory, Special skills or effects needed, a Relationship Diagram, and information about what the set needs.

For the plays themselves, we have reworked every scene to make sure that all required entrances and exits are given, that all names are unified, that unnamed characters get names, that all actions get some indication as to why they are done, and more. We have sometimes split scenes to allow for more timely entrances, or otherwise help with dramatic playability. Along with this we have sometimes added a scene here or there to allow characters to supply back-story, take actions implied by later scenes, or simply for two characters to show a developing relationship justifying their marriage, or some other event, at the end.

Speaking of the end, the Flaminio Scala comedies all ended with marriages, and the ending was stated relatively explicitly. In most of these plays the ending isn't clearly expressed. There is a resolution of a big problem (usually), but sometimes characters are left looking foolish. In many of these plays, our playable version has an ending included. We mark the beginning of our invented material with a footnote, to make it clear. Groups performing these plays will certainly have their own ideas how they want to wrap it all up for the audience. It seems unlikely that Ganassa's troupe ended with a dangling plot, so they did something. Perhaps they had paired-off exits like we do, or perhaps they simply started dancing and singing. Perhaps it was something that varied according to the audience. There is no known record to guide us about this.

Performer Versions

Silvia's Trick

Intermezzo: Sesto Tarquino

There are two separate plays here interwoven with each other. The first play is a history about the fall of the Kingdom of Rome and the start of the Roman Republic. This is treated as an intermezzo for the other play which is a comedy. Both plays are about accusations of infidelity, but one of them has a happy ending.

Dramatis Personae   6M-3F + Extras

Curzio	A gentleman, brother of Orazio
Orazio	Nobleman
Magnifico	The Host of an inn
Giacomo[13]	Servant of Orazio
Zani	Servant of Magnifico
Trastulo	Short man, formerly betrothed to Silvia
Silvia	Daughter of Zani
Isabella	Daughter of Magnifico[14]
Franceschina	Isabella's servant
Justice	An agent of the Signore
Tofano	Brother of Magnifico[15] (2 scenes)

Props

Necklace
Jewelry
Chest with a purple and gold toga
A dagger
A coin
Diana disguise
Wedding clothes, tabarino

Set: one House or Inn

- Magnifico's

Intermezzo Cast

Tarquino the superb	Last king of Rome
Sesto Tarquino	Son and heir of Tarquino
Arunto	Son of Tarquino
Tito	Son of Tarquino
Bruto	Nephew of Tarquino
Priest/Oracle	
Colatino	A Roman citizen
Lucrezia	Wife of Colatino

Intermezzo Set

- The camp
- Colatino's house
- Banquet house
- Oracle's cave

---

[13] In the manuscript this is Orazio's unnamed servant, here named Giacomo.
[14] This relationship is not in the manuscript but is plausible.
[15] This relationship is not in the manuscript but is plausible.

Porcia	Servant of Colatino
Lucrezio	Father of Lucrezia (one scene)

Special Skills & Effects

In the intermezzi, there is a lot of blood and violence.

In the main play,

- There is a door knocked to the ground.
- Silvia disguises herself credibly as the goddess Diana.

Performance Considerations

- Several of the plays in this collection are essentially two plays running concurrently. The intermezzo play is a history about the fall of the Kingdom of Rome and the rise of the Republic, brought on by the 'Rape of Lucrezia'. The second play is about a high nobleman two thousand years later who falls in love with a servant-class woman and his brother deceives him that she has been unfaithful. The history ends in suicide, and the comedy ends in marriages. The sets, costumes, and props must be very different, so it will be interesting to see how this could be performed. The cast sizes are the same, so assume that the same 9+ people are in each play.
- **Note well!** Trigger warning: this play includes an offstage rape, an onstage suicide by the rape survivor, an onstage murder, an offstage murder, and someone ordering the murder of a young woman.
- It may be that the Intermezzo scenes are abbreviated but were more fleshed out on stage. The stories they are associated with provide much more detail. It is up to the actors to give that story enough depth to the audience that they understand it. The actors, especially Tarquino, should be well versed in actual history so that they can tell their stories clearly.
- In this play, class distinction is very important. Orazio, Curzio, and the Justice are above everyone else. Magnifico and Tofano are above the servants. The servants have their own pecking order within the play.
- It is possible, with costume changes, for the same actor to play Giacomo, the Justice, and Tofano.
- Effort must be taken by the actors playing the brothers to reform themselves well enough for an audience to think they deserve the happy ending in this play.
- Scene 1.11 Orazio knocks the door to the ground "*fa getar la porta a terra*" but this makes Orazio seem like too much of a hothead. If there is a dramatic reason to do this, we haven't discovered it yet.
- Curzio's confession at the end should somehow reflect Sesto's scene at the end of the Second Intermezzo.
- Sylvia, in this scenario, doesn't get to talk about her motives, unless the actor inserts monologues or asides into her scenes.

Relationship Diagrams

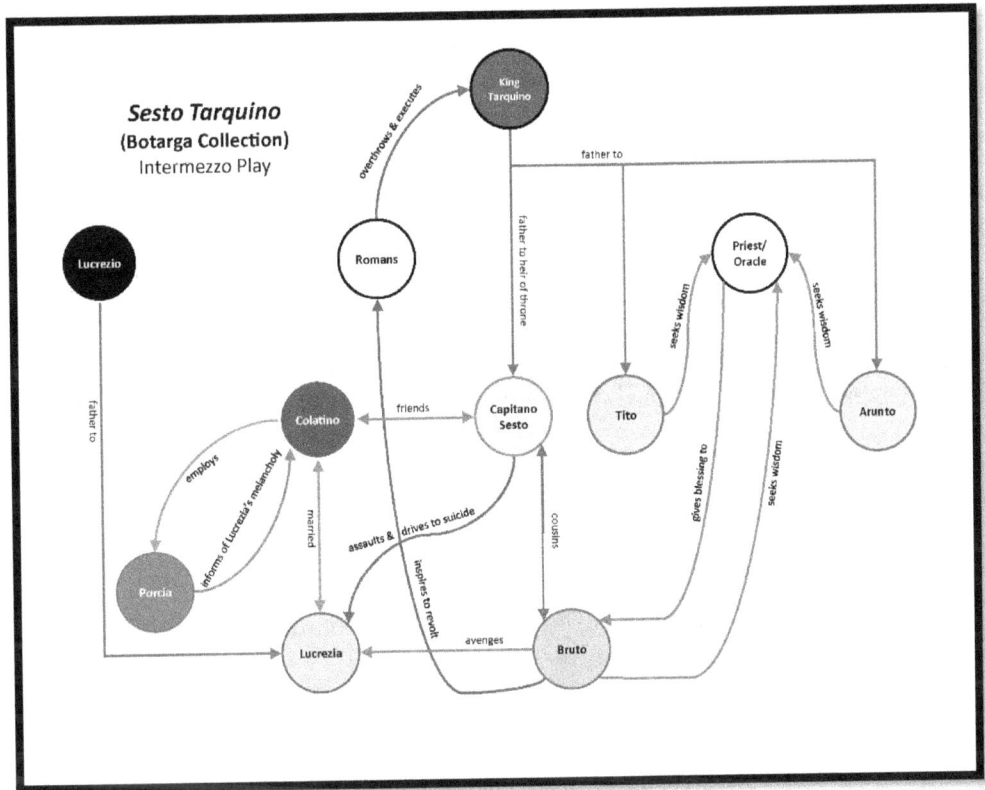

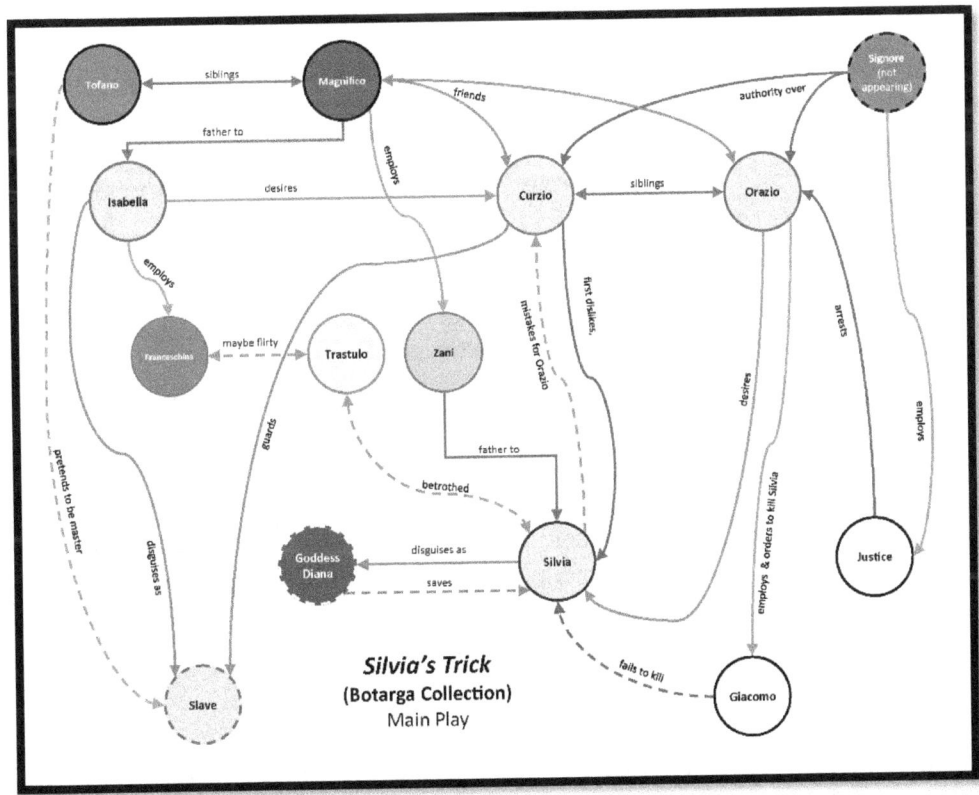

Backstory (Argomento)

Orazio and Curzio are noble brothers. Orazio has come to this town and fallen in love with Silvia, but she has been promised to the servant Trastulo. Curzio wants to protect his brother from marrying too low below his station. Meanwhile another woman, Isabella, has fallen in love with Curzio. Magnifico is the host of an inn.

Two thousand years earlier, Tarquino the superb was King of Rome (a city). His son Sesto (Tarquino the sixth) is heir to the throne. Sesto's cousin Bruto is quite smart but acts insane and comic to avoid being killed to simplify inheritance.

First Intermezzo

A.01	**Tarquino** **Capitano Sesto** **Arunto** **Tito** **Bruto**	Tito, Arunto, and Bruto anxiously discuss the serpent that appeared during court.[16] Tarquino sends Tito and Arunto to Apollo's Oracle. **Tito and Arunto exit.** Bruto acts crazy. **Bruto exits** following Tito and Arunto. Tarquino talks to Sesto about having made the line of succession clear by murdering all of Sesto's cousins, except for Bruto, who he saved because he (Bruto) is mad and amusing. Tarquino tells the story about his enemies in Rome who want revenge by sacking Ardea (in the Southern outskirts of Rome) To defend Ardea, he makes Sesto a capitano. **Tarquino and Sesto exit.**
A.02	**Tito** **Arunto** **Bruto** **Priest/Oracle**	[Carrying their offerings] Tito, Arunto, and Bruto kneel and ask the Oracle of Apollo what the oracle meant by the serpent who appeared in the royal court. Oracle replies: "**At the entrance of the proud serpent, Rome will be seen in great pleasure and, presently, laughter turns into pain, and the game into tears and death.**"[17] They interpret the death of the king; they ask whoever will succeed their father in the kingdom. Tito offers a necklace, Arunto some jewelry; Bruto, a chest. The oracle replies: "**Who of you first kisses the mother will succeed the father.**" Bruto kisses the earth. Priest is in awe and opens the chest. The oracle finds a toga of royal purple and gold. He praises Bruto's cleverness. **Everyone exits.**

Act I

1.01	**Curzio** **Orazio**	Curzio argues that Orazio should not marry Zani's daughter Silvia. Curzio points out that Orazio is noble. They are interrupted.

---

[16] This plot point is added to help support the second scene and justify Tarquino sending them away.
[17] This is an allusion to the upcoming rape leading to the fall of the kingdom of Rome.

1.02	**Magnifico** **Giacomo**	Magnifico praises Orazio and exhorts him to this marriage. Curzio contradicts Magnifico. **Curzio exits**. Orazio orders Magnifico to have the house prepared for a wedding. Orazio then asks Magnifico to tell Zani how much he wants Zani's daughter Silvia to be his wife. **Orazio exits**. Magnifico calls the servants.
1.03	**Trastulo** **Franceschina**[18]	Magnifico says that arrangements must be made.[19] He orders Franceschina to go to the house and Trastulo to go to the field to find Zani. **Franceschina exits** into the house. **Trastulo exits** up the street.
1.04	**Zani** **Trastulo**	Magnifico talks about wedding and that Zani must give Silvia to Orazio. They call her.
1.05	**Silvia**	Silvia has been promised to Trastulo and refuses to marry Orazio; Silvia asides that she is loyal, but it is true that Orazio is very appealing.[20] Zani yells at her refusal and shoos her into the house. **They all exit**.
1.06[21]	**Isabella** **Franceschina**	Isabella monologues about how wonderful Curzio was last night, but Curzio has left her alone. She asks Franceschina for advice on romance. They note handsome Orazio's interest in sweet young Silvia. They do a lazzo about women and men's interests. **Isabella and Franceschina exit** into the house.
1.07	**Curzio**	Upset about Orazio's desire to wed below his station, Curzio monologues about his worries of the wrath of the Signore. He blames Cupid and women. He is interrupted.
1.08	**Franceschina**	Franceschina tells Curzio about how Isabella is in love with him. She begs him to love Isabella. Curzio dismisses her and **Franceschina exits**.
1.09	**Zani** **Trastulo**	Zani and Trastulo talk with Curzio about the wedding. (*Important: In this scene Trastulo must stay unaware that his Silvia is the bride.*) They are interrupted.
1.10	**Magnifico**	Magnifico asks them about Silvia accepting the Signore's son Orazio. It erupts into an animated argument.
1.11	**Franceschina** **Silvia**	They arrive, and hearing the argument, they agree to go into the house and lock the door. **Franceschina and Silvia exit** into the house.

---

[18] The manuscripts entrance says "servi". If this includes Silvia, then the dialog should avoid telling her too much about her wedding in this scene. Do we also need additional unnamed servants?
[19] This 'arrangements' plot point seems implied but is not in the manuscript.
[20] This plot point is not in the manuscript but is needed to let Silvia later be in love with Orazio.
[21] Added Scene to give Isabella a scene in Act I and to establish backstory for Curzio and Isabella.

| 1.12 | **Orazio** | Orazio asks where Silvia is. Magnifico tells him. In his enthusiasm to see her, Orazio breaks the door from its hinges.[22] The argument reaches a peak. **Curzio exits** to get the Justice[23]. |
| 1.13[24] | **Silvia**
 Franceschina | Silvia asides about the foolishness of men.[25] Silvia calms them down. Orazio tells everyone what he sees in Silvia, and her worth as his wife[26]. Orazio tells Trastulo[27] to accept the situation and that they will give another wife to Trastulo. Now all happy, **they all exit** toward town. |

Second Intermezzo

B.01	**Capitano Sesto** **Colatino**	Sesto and Colatino have come from the battles in Ardea. They have come to Colacio (Colatino's home) to see what their wives are doing. The wives are next door at a banquet[28], and they have found the wife of Sesto in celebration and having fun. They go toward Colatino's house.
B.02	**Porcia**[29]	Porcia (the servant) gives them news of Lucrezia's melancholy due to Colitino's absence. They approach the house. **Porcia exits** into the house. The men step aside to discuss the qualities that make good wives, each praising Lucrezia.
B.03	**Lucrezia**	Not noticing the men, Lucrezia complains and comes out to do chores. Sesto asides that he has suddenly fallen in love with her. Colatino introduces his wife and sends Lucrezia inside. **Lucrezia exits**. Giving in to his desire, Sesto pretends that he will join his wife at the banquet and sends Colatino to invite the King (Tarquino) to the banquet. **Sesto exits** to the banquet house.[30] **Colatino exits**.

---

[22] The manuscript simply says that Orazio knocks the door to the ground. This makes him look less abusive.

[23] This plot point is not in the manuscript but is implied by their mutual entrance later.

[24] Scenes 1.11 and 1.12 were a single scene in the original but are split here to give the servant women an explicit entrance.

[25] Added plot point to show Silvia as having some agency, to help set her up as able to do the trick at the end.

[26] This is not in the manuscript but is an added plot point to make the rest of the scene less authoritarian.

[27] This is Zani in the manuscript, but Trastulo makes more sense.

[28] In the traditional story, it is the men having a banquet, and Lucrezia is the only wife present. This version may have been put in to make the drama require fewer scenes.

[29] In the original this is an unnamed servant.

[30] In the manuscript, it isn't clear that there are two houses, and which house anyone enters or exits from.

B.04	Capitano Sesto	Sesto quickly returns. He asides that he is in love with Lucrezia. He stops himself saying: "**Pleasure passes, enjoy, foolish, sweet times of love, that whoever tastes a pleasure does not always restrain himself**". He becomes agitated. He adds: "**Repentance! the pleasure will be short, the contentment short, because after the pleasure there is repentance**". He gets strong feelings; and again agitated. **Sesto exits** into Colatino's house.

Act II

2.01	Isabella Franceschina	Isabella tells Franceschina to tell her lover (Curzio) that she (Isabella) has become a nun (a lie). She continues, telling Franceschina to find Tofano and send him through the back door. **Isabella exits** into the house.
2.02	Curzio	Franceschina tells Curzio that Isabella has become a nun. He laughs and drives her away. **Franceschina exits**. Curzio asides that the Signore needs him to prevent the wedding.[31] He is interrupted.
2.03	Magnifico	Magnifico gives the news to Curzio about the wedding that is supposed to happen. Curzio, becomes angry, and plans to disturb the wedding[32], **Curzio exits**. Magnifico arranges the chairs. He hears noise of people about to enter.
2.04	Orazio Silvia Zani	[Franceschina is carrying beautiful clothes[33]] They bring food to eat. Franceschina puts the beautiful clothes on the bride and groom. Zani presents Silvia as bride to Orazio[34]. Silvia and Orazio each declare their deep and sincere love of each other.[35] The moment they are declared husband and wife, they are interrupted.[36]

---

[31] Added plot point to clarify why Orazio is later arrested.
[32] In the original, it merely says that Curzio becomes disturbed.
[33] This includes an ornate tabarino for Orazio.
[34] In the manuscript this line was cut for the binding. This is a guess as to what was written.
[35] This is an added plot point to help explain Silvia's actions and the happy ending.
[36] It isn't clear whether they are married at this point in the manuscript.

2.05	Curzio The Justice	The Justice arrives to take Orazio to prison on the part of the Signore. Silvia and Zani grieve. Orazio consoles them and puts Silvia, his wife, in the care of Curzio, his brother. Orazio removes his wedding tabarino and gives it to Franceschina.[37] **Orazio and the Justice exit.** To plea for Orazio and true love, **Zani and Franceschina exit**[38]. Silvia goes into anguish (faints) into Curzio's arms. To get water **Magnifico exits.** Curzio suddenly falls in love with Silvia. He embraces her to kiss her. She recovers from her swoon, and thinking Curzio is Orazio, she embraces him and says loving words to him. They are interrupted.
2.06	Magnifico	Magnifico sees the situation, Magnifico asides that he will tell Orazio. **Magnifico exits.**
2.07	Curzio	Curzio reveals his love for Silvia. She shoos him away, fleeing into the house. **Silvia exits** into the house. Chasing her, **Curzio exits** into the house.
2.08	Trastulo	Trastulo monologues that he is searching for a wife.
2.09	Franceschina	[Franceschina has the tabarino] They do the lazzo of the tabarino[39]. **Trastulo and Franceschina exit.**

Third Intermezzo

C.01	Capitano Sesto	Sesto asides about having forced himself on Lucrezia and now will return to the camp. **Sesto exits.**
C.02	Lucrezia Porcia[40]	Grieving, she sends Porcia for her father, husband, and relatives. **Porcia exits.** Lucrezia sobs and is interrupted.
C.03	Lucrezio (her father) Colatino Bruto And others	She tells them the facts. She kills herself. Bruto tears off his madman's clothes (reveals that the madness was feigned) and swears on Lucrezia's blood, to avenge her. They carry her remains all over Rome. Lazzo of horror and noise.[41] Raising the alarm, **All exit.** (Noise continues off-stage)

---

[37] Not in the manuscript, this action sets up the lazzo of the tabarino at the end of the act.

[38] Zani must exit, but the manuscript didn't say when. His reason for leaving was our invention.

[39] Most likely, this lazzo, involves Franceschina using the wedding tabard from Orazio, to make Trastulo into her (Franceschina's) husband with an improvised ceremony.

[40] Porcia's entrance is not in the manuscript, but is implied by Lucrezia sending for her father et al.

[41] This lazzo is not mentioned in the manuscript but is needed.

C.04	Tarquino	Monologues about the surprising noise.
C.05	Bruto Colatino Other Romans	Tarquino is horrified at the spectacle. The Romans confront Tarquino with the facts about Lucrezia and kill him. They make Bruto the proconsul and create the Republic of Rome. **All Exit.**

Act III

3.01	Curzio	Curzio is irritated that he could not have Silvia, who locked herself in a room. He is desperate.
3.02	Tofano Isabella	[Isabella is dressed as a slave] Tofano introduces her as Fatima and asks Curzio to guard her. **Tofano exits** up the street. Isabella tells Curzio that he can guard her all he likes in the house. She entices him and he responds favorably. **Curzio and Isabella exit** into the house.[42]
3.03	Orazio Zani[43]	[Orazio has a coin] Orazio thanks Zani for his impassioned words to the jailer. Orazio gives Zani a coin. To spend it, **Zani exits** up the street. Orazio monologues about being happy to be free and to see his bride.
3.04	Magnifico Curzio	[Curzio is hiding to observe, has a dagger] Curzio asides about discovering Isabella's trick, and the way he left her in the house.[44] Magnifico tells Orazio that Silvia is in love with Curzio. **Magnifico exits**. Orazio is sad. Curzio, having heard everything and with a dagger in his hand, **steps forward**. Curzio (lying) condemns Silvia saying she looked at him with love in her eyes. They do a lazzo of escalating anger at her betrayal[45]. **Curzio steps aside**. Orazio calls Silvia.
3.05	Silvia Isabella[46]	[Isabella hides at her window to observe] Silvia welcomes Orazio with love. Orazio drives her away, threatening her. **Silvia exits** into the woods. Orazio calls Giacomo to get Magnifico.

---

[42] In the manuscript, After Tofano exits, they simply go into the house. Here we added something to better set up the happy ending in act III.

[43] Zani's entrance was added by us to explain Orazio's release from jail.

[44] This is an added plot point to explain why he no longer has Isabella (dressed as a slave) with him.

[45] This lazzo was added to help justify Orazio wanting to have Silvia killed.

[46] This is an added entrance, to let Isabella see Silvia's plight and act on it shortly afterward.

3.06	**Magnifico** **Giacomo**[47]	Believing his bride was unfaithful on their first day of marriage, Orazio gives an order to Giacomo to kill Silvia in the woods. **Curzio**[48]**, Orazio and Magnifico exit.**
		Giacomo asides about the error of what he is about to do.[49] **Giacomo exits** to find Silvia.
3.07[50]	Isabella	[Carrying a bundle] Isabella asides that she can fix this. **Isabella exits** chasing Giacomo.
3.08	Zani	Back from spending the coin, Zani asides about enjoying the freedom of Orazio.
3.09	Magnifico	Magnifico gives him the news that Orazio has ordered his daughter to be killed as an adulteress. Zani reacts. They are interrupted.
3.10	Giacomo	[Giacomo carries a naked dagger] The dagger seems to confirm her death. Zani goes into a rage. Magnifico flees. Zani, follows. Beginning a series of run-through bits[51], **Magnifico and Zani exit.**
		Giacomo (perhaps lying) recounts that when he tried to kill Silvia, she disappeared, and he does not know how. **Giacomo exits.**
3.11	**Silvia**[52] **Magnifico** **Zani**	[Silvia is disguised as the goddess Diana[53]] Magnifico and Zani stop running. Diana says that Silvia was saved for her chastity. Silvia's case was presented to a tribunal of justice to prove her innocence. **Silvia (as Diana) appears to exit** but hides to observe.
		Zani exits to get the others.
		Hearing the brothers, **everyone stands to the side.**
3.12	**Curzio** **Orazio**	Curzio is happily relieved to have prevented Orazio from taking the servant-girl as a wife. Orazio mourns the death of Silvia[54]. They are interrupted.

[47] In the manuscript this is Orazio's unnamed servant.

[48] In the manuscript Curzio has no exit.

[49] The manuscript does not demand that Giacomo express himself here, but it seems implied.

[50] Added scene to show origin of the Diana costume.

[51] The run-throughs are not specifically mentioned in the manuscript but are implied by the presence of Magnifico and Zani even after they have exited.

[52] It isn't clear (for lack of a comma) whether Diana is the Justice, or whether Diana is with the Justice on entrance. Here we've chosen that she's with the Justice.

[53] Note that the manuscript hints at this but doesn't say it explicitly. It is possible that Diana and Silvia are two separate characters, but "Silvia si scopre" in the final scene implies that she reveals her deception, not that she's been hiding and watching.

[54] In the manuscript this scene is that the two brothers are celebrating the death of Silvia, which is hard to reconcile with a happy ending.

3.13	Zani Trastulo[55] **The Justice** Isabella **Franceschina**	Zani is desperate, he accuses the brothers to the Justice. Orazio confesses. The Justice scares Curzio. Curzio confesses his corrupt intent. Curzio's desire and treachery is revealed to Orazio. Curzio weeps and apologizes for the irreparable harm he caused. Silvia reveals her trick and embraces Orazio. The Justice agrees to the marriage. **Orazio and Silvia exit.**[56]
		Isabella praises Curzio's remorse and apology.[57] Curzio realizes his true love. Curzio and Isabella do a love scene, and they marry. **Curzio and Isabella exit.**
		After a lazzo, Trastulo and Franceschina declare their marriage[58]. **Trastulo and Franceschina exit.**
		Talking business, **Magnifico, and the Justice exit.**
		Zani asides to the audience and then **Zani exits**.

---

[55] A lot of things were added to this last scene, including entrances Trastulo and Franceschina,
[56] The manuscript does not include exits. They are provided here if you want them. End the show in a way that suits your audience and venue.
[57] This is an added plot point to help justify the happy ending for Curzio.
[58] This final pairing is not in the manuscript.

The Wheat

Intermezzo: Epaminondas[59]

This is one of the five scenarios with two separate plays that are interwoven, though in this case the History is only two short acts. The main play is a comedy about a vengeful son who has been kicked out of the house and tries to ruin his favored adopted brother. The Intermezzi play is a history about a Greek statesman who gives advice to a father of unruly children.

Dramatis Personae   7M-1F

Magnifico	A wealthy old man
Trastulo	Magnifico's servant
Zani	Magnifico's servant
Orazio	Magnifico's foster son
Curzio	Magnifico's exiled son
Capitano Gamberro[60]	A soldier and hired thug
Ortenzia	Daughter of Magnifico
Cassandro	Real father of Orazio

Props

3 sacks of wheat
Disguise for Magnifico
Sticks for beating people
Coins

First Intermezzo Cast

Vecchio	An old man
Messenger	A messenger from the king
Apion[61]	Son of Vechio
Florus & Gallus	Two rascally thugs

Set: one house
• Magnifico's inn

Second Intermezzo Cast

Epaminondas	Wise old man
Pelopida	A Famous General

---

[59] In the manuscript, the intermezzi play is not given a name. Here we've named it after the main character.

[60] The Capitano is nameless in the manuscript. Here provided a name which means "thug", or "Shrimp".

[61] Apion, Florus, Gallus, Aktis, Belos, and Cilix are unnamed in the manuscript, but have names here for clarity.

Aktis	Oldest son of Pelopida
Belos	Second son of Pelopida
Cilix	Pelopida's youngest child

Special Skills and Effects

- Need three bags that appear to be filled with wheat.
- Need a costume for Magnifico to wear and appear to be Curzio in disguise.

Performance Considerations

- The two Intermezzi could be independent of each other, but both tell stories of fathers who should discipline their children with love rather than abuse, so that they learn to treat all people with dignity. This theme is echoed in the main play, in which Magnifico has kicked Curzio out of the house, and treats him with physical abuse, and this has resulted in Curzio developing a murderous sensibility. Thus, Cassandro should echo things that Epaminondas says in the 2nd intermezzo.
- In the first intermezzo, the Messenger has a chance to really give the backstory to explain the connections.
- Scene 2.03 – Should Curzio show some remorse when he hears that Orazio has been killed? It might help his apparent rehabilitation at the end.
- Zani still holds some affection for Curzio, and it is important for Magnifico in the end to realize his error and embrace the return of his exiled son. The text of the play only hints at this, but it is a core part of the drama that the characters should improvise on through the play.
- Gamberro is not in Act III, and Cassandro is not in Acts I & II. They can be played by the same actor.

Relationship Diagrams

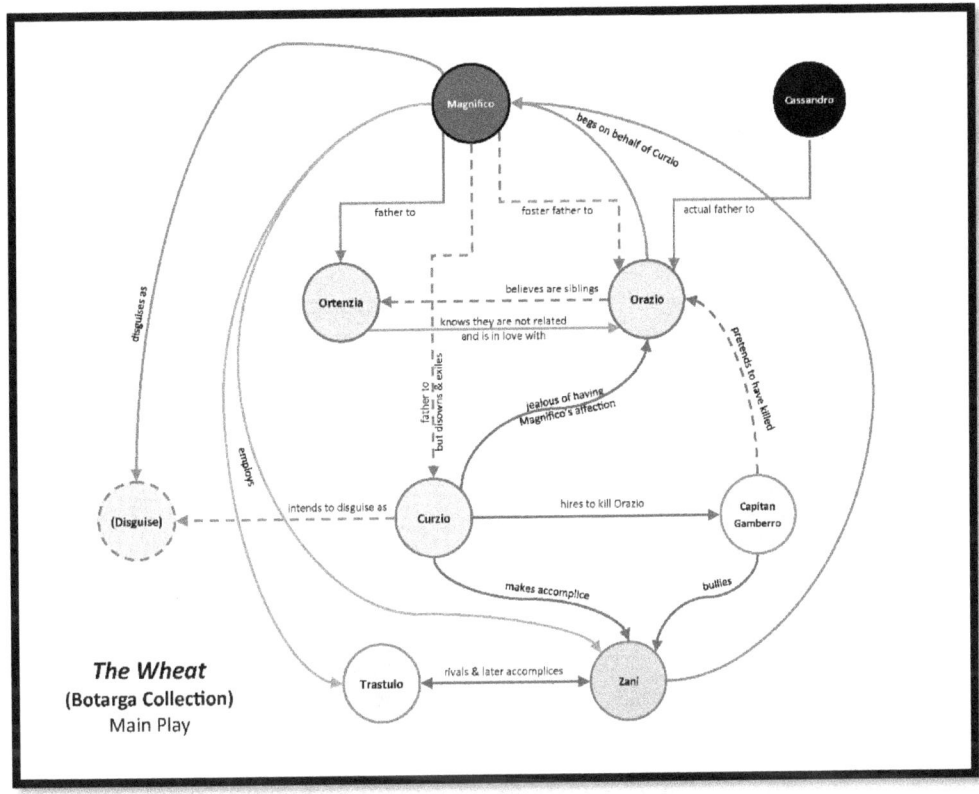

The Wheat
(Botarga Collection)
Main Play

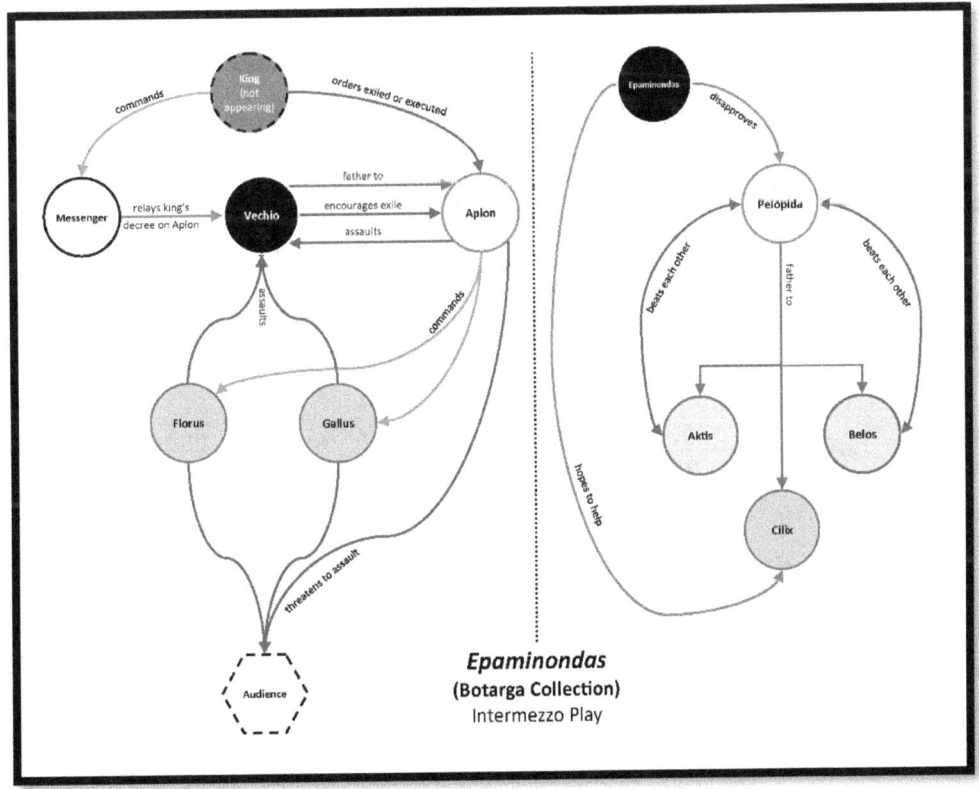

Epaminondas
(Botarga Collection)
Intermezzo Play

Backstory (Argomento)

Orazio and Ortenzia lived as brother and sister in the house of Magnifico but held a great affection for each other. Curzio was also a son of Magnifico but had been removed from the house for his bad response to Magnifico's strictness. Jealous that Orazio was getting all of his father's approval, Curzio plotted his revenge. Unbeknownst to Orazio, Ortenzia discovered that Orazio was a foster child, and not her brother by blood.

Act I

1.01	**Magnifico** **Trastulo** **Zani**	Zani and Trastulo argue about which of them is more loyal (Trastulo or Zani). Magnifico makes peace between them. **Trastulo exits** into the house. Zani begs Magnifico on behalf of Curzio. Magnifico threatens him. **Zani exits**.
1.02	**Orazio**	Magnifico welcomes Orazio. Orazio begs his father on behalf of his brother Curzio. Magnifico does not want Curzio in the house. **Orazio and Magnifico exit** for (*account?*) books.[62]
1.03	**Zani**	Zani asides that he sees Curzio coming and that he wishes Magnifico had not exiled his own son.[63]
1.04	**Curzio**	Curzio complains with Zani. He ordered a capitano to kill Orazio, and Zani must give three sacks of wheat to Curzio to give to Gamberro.
1.05	**Capitano Gamberro**	Gamberro bullies Zani. Zani promises to get the wheat to Curzio. **Gamberro and Zani exit**.
1.06	**Magnifico**	Curzio humbles himself to Magnifico. Magnifico kicks him away. **Curzio exits**. **Magnifico exits**.
1.07	**Ortenzia**	Ortenzia monologues about her love of Orazio.
1.08	**Orazio**	She declares her love to him. They circle around each other (make the figure)[64]; she says she is not his sister. Orazio is excited but needs proof. **Orazio and Ortenzia exit** to see proof.[65]
1.09	**Zani**	Zani asides that he wants to deceive Trastulo to get the key for the granary. Zani calls Trastulo.

---

[62] They go for 'librii' books? Freedoms? Beverages? We think it is account books to show why Curzio is unwelcome.

[63] This plot point is implied but added here to show why Zani is willing to steal the wheat.

[64] "Fano la figura" is a recurring idiom in these plays. It may be dancing or embracing. It appears to be something graceful and loving.

[65] We think it is proof of this non-relationship that they exit to see. The original is ambiguous.

| 1.10 | Trastulo | Zani makes his case.[66] Trastulo says that if he learns that the wheat was stolen, Magnifico would put Zani in prison. They agree to steal the wheat. **All exit**. |

First Intermezzo

A.01	**Vechio**	Vecchio complains about his bad son.
A.02	**Messenger**	The messenger tells Vecchio that by order of the King, His son Apion must be exiled or burned at the stake. **Messenger exits**.
A.03	**Apion** **Florus** **Gallus**	Vecchio tells him to go into exile. Apion threatens the father. They test the wooden bats on Vecchio. **Vecchio exits**. Once tested, they threaten to beat people in the audience.[67]

Act II

2.01	**Orazio** **Ortenzia** **Capitano Gamberro**	[Gamberro is hiding to observe] Having seen proof that he is only Magnifico's foster son, Orazio wants to leave to go to Napoli to visit his father. Ortenzia is sad that he's leaving. Gamberro asides that he is supposed to kill Orazio. Gamberro silently rejoices. **Ortenzia exits**. **Orazio exits** to Napoli.
2.02	**Capitano Gamberro**	**Gamberro steps forward**. Gamberro asides that he will give the impression that he has killed Orazio. Gamberro calls Cuzio.[68]
2.03	**Curzio**	Gamberro pretends to Curzio that he killed Orazio. **Gamberro exits**. Curzio comments. He is interrupted.
2.04	**Zani** **Trastulo**	[Trastulo hides at his window] Curzio says that he (Curzio) needs to be disguised to minimize the risk of witnesses when he gets the wheat.[69] Zani says that at the second hour he will bring three sacks of wheat. Zani specifies a gesture to identify disguised Curzio when he hands over the wheat. They are interrupted.
2.05	**Trastulo**	**Curzio exits**. **Zani exits** into the house. Trastulo asides that he heard everything. **Trastulo withdraws**.
2.06	**Magnifico**	[From the street] Magnifico is going to his house.

---

66 This little plot point is assumed but wasn't in the manuscript.
67 In the manuscript they see children and exit to beat them.
68 This plot point was implied by Curzio's convenient entrance.
69 This is not in the manuscript but is implied because of scene 2.10.

2.07	Trastulo	Trastulo complains telling everything about Zani, the disguise, and the gesture. Magnifico is grateful and sends him into the house **Trastulo exits.**
		Magnifico asides that he has a plan to save the wheat.[70] He calls Zani.
2.08	Zani	Magnifico tells Zani that he will not be home tonight. **Magnifico exits** into the house.
		Zani asides that he can't have witnesses for the transfer.[71] Zani calls Ortenzia.
2.09	Ortenzia	Zani orders Ortenzia to be home early. Zani pretends that it is dark. **Zani and Ortenzia exit** into the house.
2.10	Magnifico	[Disguised as Curzio] Silently, Magnifico gestures with his hands.
2.11	Zani	[Zani has three sacks of wheat] Zani gives Magnifico the sacks of wheat. **Zani and Magnifico exit.**

Second Intermezzo

B.01	Epaminondas Pelopida Aktis	(**Note:** *Plutarch described Epaminondas as a brilliant, well-spoken politician from Thebes, who had previously been the military genius that freed Thebes from Spartan rule. He had once saved the life of Pelopida, a brutish Theban general. This story about Pelopida's children may be an invention for this play to help emphasize Magnifico's forgiveness of Curzio in the end of the main play.*)
		Epaminondas admonishes Pelopeda about his vices and of the undisciplined children that he has. Pelopida defends himself saying that he beats his sons only when they misbehave. Aktis looks sheepish for what he had done while Epaminondas makes his case.[72] They are interrupted.
B.02	Belos Cilix	[Hand-in-hand with Cilix] dragging the child to Pelopida. Pelopida and the children beat each other.[73] Epaminondas scolds Pelopida again. Epaminondas says that the little son will later mistreat people this same way. Epaminondas dismisses Pelopida and his older sons.[74] **Pelopida, Aktis, and Belos exit.**

---

[70] This plot point is not in the manuscript but is needed to let the audience know what is happening.
[71] Added plot point to let the actors to know what's happening.
[72] Added plot point to force the actors to bring out more of the backstory.
[73] Added plot point to tell the actors to do something.
[74] This plot point is implied but added here explicitly.

		Cilix embraces Epaminondas and goes with him. **They exit.**

Act III

3.01	**Curzio**	Curzio calls Zani and asks for the grain.
3.02	**Zani**	[Sleepy] Zani says that he already gave it to him. They shout. Curzio says Orazio is dead. **Curzio exits.**
3.03	**Magnifico**	[Magnifico has coins] Magnifico asks about the shouting. Zani tries to hide the facts. Magnifico threatens Zani and Zani confesses. Zani says Curzio has arranged to kill Orazio, but now Curzio can't pay Gamberro[75], and may get killed himself. Magnifico gives money to Zani so that Curzio may be saved. **Zani exits** up the street.
3.04	**Ortenzia**	[Sorrowful] Ortenzia overheard about Orazio's death. Magnifico, says that Orazio is not his son, and he has written to Cassandro, Orazio's father in Napoli. They are interrupted.
3.05	**Cassandro**	Orazio's father introduces himself to Magnifico. Magnifico gives him the news of his son's death. He laments, Magnifico invites him into his house.[76] Ortenzio escorts Cassandro into the house. **Ortenzia and Cassandro exit** into the house.
3.06	**Orazio**	Orazio asides that he met someone who gave him the news that his father has come. Magnifico thinks Orazio is a ghost. Magnifico is terrified.
3.07	**Curzio**	gets scared.
3.08	**Zani**	gets scared.
3.09	**Trastulo**	gets scared.
3.10	**Ortenzia**[77]	gets scared. Orazio is surprised by the reactions. Magnifico recognizes that he is alive. Magnifico calls Cassandro.
3.11	**Cassandro**	Cassandro reveals to Orazio that he is his father. Orazio asks Cassandro to let him marry Ortenzia. Cassandro agrees. Magnifico gives the couple his blessing. They plead for Curzio. Magnifico stands firm against Curzio. Cassandro promotes the idea of showing love and forgiveness to one's children.[78] Magnifico forgives Curzio and Zani.

[75] Telling Magnifico about the threat to Curzio is implied, but not in the manuscript.
[76] Added this exit. Ortenzia had no exit but enters later.
[77] The entrances of Trastulo and Ortenzia are reversed from the manuscript to let her be last.
[78] This is an added plot point implied by Magnifico standing firm against, and then forgiving Curzio right at the end.

The King Artaxerse

This is a single history play with no intermezzi. This is a play about a great but old king being undermined by power-hungry deceivers in his court, and the difficulty in distinguishing fact from cleverly presented fiction.

This play is unique in the collection in that there are two speech fragments provided for this play in the notebook. The other speech fragments are either generic, or otherwise not identifiable as to which play they belong to. Translations of these fragments appear at the end of this Performer Version of this play.

Dramatis Personae   8M-3F

Artaxerse	King Artexerse II of Persia
Dulipo	Satrap (Governor) of Lydia
Ariobarzane	Chief Administrator[79] for Artexerse
Drusila	Pregnant daughter of Ariobarzane
Daria	Younger sister of Drusila
Zani	A servant
Ciro	Son of Artexerse
Trastulo	A servant
Franceschina	A mute servant
Magnifico	A medical doctor
Polione	Satrap of Phrygia, bro. of Ariobarzane

Props

Seneschal's staff
Bottle of poison
A letter
Packet of deafness powder

Set: three houses
• Ariobarzone's house
• The palace
• Zani's house

Special Skills and Effects

There is some violence, and an unmarried pregnant woman.

Performance Considerations

- **Trigger warning**: A character is said to have killed herself with poison. There is also some 'comic' wife-beating.
- The characters Artaxerse and Magnifico could be played by the same actor.
- The characters Drusila, Trastulo, and Polione could be played by the same actor.
- Note that the names, and relationships in the play do not match up with those of the real history of the Satraps' revolt. Just play the play and remember that in this time troupes were loose with history for the sake of increased drama and decreased cast size.

---

[79] The word used was Seneschal. Chief administrator is a similar title.

- The character Ariobarzane should be played as someone careful to the point of obsession about courtesy and protocol.
- The character Dulipo is a manipulative conniving bad guy. Best if it doesn't look that way until Act II.
- The character Artaxerse should be old, well-meaning, and outwardly look easily manipulated.
- We don't understand the law that Drusila uses about first-born sons. You will need to invent something that works enough for the audience to follow.

Relationship Diagram

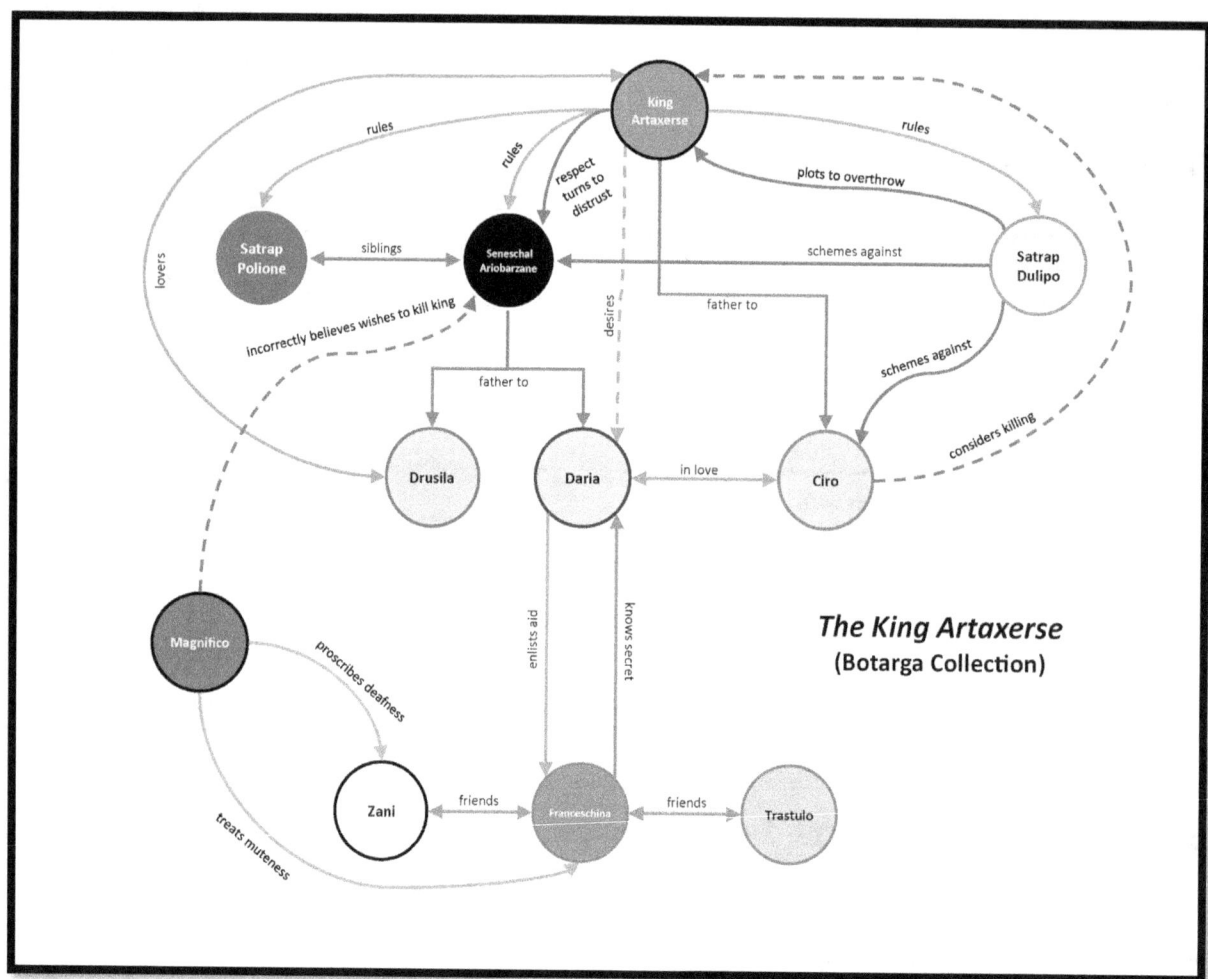

The King Artaxerse
(Botarga Collection)

Backstory (Argomento)

King Artexerse II had loved Drusila (daughter of his seneschal), and she was now ready to give birth to the next of Artexerse's 120 children. Drusila's younger sister Daria loves and is loved by Artexerse's son Ciro. Ariobarzane, father of Drusila, is the seneschal for Artaxerse and has a claim to the kingdom of Lydia, which Dulipo has been running while Ariobarzane runs things under Artexerse. Governors (Satraps) of some Persian states are visiting the court. Dulipo, Satrap of Lydia, has a plan to advance himself.

Act I

1.01 [80]	**Dulipo, Satrip of Lydia**	[With a letter] Dulipo monologues about having intercepted a love letter that he can leverage to become the next King of Persia. He hides the letter.
1.02	**King Artaxerse**	Artaxerse asks Dulipo about his happiness. Dulipo praises him. Artaxerse says he would be happy if he could win the favor of Ariobarzane[81]. Dulipo, says he should kill Ariobarzane. Dulipo makes the figure of the falcon[82]. Artaxerse refuses. Dulipo accuses Ariobarzane of giving Artaxerse his uglier daughter. Artaxerse calls Drusila, daughter of Ariobarzane.
1.03	**Drusila**	[Drusila is nine-months pregnant] Drusila confirms that Daria, her sister, is more beautiful. King sends her to her house, and orders her to tell Ariobarzane to send to him the other one (Daria), and for Ariobarzane to relinquish his Senechal's Staff[83] to Dulipo. **Dulipo and Artaxerse exit.**
		Drusila remains grieving and monologues that she is pregnant by Artaxerse, her only lover[84]. At that:
1.04	**Zani**	Drusila sobs to Zani. Zani, hearing Drusila's grief[85], calls Daria.
1.05	**Daria**[86]	Drusila tells Daria and Zani the will of the King. They grieve and **Zani and Drusila exit** into Ariobarzane's house.
		Daria monologues about honor and her love of Ciro[87].
1.06	**Ciro**[88]	Daria and Ciro do a love scene, that ends when Daria tells Ciro that Artaxerse wants her. Ciro wants to poison himself. **Ciro and Daria exit.**

---

[80] This is an added scene that shows Dulipo as a bad guy right away and explains where the letter from the end of Act I comes from.

[81] Historically, Ariobarzane was an administrator (under-Satrap) of Anatolia. Pharnabazos came to woo and hopefully marry Apama, daughter of Artaxerse, and and Ariobarzane succeded him as Satrap of Phrygia and the Hellesponte. He was joined by Nepos, Satrap of Lydia and Ionia, Mausolus of Caria, Orontes I of Armenia, Autophradates of Lydia and Datames of Cappadocia in a revolt against Artaxerse II. Ariobarzane's son Mithradates betrayed him to Artaxerse, and Ariobarzanes was crucified. Artaxerse died of old age a year later.

[82] In the old story this is based on, Dulipo made Ariobarzanes seem dangerous, and a plan was afoot to kill him while out falconing.

[83] Seneschal is the administrator for a high office. This seems to imply Dulipo is replacing Ariobarzane as Seneschal (a slight increase in power over Satrap of Lydia).

[84] This plot point is not in the manuscript, but it is implied.

[85] The reason for Zani calling Daria is implied but not written in the manuscript.

[86] In the manuscript there is also an entrance here for Drusila, but she never left the stage.

[87] This monologue is implied but not specified in the manuscript.

[88] Historically, Ciro was the younger brother of Artaxerse who led an unsuccessful revolt against him early in the 53 year reign, but in this play may be the son of Artexerse named for his uncle.

1.07	Trastulo Francheschina Zani	[Franceschina is mute] They tease each other in a word-and-gesture dance. **Franceschina and Trastulo exit**. Zani stays.
1.08	Magnifico	Magnifico, a medical doctor, says that he can heal Franceschina's muteness.[89] Zani leads Magnifico into the house to heal her (Mute Franceschina). **Zani and Magnifico exit** into Zani's house.
1.09	Ariobarzane	[Carrying the Seneschal's staff, has a vial of poison] Ariobarzane monologues cheerfully about his situation (not knowing what Artaxerse and Dulipo have arranged).
1.10	Dulipo	Dulipo, by order of the King demands the Seneschal's staff. Ariobarzane willingly gives it to him. Dulipo tells him that Artaxerse sent Drusila home and now desires Daria. **Dulipo exits** up the street.
1.11	Daria	Daria tells Ariobarzane (her father) that Drusila is in bed to give birth. Ariobarzane tells her that it is necessary that she go to the king. She does a scene of misery for being in love with Ciro. Ariobarzane consoles her and gives her a poison which can kill her before she could please the King. At that: **Daria exits** into her house.
1.12	Magnifico	Ariobarzane mutters something about poison[90]. **Ariobarzane exits** up the street. Magnifico has overheard something about the poison and the King. He thinks they want to poison Artaxerse. To learn more, **Magnifico exits** up the street.
1.13	Zani	Zani is cheerful because Franceschina can now speak. **Zani exits** up the street.
1.14	Artaxerse Dulipo Ariobarzane	Artaxerse reprimands Ariobarzane for his pride, and for trying to be the king's equal in charity and grace. He accuses Ariobarzane of trying to acquire nobility through hollow considerations. Ariobarzane says that he will give Artaxerse the most beautiful sister. Ariobarzane calls Daria:

---

[89] This is added to give more basis for the next plot-point.
[90] Added plot point to make it clear that Magnifico overhears imperfectly about the poison.

1.15	Daria	Ariobarzane introduces her to the King. Very pleased, Artaxerse sends her into the palace. **Daria exits** into the palace.
		Ariobarzane exits up the street.
		Dulipo gives Artaxerse a letter[91]. Artaxerse makes Dulipo read the letter. It says that Ciro is in love with Daria. Artaxerse calls Ciro. Dulipo asides that the House of Artaxerse is about to fall.[92]
1.16	Ciro	Ciro asides that he has to poison his father so that Daria can be free.[93] Artaxerse finds the poison around Ciro's neck. Artaxerse scolds Ciro[94]. Ciro is afraid. Artaxerse tells his son that killing himself is a terrible answer when love is involved. Artaxerse grants Daria to Ciro. Artaxerse sends Ciro into the palace to be with her. **Ciro exits**.
		Dulipo gets upset. Artaxerse calls Ariobarzane.[95]
1.17	Ariobarzane	Artaxerse embraces Ariobarzone. Ariobarzane gives his daughter Daria to Artaxerses along with his claim on the kingdom of Lydia. Artaxerse refuses the dowry. Artaxerse gives Daria to Ciro along with his (Artaxerse's) own fortune. Desperate **Dulipo exits** up the street.
		Happily, **Artaxerse and Ariobarzane exit** into the palace.
1.18	Zani Franceschina Trastulo	Franceschina shouts, speaks, and is happy that Drusila has had a son. They do a lazzo of too much talking and teasing. **They exit**.

Act II

| 2.01 | Dulipo | Dulipo monologues lamenting his misery caused by his plan not working yet. |

[91] In the manuscript, the letter was carried by Ariobarzane, not Dulipo. This change was made reflecting the several times that Dulipo gets upset or satisfied when his plan hits a setback or succeeds. The letter seems more consistent as part of Dulipo's scheming.
[92] This aside is not in the manuscript but sets up Dulipo for the comic climbing the ladder before the fall.
[93] This aside is not in the manuscript but is implied but other actions later in the play.
[94] Either he grabs the poison, or simply scolds Ciro.
[95] This summoning is an implied plot point from the original. It explains Ariobarzane's arrival in the next scene.

2.02	**Magnifico**	Magnifico tells Dulipo (his wrong belief) about Ariobarzane and the poison. Dulipo explains that Ariobarzane was ordered to give Daria to the King. Dulipo is happy, **Dulipo exits** up the street.
		Magnifico asides some concerns[96]. **Magnifico exits** down the street.
2.03	**Zani** **Franceschina** **Trastulo**	Franceschina shouts that she wants to reveal the secret of the son who was born of Drusila. Zani tells her to shut up. She talks a lot. They shout. **Franceschina and Trastulo exit** into Zani's house.
2.04	**Magnifico**	Zani asks Magnifico for a remedy. Zani doesn't want to listen to Franceschina. Magnifico offers to get Zani a powder to make him deaf. **Magnifico exits** up the street.
		Zani exits into his house.
2.05	**Artaxerse** **Dulipo**	Dulipa (lying) tells Artaxerse about Ariobarzane's betrayal. He tells him that he will find the poison on Daria. Artaxerse summons Daria.[97]
2.06	**Daria**	Artaxerse finds the poison on Daria. He summons Ariobarzane.
2.07 [98]	**Ariobarzane**	Artaxerse condemns Ariobarzane to the fire. **Artaxerse, Ariobarzane, and Daria exit** into the palace.
		Dulipo, again, is cheerful. **Dulipo exits** up the street.
2.07	**Zani**	With his ears hurting from Franceschina's constant chatter, Zani wants to get the remedy. Zani calls Magnifico.
2.08	**Magnifico**	Magnifico gives the powder to Zani and **Magnifico exits** up the street.
		Zani asides that he will pretend to be deaf. He calls Franceschina.
2.09	**Franceschino** **Trastulo**	Zani pretends not notice her and doesn't respond to her calls.[99] She slaps him with the back of her hand. Surprised, Zani turns and slaps her with a stick. She faints. They splash water on her, but it doesn't help (she pretends to be unconscious). They play a lazzo of fire and kindling. Franceschina gets up and chases the men. **Zani, Trastulo, and Franceschina exit** into their house[100].

---

[96] Added plot point to give a beat between exits.
[97] Added plot point that was implied.
[98] Split a scene to allow Ariobarzane to have an entrance.
[99] This trick is implied but not specifically stated in the manuscript.
[100] This exit is only implied by the manuscript.

Act III

3.01	**Zani**	Zani asides that Franceschina has calmed down. He is cheerful now.
3.02	**Magnifico**	Magnifico asks Zani for payment. Zani pretends to be deaf. They argue and **Zani exits** into his house. **Magnifico exits** up the street.
3.03	**Polione** **Ciro**	Ciro asides that he believes Daria must have killed herself by now and he mourns her death. Polione promises Ciro to save his life and, also to save the life of his (Polione's) brother, Ariobarzane, on the condition that he (Ciro) confesses the truth. Ciro agrees to this. At that:
3.04	**Artaxerse** **Dulipo**	Dulipo asides anger at seeing Polione, a meddler, here.[101] Polione asks Artaxerse for the life of Ciro as a gift. Artaxerse promises it to him. Ciro confesses that he had wanted to poison him (Artaxerse) for the love of Daria. Artaxerse is surprised. Artaxerse gives Ciro to Polione! Polione asks for a hearing for Ariobarzane. The King summons Ariobarzane. Dulipo demands that the traitor Ariobarzane be thrown in the fire.
3.05	**Ariobarzane** **Daria**	Dressed for execution. Ariobarzane tells Artaxerse that, if he had wanted to kill him (Artaxerse), that he would have let Ciro poison him, but that the poison he gave to Daria was because she wanted to kill herself before Artaxerse could take away her honor. Further, Drusila being pregnant, came up with the idea to give birth outside court. It is the law that, if at the time of the King's death, there is a firstborn son, all the other acknowledged sons are to be killed. She saved the lives of Ciro and the baby. Polione[102] adds that Ciro preserved Artaxerse's glory by confessing the crime and preventing the unjust execution of Ariobarzane. Artaxerse rejoices. He embraces Daria and Ciro. Artaxerse confirms Drusila as his wife and takes the Seneschals staff back from Dulipo and with great humility gives it to Ariobarzane. Daria takes Ciro. Dulipo is stripped of all rank, and Ciro is made Satrap of Lydia. With Silent rage, **Dulipo exits** up the street.[103]

---

[101] This aside and the demand that Ariobarzane be burned are added plot points. Dulipo has no written plot points but is present to see his evil scheme unravel.

[102] It is unclear who says this, but this gives Polione something to do.

[103] The ending is not very clear in the manuscript. Dulipo had no written consequence, and Ariobarzane not much of a reward. This ending reflects the speeches given in fragment 175 "Del Re Artaxerse".

| 3.06 | Zani Franceschina Trastulo | They bear the son of Drusila. King embraces him. **Artaxese and the baby exit** to visit his wife.

Ciro, Daria, Ariobarzane, and Polione exit into the palace.

After one last comic bit, **Zani, Trastulo, and Franceschina exit** into Zani's house.[104] |

<hr>

[104] The exits are not in the manuscript but added here to complete the play.

Two Fragments

Monologue #18, RMB II-1586-0174.jpg (bottom), C-175

Note

Of all the plays in the manuscript, this is the only one that has obvious suggested speeches, both by King Artexerse among the monologues. We have included them here, rather than with the other 'scene fragments'.

The Suggested Speeches

[*This fragment appears to be from the first scene of the play*]

Don't you know, Oh Dulipo, that our life is like a fairy tale, that we cannot see whether it is long or short, but we can see well if it is good and well represented. So, the greatness, the power, the status, the wealth, and the dominion that I keep, I do not deny that it is great, but you can't deny that it has been possessed by many, but in the present, it is only one, but there are many who resist the domination of the power of these real forces. Yet, many have possessed it fruitlessly, and these are not worthy of being named as the Dead Sea, whose water grows no fruit. It is not a great thing to be called noble for your bloodline, but it is praiseworthy and glorious to possess these dignities because of merits, because honor is the good thing behind all virtuous acts. And this honor from your praise I cannot receive from you, nor from your will, as a gift, if my virtue does not inspire you, for nobody can deserve any honor, if his own virtue does not make him worthy of merit. But be careful as praise me as you do because it is an arrogant, and feigned, and adulating thing to praise those who do not have merit. And, because, you know, the honor of a king does not consist in title 'king' or in possessing a crown and kingdom, but instead, knowing how to be a king and make himself worthy of this title with works worthy of the greatness of this position. And we can do this by combining wisdom with power, advice with strength, and consideration and magnanimity with wealth; therefore, that the real treasure is none other than the good reputation that he leaves after himself, which is like the shadow that continually follows him even after death.

[*This fragment appears to be from the final scene of the play*]

Ariobarzane, if I don't praise you, I will appear ungrateful for having received so many benefits from you, which includes the lives of myself and my two children, and my own honor and fame that you kept for me, which are so much power that, if I want to praise them, I will be kept ignorant so as not to be able to contribute to the merit of them. However, you tell me and you command if I should either to be silent or to speak in this, because, if I remain silent, by obeying you I will not be thought ignorant, and, if you command me that I speak, I trust that you will not care that I cannot with my tongue add to the greatness of your merits, but you will accept what little of my remaining strength I am able to give.

Ramiro

This play is about a historical Spanish King. In the play, before he takes power, he pretends to be dimwitted, and influenced by the fairy folk (that no one else among the royalty believes in). He saves the queen from an abuse of her reputation, and he himself is publicly saved by ghosts and a fairy. That makes this play a little unusual, since few of the other histories or comedies involve magical characters. Magic and godly powers generally only appear in the Pastorals and Operas.

Dramatis Personae   8M-3F + Extras

Don Sancho	King of Pamplona
Don Garcia	Sancho's oldest son
Fernando	Sancho's youngest son
Don Ramiro	Sancho's bastard son, king of Navarre
Zani	Servant of Don Sancho
Dorotea	Zani's foster daughter (later a princess)
Ermisenda	Daughter of the King of Bigorre
Trastulo	Servant of Ermisenda
A Fairy	A creature with magical powers
Elvira[105]	Queen of Pamplona, wife of Sancho
Domicio	The queen's butler/majordomo
Siriamamoli	A captured Moorish King
Ghost of Alfonso I	A defeated cowardly king
Ghost of Old Woman	Mother of Alfonso the first
Dragon	A talking dragon

Props

Ermisenda's letter
Food for Zani
Food for Ramiro
Gifts from Ramiro
A ring for Ermisenda
A signet ring for Garcia
Drums and trumpets sounds

Set: palace, house, field
• The palace
• Zani's house
• The field of honor

Special Skills and Effects

- A fairy costume is needed.
- At the end of Act I is a talking dragon/serpent.
- Two players have to look like ghosts.
- Garcia and Ramiro do armed combat in Act III. Do they wear armor?
- There are a few times when drums and trumpets are sounded.

---

[105] In the manuscript she is simply called either The Queen, or The Mother depending on context. Elvira is the historic name for the wife of Don Sancho.

Performance Considerations

- The cast of characters is quite large (fifteen), though seven characters have very isolated appearances: The Dragon is one scene in Act I only. The two ghosts are one scene in Act 3 only. Domicio is a few scenes in the middle of Act II only. Trastulo has one brief scene in each of Act I and Act II. Fernando has two scenes, one in Act 2, one in Act 3, Siriamamoli appears only at the beginning and end of Act III.
- The actor playing Trastulo can also play: The Fairy, The Dragon, Domicio, and Siriamamoli.
- The actor playing Ermisenda can also play: Ghost of Alfonso's mother, and Fernando.
- The actor playing Zani can also play the ghost of Alfonso.
- There is a Lope de Vega comedy version of this play "El testimio vengado", but it postdates the manuscript by about 15 years, so it was unknown to this troupe.

Relationship Diagram

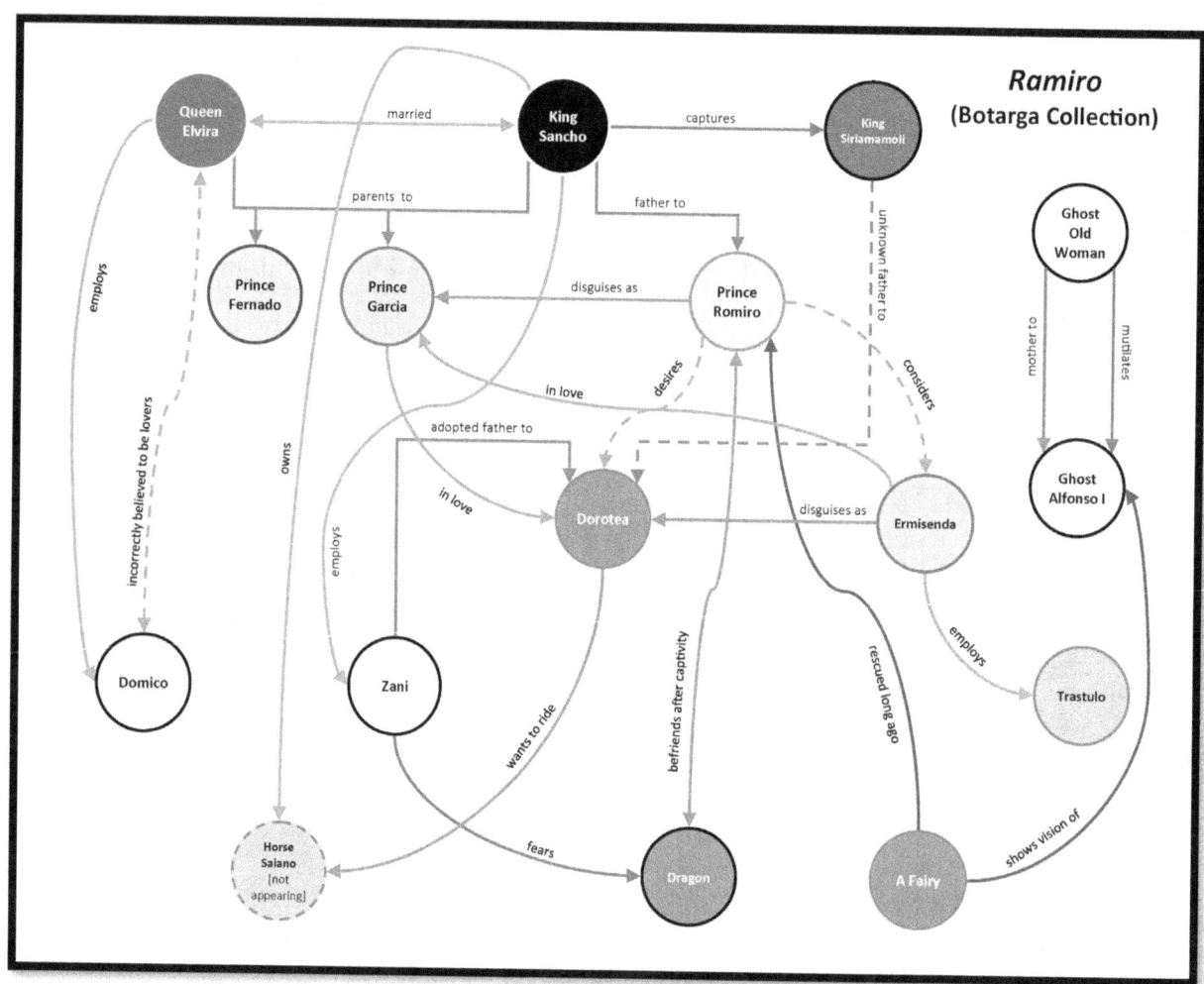

Backstory (Argomento)

Shortly after the turn of the first millennium, in what is now Spain, Don Sancho, king of Pamplona, married Elvira, the heir of Aragon, and had several children. Sancho's oldest was an acknowledged bastard child named Ramiro, who was king of Navarre, but considered to be a witless fool for his stories of dragons and fairies. Don Sancho's next son Don Garcia had ambitions to be king of everything as soon as possible, and he was still an eligible bachelor!

Dorotea is the foster daughter of Zani but doesn't know he is not her father.

Issues

Ramiro's trick on Ermisenda could imply a bed-trick which today is a form of rape.

Act I – Kingdom of Pamplona

1.01	**Don Sancho** **Garcia** **Elvira**[106] **Fernando** **Domicio**	[Holding Court] Don Sancho says that, because the Moors have risen up in Córdoba, it is necessary for him to go in person. He leaves to Garcia's custody: the kingdom, the kingdom that goes to Ramiro (Navarre), who is lacking intellect; and the care of young Prince Fernando and Queen Elvira. Elvira asides that she does not trust the ambitious Garcia.[107] Don Sancho will go stain[108] the field with Moorish blood and says that he needs to leave. He is interrupted.
1.02	**Ramiro**	[Ramiro, king of Navarre, acts witlessly] Ramiro makes peace with Don Sancho. Ramiro wants to go hunt. Don Sancho orders that they take Ramiro out to hunt and that young Fernando start to learn to follow orders in the field[109]. **Don Sancho, Garcia, Fernando, and Ramiro exit**. Elvira worries about her boy Fernando. Domicio is supportive. **Elvira and Domicio exit** into the palace.
1.03	**Zani** **Dorotea**[110]	[Dorotea is Zani's foster daughter] Zani questions her about whether she is still chaste. Because Zani wants to join the hunt in the woods, she will send a snack to him. **Zani exits**. **Dorotea exits** into the palace.

---

[106] We added Elvira, Fernando, and Domicio to this scene to give an opportunity to establish some background for things that happen later.
[107] This plot point added to explain her fears in scene 2.05.
[108] In the manuscript this is 'mark the field' (marchiar il campo), here we gave a more visceral translation.
[109] We've guessed what is in a missing few words of the manuscript.
[110] There is no known historical counterpart to Dorotea. Her storyline is an invention to make interesting drama.

1.04	Ermisenda[111] Trastulo	[Has a letter] Ermisenda asides about her love with Garcia. She gives Trastulo a letter to give to Garcia. **Ermisenda exits** into the palace. **Trastulo exits** looking for Don Garcia[112].
1.05	Garcia	Garcia monologues about his desire for Dorotea, and also that he was the source of the reports of Ramiro's madness[113] which he exaggerated to help eliminate Ramiro as a candidate to inherit the kingdom. Hearing Dorotea, he anticipates her arrival.
1.06	Dorotea	Dorotea complains about her father's queries.[114] Garcia reveals his love for her. He begs her. She modestly refuses. At that:
1.07	Trastulo	[Carrying a letter] Trastulo gives the letter from Ermisenda to Garcia. Garcia, without reading it, tears it up in front of Dorotea. Trastulo is upset and **Trastulo exits**. Dorotea does not want to give her honor to anyone except to her husband. **Dorotea exits** into the palace. **Garcia exits**.
1.08	Zani	[Carrying dry things to eat] To get some water, **Zani exits**.
1.09	Ramiro Zani	[Ramiro has food] Back from hunting, Ramiro is eating. **Zani comes back** with water, he also eats. They are interrupted.
1.10	Dragon	Zani wants to kill the dragon; Ramiro defends the dragon. The dragon speaks and leads Ramiro with him. **Ramiro and the Dragon exit** up the road. **Zani exits** down the road.

Act II

2.01	Fairy Ramiro	[Ramiro no longer seems foolish] The Fairy predicts, telling Ramiro that he (Ramiro) will be next after twenty-two crowned kings of his kingdom. **The fairy exits**. **Ramiro exits**.
2.02	Zani	Zani does a lazzo[115] of still being frightened of the serpent.

---

[111] The historical Ermisenda was the daughter of Bernard-Roger Count of Bigorre.
[112] In the manuscript it is not clear if Trastulo exits, but flow of the play dictates that he must.
[113] There's an opportunity for a terrific bit of backstory here.
[114] This is an added plot point.
[115] The manuscript doesn't call this out as a lazzo, but it is implied by Zani being alone on stage.

2.03	**Garcia**	[Garcia has a signet ring] Garcia asides that he is resolved that he wants Dorotea to be his wife. Garcia asks Zani for her. Zani is unrelenting at first but eventually likes the idea. Zani calls Dorotea.
2.04	**Dorotea**	Dorotea refuses, unless she can ride on Saiano[116], Don Sancho's horse. He promises that to her. **Dorotea exits** into Zani's house.
		Garcia gives his signet ring[117] to Zani, so that he can get as much money as he wants to put himself in order. **Garcia exits** up the street.
		Cheerful, **Zani exits** down the street.
2.05	**Queen Elvira** **Domicio**	Queen Elvira is afraid of an ambush from Garcia's henchmen, and for the well-being of her boy, Fernando. Domicio, the majordomo, tries to comfort her. Her panicking escalates and she faints into the arms of Domicio.[118]
		The noise of trumpets & drums. Just then:
2.06	**Garcia** **Fernando**	They see her in Domicio's arms; they are surprised. She comes back to consciousness. Garcia asks her for the horse Saiano. She grants it to him. Domicio reminds her that Don Sancho ordered that the horse not come out of the palace. She takes back the agreement. Garcia is angry at Queen Elvira and Domicio. Queen Elvira argues with Garcia. **Elvira and Domicio exit** up the road.
		Garcia and Fernando discuss wanting to accuse their mother of adultery. **Garcia and Fernando exit** into the palace.
2.07	**Ramiro**	[Ramiro has gifts to give] Ramiro monologues about his cheerful situation. He is interrupted:

---

[116] Note: 'Saiano' would stand out to the audience as the name of a horse that was bad luck and tragedy to everyone that owned it, from a story about Marc Antony. In this play Don Sancho has a horse with that name, and that horse needed to stay in Sancho's bedroom when not in use for quick access in an emergency.

[117] Siglio in the manuscript. Signet ring is an informed guess as to the meaning.

[118] In the manuscript, it says that the queen gives the horse, but it is repeated in the next scene, so we omit it here.

2.08	Dorotea	Dorotea monologues lamenting her sudden rise in status, and that Zani has not returned. Ramiro sees her sadness, and praises her worthiness to be a queen, perhaps his queen. Her mood lifted, she teases him as if he is crazy, and rejects him.[119] **Ramiro withdraws** to observe.
		Dorotea exits into the Zani's house.
2.09	Zani	Zani is dressed as a gentleman and does a proud lazzo[120]. He is interrupted.
2.10	Trastulo	Trastulo leads Zani to Ermisenda.
2.11	Ermisenda	Ermisenda (lying) tells Zani that Garcia is her (Ermisenda's) relative[121], and that Garcia wanted to take Dorotea's honor and then her life. To protect Dorotea, Ermisenda makes Zani put her in Dorotea's place, in disguise[122]. Zani agrees and starts pretending she is his daughter. At that:
2.12	Ramiro	[Ramiro steps forward, disguised as Garcia] Ramiro asides that he has heard everything. Ramiro (as a trick) acts like Garcia and begs Zani to introduce him to his (Zani's) daughter. Ermisenda thinks this is Garcia and asides that her trick is working. Ramiro gives them gifts. Zani introduces Ermisenda as Dorotea. Ramiro asides that he knows his double-trick is working and that this is really Ermisenda, whom he wants.[123] **All exit** into Zani's house.

Act III

3.01	Ermisenda	[With a ring on her finger] Ermisenda is cheerful thinking she was with Garcia[124]. **Ermisenda exits** into the palace.
		Just then: Trumpets.
3.02	Don Sancho Siriamamoli	The Moorish king Siriamamoli was captured in war. Don Sancho grants him his life and sends him to rest and freshen up in the palace. **Siriamamoli exits** into the palace.
		Don Sancho asides that he wonders why Prince Garcia did not come to meet him. Just then:

---

[119] This plot point is changed to allow the final ending of the play. In the manuscript, Ramiro appears to be sincere in his love for Dorotea, but later is sincere in his love for Ermisenda.
[120] This lazzo is implied by the manuscript.
[121] Reminder: she is jealously in love with Garcia.
[122] "in disguise" is a guess as to the few missing words in a short gap in the manuscript.
[123] This plot point about the asides was added for clarity.
[124] She was actually with Ramiro.

3.03	**Garcia** **Fernando**	Garcia and Fernando accuse Queen Elvira of adultery with Domicio, and that Garcia will keep Domicio from returning to the palace.[125] **Garcia exits**. **Fernando exits** into the palace.[126] Don Sancho grieves. At that:
3.04	**Ramiro**	Ramiro talks to Don Sancho about what he has seen. Don Sancho wonders, then realizes that Ramiro is wise[127]. Don Sancho tells Ramiro the accusations of the sons about Queen Elvira. Ramiro says that he wants to defend her. Don Sancho calls Queen Elvira.
3.05	**Queen Elvira**	Ramiro announces that he wants to enter the field for her. To get ready for combat, **Ramiro exits**.[128] Queen Elvira wants to apologize to Don Sancho. He doesn't listen to her.
3.06	**Garcia**	[Dressed for combat] Enters the field. Queen Elvira begs him to tell the truth. He asserts again that she is adulterous and threatens her. Just then: drums.
3.07	**Ramiro**	[Dressed for combat] In the field, Ramiro challenges and will disprove Garcia. Don Sancho makes them start when the Sun lights the West wall of the palace (noon). They draw their weapons and begin to fight. They are interrupted.

---

[125] "keep him in the field" might mean that he's being sent to the war, or maybe just exiled from the castle. Here we chose a simple meaning.

[126] This exit is implied by lack of Fernando plot points in the rest of the play. Garcia returns, but Fernando doesn't.

[127] Ramiro has been falsely portrayed as crazy until now.

[128] This exit is implied.

3.08	**Fairy** **Ghost Alfonso 1st** **His Mother**	[Alfonso is heavily wounded] The mother cuts off his tongue. **The ghosts disappear**.
		The fairy narrates about ungrateful Alfonso the First to Don Sancho.[129] The fairy scolds Garcia. Garcia declares the truth. The fairy tells Ramiro that he/she is the fairy that freed him from the dragon years ago.[130] **The fairy exits**.
		Garcia exonerates Queen Elvira. Don Sancho wants to kill Garcia, but Ramiro restrains him. Garcia tries to flee but is captured by Ramiro. Garcia begs Ramiro to ask Queen Elvira's forgiveness for him. Queen Elvira embraces Ramiro, and gives Ramiro the kingdom of Aragon, which is her dowry. Ramiro releases Garcia and asks him to be forgiven. Don Sancho and Elvira do so.[131] **Garcia exits** into Zani's house.
		They are interrupted.
3.09	**Don Sancho** **Siriamamoli** **Zani**	[Zani is bound with ropes] Siriamamoli tells how Zani[132] stole from him a little daughter. Zani confesses that she is Dorotea, Daughter of the Moorish Prince, whom he found alone on a beach and saved. Zani begs that she be allowed to convert.[133] Siriamamoli allows that she can become a Christian if Garcia marries her. Don Sancho promises that; they call Garcia and Dorotea.
3.10	**Garcia** **Dorotea**	Don Sancho and Siriamamoli say that they want Garcia and Dorotea to marry. They are interrupted.
3.11	**Ermisenda**	Ermisenda declares that Garcia is her husband. Ramiro reveals the deception, Ramiro marries Ermisenda. With her consent Garcia takes Dorotea as his own bride[134].
		Celebration, and **everyone exits**.[135]

---

[129] Alfonso the first was a famously ungrateful son. This scene is to show how unworthy Garcia is for his ambitious false accusations.

[130] In the manuscript, "freed him from death". Given the mysteries of the dragon in this play we changed this to unite the ideas.

[131] This plot point is implied but not stated in the manuscript.

[132] Zani stole the young daughter.

[133] We supplied these two details, as a story for the actor playing Zani to give. Other stories are welcome.

[134] The historical Garcia married Stephanie of Foix, the youngest sister of Ermisenda.

[135] The final exit is implied or might have been in the lost line of the manuscript.

Constant Love

This is a comedy about two men, who when they were young loved each other's sisters, resulting in an attack in which one was left for dead, and the other ran from the law. Now, years later, they are companions, but don't recognize each other. They both still love the same women after all these years, but much needs to be resolved before anyone can be happy.

Dramatis Personae   6M-3F

Curzio	Young man, formerly Decio
Orazio	Young man, formerly Sigismondo
Cipriota	Sister of Curzio, loved by Orazio
Magnifico	Father of Isabella and Orazio
Zani	Servant of Magnifico
Isabella	Sister of Orazio, former lover of Curzio
Agnese	Traveling companion/nurse of Isabella
Trastulo	Servant of Isabella
Capitano Gamberro[136]	Hired protection for Orazio

Props

A note
Cups of foamy beer
Food
A sword

Set: two houses
• Magnifico's house
• Cipriota's house

Special Skills and Effects

Some scenes involve cups of foamy beer, possibly some of it getting spilled. Some scenes will require people to act drunk.

Performance Considerations

- Does Cipriota have enough money and income to keep living in her dead father's house? It isn't stated but can be another source of drama.
- It isn't specified in the scenario how it is that Orazio has been following or trying to love Cipriota but note that she has fairly recently come from Napoli, and he appears to have followed her, and yet he somehow doesn't realize until Act III that she wants him dead. This is a bit of backstory that needs development by the players own inventions.
- In this play, two people thought dead are revealed to be alive. One of them "pretends to be a necromancer" (finge il negromante). This seems to be a running joke, and probably implies a lot of use of the idea of raising the dead in speeches throughout the play.
- In this version, Vecchio is Agnese, Isabella's nurse/chaperone, and she is sought romantically by Trastulo and Zani as a way to give these characters more drama and parallelism with the rest of the play.

---

[136] The Capitano has no name in the manuscript. He's given one here to help the actors.

- Pietro's porter disguise is to help keep anyone from recognizing him as long-lost Decio.

Relationship Diagram

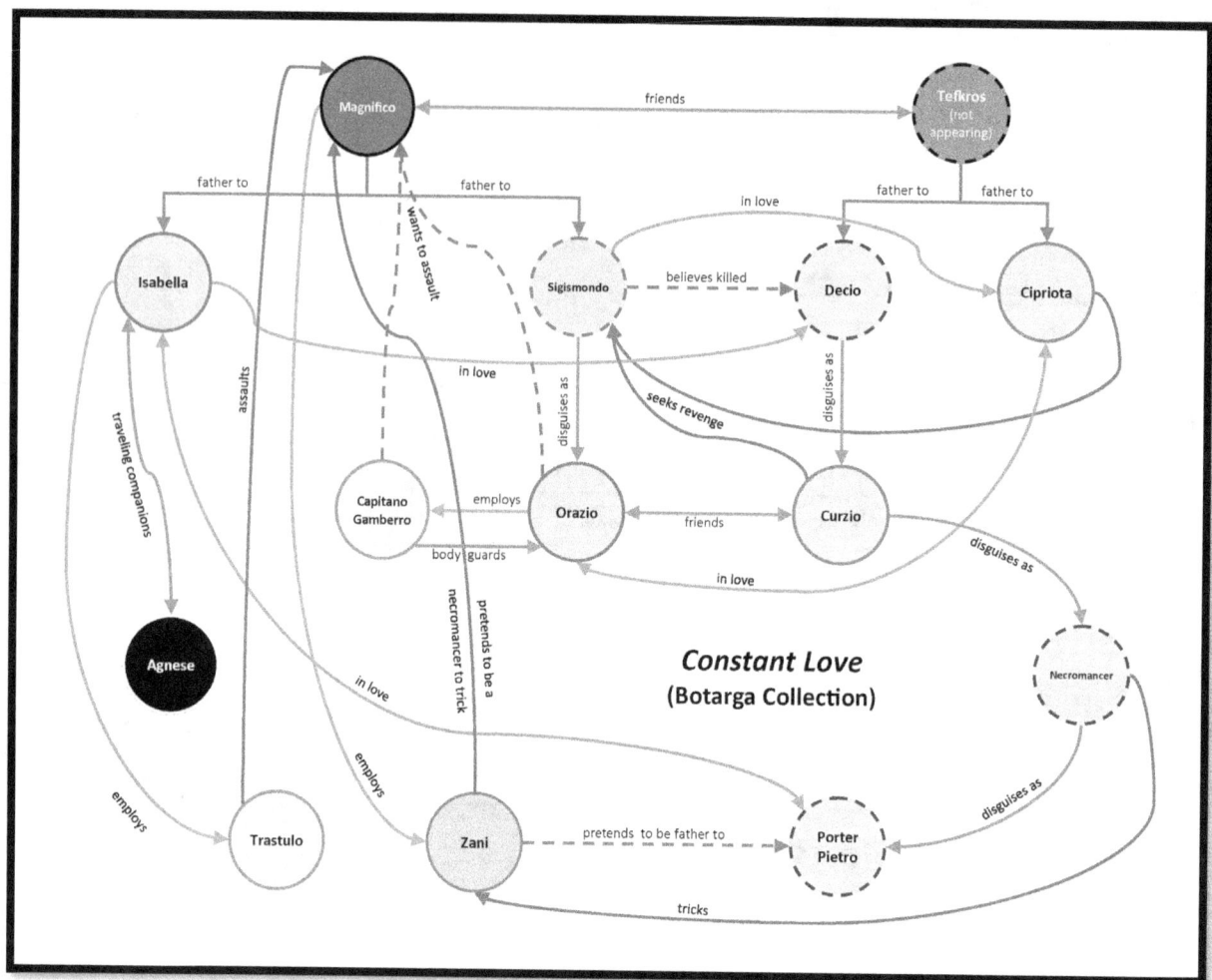

Backstory (Argomento)[137]

Magnifico and the Cypriot Tefkros[138] were friends in Venice, each with a son and a daughter. Ten years before the time of this play, Sigismondo loved Cipriota. Sigismondo's sister Isabella loved Cipriota's brother Decio. Sigismondo got into a fight with Decio and thought he had killed him. Decio ran away and was presumed dead. Sigismondo faked his own death and ran away rather than face the consequences.

Drawn together by tragedy, Magnifico and Tefkros moved to Rome with their daughters. Later, Cipriota moved to Napoli looking for the killer of her brother Decio. Decio, secretly living in Napoli, observed her, but stayed hidden. Having heard rumors, Isabella made occasional

---

[137] There are no backstories in the manuscript. The one constructed here answers the questions of how the characters knew each other, traveled at the same time, and yet didn't recognize each other until the play starts. It is possible to answer these questions with some other backstory if you are motivated to do so.
[138] This name does not appear in the manuscript was added for an easy reference for the actors.

month-long trips to Napoli looking for word of her lost lover, Decio. Sigismondo was also incognito in Napoli and was quite taken with a woman he had seen there who looked like his former lover. Hearing of her father's failing health Cipriota recently came back to Rome and was with Tefkros when he passed from this Earth one week ago.

Act I

1.01	**Magnifico** **Zani**	Magnifico monologues about waiting for his daughter from Napoli. He tells Zani to watch from the door. **Magnifico and Zani exit** into the house.
1.02	**Curzio** **Orazio**	The two became friends during a week of traveling on foot from Napoli to Rome. Curzio asks Orazio the reason he left his home. Orazio says that he escaped from Venice after wounding his friend Decio, a Cypriot. He thinks he killed him. That was ten years ago, and his family thinks he (Orazio) has drowned[139], and that his real name is Sigismondo. Curzio asides that he is Decio, and he now realizes that Orazio is his enemy. Not revealing why, Curzio says angry words to Orazio. He tells him that he wants to punch him. Orazio won't fight his friend[140] and **Orazio exits** up the street. Curzio monologues that he should have killed Orazio, also that he (Curzio) came secretly after his sister, who has come from Napoli, and that she has to come to Rome to visit their dying (now dead)[141] father, and that he needs to learn where the house is.
1.03	**Zani**	[Zani has some food] Curzio recognizes Zani as the servant of his beloved's father. Suddenly he is obsessed with finding a way to reunite with Isabella. Curzio pretends to be a necromancer. In a lazzo, Curzio gets Zani to reveal which house is Magnifico's. Zani also lets it slip about Magnifico's secret treasure.[142] Curzio reveals who he is, and demands Zani keep it a secret, lest something happen to the treasure.[143] They both agree that Curzio will be called Pietro and pretend to be Zani's son[144]. **Curzio exits** up the street.

[139] "perche casso nel aqua", Cancelled himself in the water? Pretended to drown, faking his own death?
[140] A word is omitted from the manuscript. Here we inserted 'friend' as the missing word.
[141] The manuscript doesn't say that the father is dead, but she is here, and the father isn't.
[142] This is the first and only mention of the treasure. This is probably a que for a lazzo of telling too much.
[143] Added plot point to help explain why Zani agrees to everything that follows.
[144] The plot point about the son is invented here to support the events in 1.10.

1.04 [145]	**Trastulo**	Trastulo has arrived ahead of Isabella to let Magnifico know that she will arrive shortly. They speak excitedly of a servants' view of the travel. Trastulo is excited about having travelled with Agnese. Zani is jealous. Zani gives Trastulo some food and drink, and Trastulo races off to let Isabella know that Magnifico is ready for her. **Trastulo exits** up the street. Zani knocks at the door of the house and calls Magnifico.
1.05	**Magnifico**	Zani tells Magnifico that his daughter is coming. They agree that Cipriota should be told that her old friend Isabella is returning.[146] They go to knock at the house of Cipriota[147].
1.06	**Cipriota**	She shoos them away. Magnifico goes back to his door and **Magnifico exits** into his house. **Zani exits** up the street.[148] Cipriota gives a monomaniacal monologue that she is looking for revenge one day for her brother Decio who was treacherously killed. **Cipriota exits** into her house.
1.07	**Orazio** **Capitano Gamberro**	Orazio asides his worry that he wants to avoid Curzio who wants to fight him.[149] Orazio hires Gamberro as protection.
1.08 [150]	**Cipriota**	[At her window] Orazio sees Cipriota, he recognizes her as the one he has been following for love in Napoli[151]. Orazio greets her. She receives his greeting and thanks him for his offers. She says that she loves him, but that she can only marry the one who will put the head of her enemy into her hands. Orazio offers himself. She says there will be time. She bids goodbye, they split. **Cipriota exits** into her house. **Orazio and Gamberro exit** up the street.
1.09	**Isabella** **Agnese**	Isabella and Agnese, give details about their trip from Napoli. (*This is an opportunity for Isabella to be upbeat and convinced that it is time to put Decio aside and look for new love*).

---

[145] This scene is not in the original but is inserted to justify Zani knowing that Isabella will soon arrive, plus it gives Trastulo a little extra stage time.

[146] In the manuscript, no reason is given for them to knock on Cipriota's door.

[147] They must just be planning to look for her, because she arrives, and they are both still there.

[148] In the manuscript it is not clear what door Zani goes to, or whether he stays at the door to overhear or not. Context says that he doesn't overhear.

[149] This aside is inserted to make it clear why Orazio and Curzio don't have scenes together after 1.02 until the finale.

[150] We split 1.07 to give Cipriota a chance to exit and reenter.

[151] The manuscript doesn't mention that his following happened in Napoli, but that is inserted here to match our backstory.

1.10 [152]	**Trastulo**	Trastulo lets them know the house is ready to receive them. Trastulo flirts with Agnese.
1.11	**Zani**	Zani flirts with Agnese, Trastulo reacts. Zani leads them to the house of Magnifico.
1.12	**Magnifico**	Magnifico, at his door, welcomes them. **Isabella, Agnese, and Trastulo exit** into Magnifico's house. Zani and Magnifico begin to discuss plans for hospitality. They are interrupted.
1.13	**Curzio/Pietro**	[Disguised as a porter] Zani pretends that Curzio is his (Zani's) son, Pietro; Magnifico receives him in the house. Happily, **Zani, Curzio, and Magnifico exit** into Magnifico's house.

Act II

2.01	**Zani** **Trastulo**[153]	[Zani has beer[154]]. Zani cheers. Trastulo is opposed to beer. They speak competitively about Agnese.
2.02 [155]	**Curzio/Pietro** **Isabella** **Agnese**	[Pietro and Agnese have beer] Pietro offers Isabella beer from his cup, Isabella is taken by love, because Pietro resembles her lover (*Note: He is her former lover, now with a new name*). Pietro asides about his delight. She drinks from the cup. Trastulo complains that they should not be drinking beer.
2.03	**Magnifico**	Magnifico drives away Pietro. Magnifico is angry at Trastulo for Isabella's condition and fires him. Tipsy Isabella says to Agnese, let's visit my friend Cipriota. Trastulo follows. **Isabella, Agnese, and Trastulo exit** into Cipriota's house. **Curzio (as Pietro) exits** up the street. Zani, fearing also being fired, pretends to be a necromancer, says that he will use his powers to get Magnifico a lover. Magnifico does a lazzo of imagining caressing a woman[156]. Magnifico orders Zani to go and find her in the square. Zani has a cup of beer. **Magnifico exits** into his house.

---

[152] Scene 1.09 has been split into three scenes to allow characters to establish themselves a few at a time.

[153] Trastulo and his plot point were added to this scene to give him more stage time, and to add to the implied beer lazzo.

[154] Schiuma, literally "foam". From context we guess this means Beer/Ale? It makes characters happy and sloppy.

[155] Scene 2.01 has been split to allow Zani and Trastulo to establish more of their competition to romance Agnese.

[156] In the manuscript Magnifico caresses Zani.

2.04	**Cipriota**	Zani tells her about Pietro as his (fake) son. She should meet him.[157] (*Note: what Zani says cannot include that Pietro is really her brother Decio*). She sends him away. **Zani exits** up the street.
2.05	**Orazio** **Cap. Gamberro**	Orazio begs her (Cipriota) to tell him the name of her enemy. She says that she will give it to him in writing later. Orazio should send Gamberro for the note and punish Magnifico[158] for sending Isabella and Trastulo to her house. To kick out the interlopers, **Cipriota exits** into her house. Orazio asides that he doesn't want to encounter Magnifico, because Magnifico is his father, and he doesn't want to reveal himself just yet. Orazio tells Gamberro to do as the lady asks and harass Magnifico about the drunken revelers in Cipriota's house.[159] **Orazio exits** up the street. Gamberro begins talking about his glorious past[160] but is interrupted.
2.06	**Trastulo** **Isabella** **Agnese**	[From Cipriota's house] Agnese takes the tipsy Isabella to Magnifico's house. **Isabella and Agnese exit**. Trastulo complains that Magnifico mistreated him by firing such a loyal servant. Trastulo wants revenge against Magnifico. Gamberro asides that this man (Trastulo) will beat Magnifico, saving him the trouble. **Gamberro exits** up the street. Trastulo hears noises and stands aside.
2.07	**Magnifico** **Curzio/Pietro**	Magnifico and Pietro do the lazzo of weak fighting[161]. When Magnifico is exhausted, Magnifico asks for Trastulo's help. Magnifico rehires Trastulo, Trastulo beats Curzio and **all exit** in a chase.

Act III

3.01	**Isabella** **Agnese**[162]	Isabella monologues that she wants to reveal her love to Pietro. Agnese cautions her against trusting her feelings when drinking beer.[163]

---

[157] It is not clear what Zani tells her.

[158] Stefanello in the manuscript (same character)

[159] This seems to be Cipriota's plan, but how will a beating help? Perhaps because Magnifico was a poor host, and his drunken daughter came to her house.

[160] Gamberro's monologue is an added plot point to fill the gap before Trastulo's entrance.

[161] This is the lazzo of weak defense. Both men are pathetic fighters.

[162] Trastulo is not in this scene in the original.

[163] Added plot point, to help give Trastulo an adversarial role here.

3.02	**Curzio/Pietro** **Zani** **Trastulo**	Isabella declares her love to Pietro. Pietro asides to her that he is Decio and has loved her constantly.[164] Zani from the window lifts his beer[165]. Pietro promises to receive her as a wife. **Curzio (as Pietro) and Isabella exit** to get married.[166] Zani and Trastulo competitively alternate wooing Agnese. **Agnese exits.** **Trastulo and Zani exit** in opposite directions.[167]
3.03	**Cap. Gamberro**	Gamberro goes to Cipriota for the note.
3.04	**Cipriota**	[Cipriota has a note] She gives the note to Capitano. **Cipriota exits**[168] into her house. Gamberro calls Orazio.[169]
3.05	**Orazio**	Seeing the note, Orazio realizes he, himself, is Cipriota's enemy. Orazio laments and eventually resolves to present himself to Cipriota. Horrified, Gamberro refuses to help and **Gamberro exits.**
3.06	**Magnifico**	Magnifico recognizes Orazio as his son. Magnifico calls Orazio by the name Sigismondo. They have a scene of reuniting. Orazio tells Magnifico that he still loves Cipriota and has unfinished business with her. Magnifico agrees to let him woo Cipriota. Orazio calls Cipriota.
3.07	**Cipriota**	Orazio presents himself to her as her enemy; Cipriota is uncertain whether to kill him. She is interrupted.

---

[164] This assertion is not in the manuscript but is implied by Isabella's actions.

[165] "Zani da la finestra che schiumi", Literally this means to be foaming the window. Does he throw beer on the window? Is it a toast to the wedding?

[166] In the manuscript Curzio exits to get dressed, and Isabella goes into the house, perhaps also to dress-up. There is no separate scene with them going off to make it official, but they show up at the end already married. Here, they exit together to avoid the issue of how they got together again to enter in 3.08.

[167] This monologue and exit are not in the manuscript. Added here to complete Trastulo's story.

[168] This exit is implied in the manuscript.

[169] This calling plot point is implied by Orazio's arrival in the next scene.

3.08	**Curzio/Pietro** **Isabella**[170] **Agnese**	Curzio says that he wants to kill Orazio. Curzio reveals that he is alive and is Cipriota's brother Decio. Decio tells Orazio that he has married Isabella. Isabella pleads for the life of her brother.[171] Orazio proposes to marry Cipriota. Everything is revealed. Cipriota accepts. Magnifico accepts the situation. **Orazio and Cipriota exit** into her house.
		Curzio and Isabella exit into Magnifico's house.
3.09 [172]	**Zani** **Trastulo**	[With beer] Magnifico complains that Zani never used his power as a necromancer to get Magnifico a lover. Zani confesses that he is not a necromancer, but that beer can help you get a lover. Trastulo says that beer will never help you get a lover. Each tries to prove their point by wooing Agnese. Agnese makes an overture to Magnifico. Magnifico accepts. **Magnifico and Agnese exit**.
		Zani and Trastulo realize their loss. Zani offers the beer to Trastulo. **Zani and Trastulo exit**.

---

[170] In the manuscript, Isabella does not enter at the end of Act III. This entrance was added for a more complete happy ending, but it means you need separate actors to play Cipriota and Isabella.
[171] This plot point for Isabella helps clarify how the people angry at Orazio begin to accept him and remember their love for him.
[172] This is an added scene to give Zani a final goodbye and wrap up a plot point.

In Between

This is a pastoral play taking place in a magical world. A Sorceress is obsessed with a handsome young shepherd and attempts to use her magical powers to get him to love her.

Dramatis Personae   5M-4F-1N + Extras

Flori	An evil sorceress
Argano	A monster
Zani	Servant of Magnifico
Sireno	A young man
Orfinio	Friend of Sireno
Laura[173]	Wife of Magnifico
Magnifico	A man
Delia	Daughter of Magnifico
Rosalba[174]	A good witch
Demogorgon	A big monster
Centaur	A centaur
Spirit	
Prisoners[175]	Released at the end of Act III.

Props

Food
A chest with Zani's head
Spell book
Magic dagger
Shield

Set: four places
• Flori's cave
• The tower-prison
• Well
• Tree

Special Skills and Effects

- A tree gets burned.
- Zani's head is in a box, and then there is a fire (in the box?)
- Zani turns into a frog.
- Animals untie a rope.

Performance Considerations

- The manuscript does not say, but it is possible to play Sireno and Orfinio as Satyrs (the manuscript calls this a 'satire') and Delia as a nymph. Alternatively, the men could be shepherds, and Delia and Laura are human.
- Several of the characters have very little stage time and few if any plot points.

---

[173] In the manuscript she is a nameless wife. Having a name is helpful to the actors.
[174] In the original, the good witch is nameless. Here we have borrowed a name from a Scala pastoral.
[175] The prisoners could be volunteers from the audience, who come out and dance at the end.

Relationship Diagram

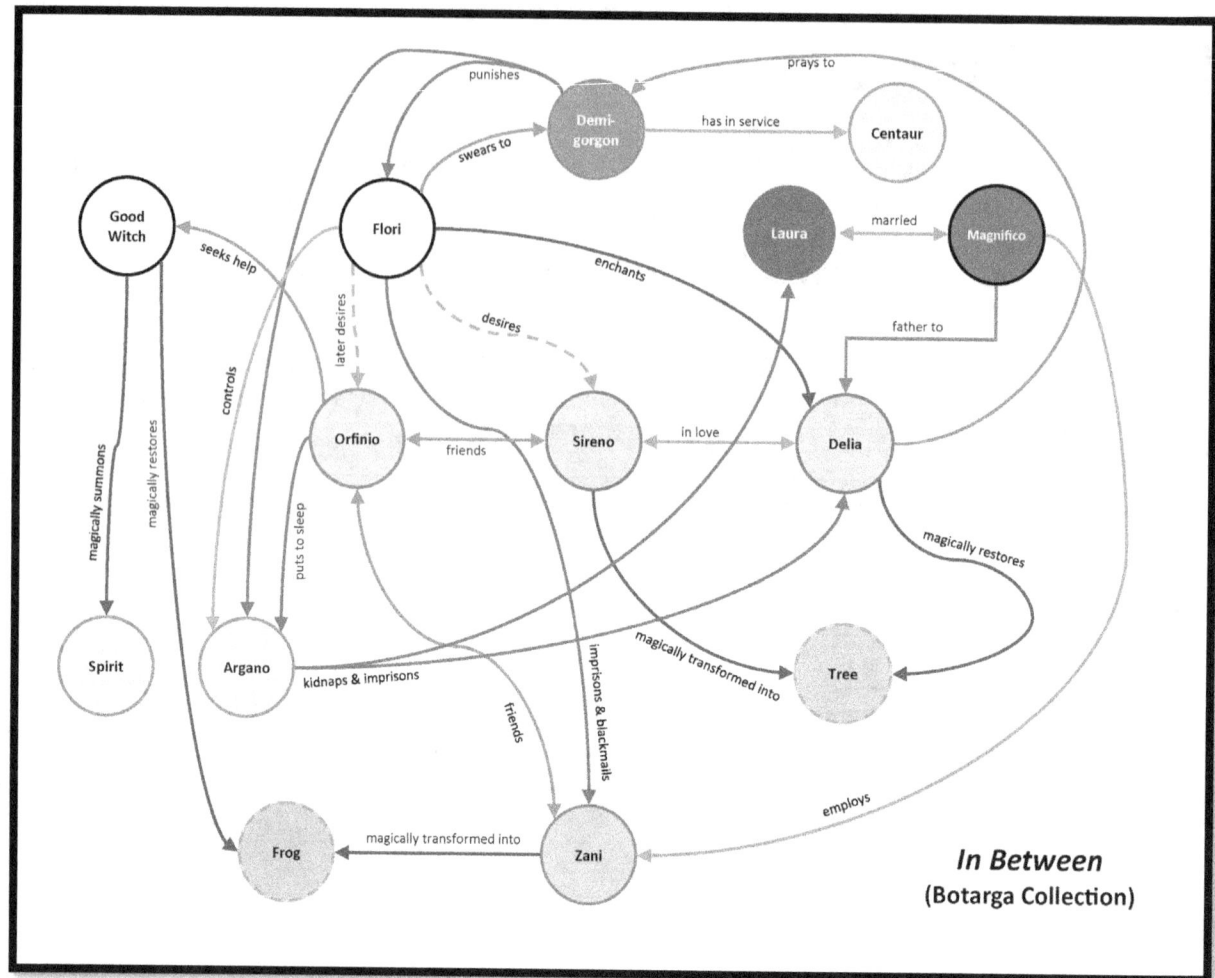

In Between
(Botarga Collection)

Backstory (Argomento)[176]

Flori, a witch corrupted by her own magic, has become obsessed with desire for Sireno, a young man. Sireno is in love with Delia, a young woman or nymph. Flori plans to use her powers to force her way in this love situation.

---

[176] There are no backstories in the manuscript. The one constructed here answers the questions of how the characters knew each other, traveled at the same time, and yet didn't recognize each other until the play starts. It is possible to answer these questions with some other backstory if you are motivated to do so.

Act I

1.01	Flori (La Maga)	Flori monologues, complaining about her unreturned love for Sireno. She wants to use her magic arts to make him do what she wants although she knows that he is in love with Delia. She calls Argano.
1.02	Argano (monster) Zani	[Zani is inside the cave] Flori commands Argano to take all the women of Arcadia as prisoners. Zani yells from inside. Flori calls him.
1.03	Zani	Zani begs her for mercy. She will free him if he promises him to convince Sireno to leave Delia and love her. He promises that to her. **Flori and Argano exit.** Happy to be free, **Zani exits.**
1.04	Sireno Orfinio	Orfinio praises eating[177] and Sireno praises love. They are interrupted.
1.05	Zani	[Dressed as a judge] Zani praises food. They do a lazzo of teasing. Zani reveals that Flori has used her magic book to imprison him but has freed him with conditions.[178] They promise each other to help and **Sireno, Orfinio, and Zani exit.**
1.06	Argano Laura	[Argano stole Laura] Laura calls out Magnifico's name pleading for help.
1.07	Magnifico	Magnifico shouts at Argano. Argano takes Laura as a prisoner. **Argano and Laura exit.** Complaining, **Magnifico exits.**
1.08	Delia	Delia monologues about the love of Sireno[179] and that Flori disturbs her. Still, Sireno loves her
1.09	Sireno	Delia and Sireno caress each other. They are interrupted.
1.10	Argano	Argano steals Delia from Sireno. **Argano and Delia exit** into the cave. Sireno becomes desperate. **Sireno exits.**
1.11	Orfinio	[Orfinio has food] Orfinio eats.
1.12	Zani	Zani and Orfinio do a lazzo about food. **Zani and Orfinio exit.**

[177] The manuscript doesn't specify who praises eating, but the story (see 1.11) suggests it is Orfinio.
[178] This is an added plot point, so that the subject of "The Book" doesn't come out of the blue in 2.06.
[179] Not clear if it is Sireno's love of her, or mutual love, but 1.09 strongly suggests that it is mutual.

Act II

2.01	**Flori (La Maga)**	[A chest is at the mouth of the cave] Flori is cheerful because Delia was taken, and she predicts that Sireno will now love her. To torment Delia, **Flori exits** into the cave.
2.02	Sireno	Sireno monologues, complaining about Delia's imprisonment. He is interrupted.
2.03	Zani	Zani promises to help him. With the food and wine, Zani wants to make Argano[180] fall asleep.
2.04	Argano	[In the tower prison] Zani praises him. Argano lowers himself from the tower. Zani and Argano are convivial. This makes Argano fall asleep. **Argano falls asleep** and snores. Zani goes to the chest where the book is. Sireno looks at the chest. He takes the chest out. They open it and find Zani's head in there. Zani panics. There is a fire[181]. **Zani transforms into a frog.**[182] **Zani exits.**
2.05	**Sireno**	Sireno despairs. The book was not in the chest.[183] He is interrupted.
2.06 184	Orfinio	Orfinio consoles Sireno and tells him that this is the hour that the sorceress sleeps. To get the book, **Orfinio exits** into the cave.
2.07	**Orfinio** **Flori**	[Flori is tied up in the mouth of the cave] Orfinio says that he has tied her up. An animal, lion, or gelding unties the rope.
2.08		[Flori is now untied] Flori laughs at Orfinio and Sireno, mocking them. She wakes up Argano and scolds him and kicks him into the tower. **Argano exits.** Sireno begs Flori to give him Delia. To torment Delia, she says that if he gives her (Flori) a kiss, that yes, she will release Delia. Sireno doesn't trust her and makes her swear on the Demogorgon god that she will release Delia if Sireno kisses her (Flori).

---

180 In the manuscript the word is savage. The next scene strongly implies that this refers to Argano.
181 What is on fire? Not certain, the manuscript is damaged.
182 Missing text, perhaps Zani is turned into a frog here.
183 This is an added plot point to make clear that the book is still in the cave somewhere.
184 This scene is split to make clear Orfinio's new entrance.

| 2.09 | **Delia** **Argano** | Sireno looks at Delia, and kisses Flori. Fiori is indignant that Sireno's attention was not on her during the kiss. Flori waves her arms and **transforms Delia into a tree**.

Flori says that Delia will not return unless she is burned. **Flori and Argano exit** into her cave.

Orfinio tells him about a witch who can counteract Flori's spells. **Orfinio exits**.

Sireno hugs the tree. **Sireno exits**. |
| 2.10 | **Magnifico** | Magnifico echoes[185] Sireno and asks the absent Flori to return Laura. He is interrupted. |
| 2.11 [186] | **Orfinio** **Sireno** **Frog-Zani** **Rosalba** | Orfinio and Sireno bring tied-up frog-Zani. Rosalba the witch summons a spirit. |
| 2.12 | **Spirit** | The spirit tells Sireno to go to a nearby well. There Sireno will find a shield. The spirit says that with the shield, Sireno can remove the strength of the sorceress and take the book from her. She will then be powerless. Rosalba frees the spirit. **The spirit exits**.

Rosalba removes the spell and Zani is human again[187]. Zani talks about his happiness with being restored to human form. **They all exit (except tree-Delia)**. |

Act III

| 3.01 | **Argano** **Flori** | Flori orders Argano to give her a magic dagger with which if she wounds Sireno, he will be compelled to love her. **Argano exits into the cave**. |
| 3.02 | **Zani** | Zani tells Flori he has spoken well about her to Sireno.[188] Flori is happy about this.[189] **Flori exits**.

Zani stays. |
| 3.03 | **Sireno** | Sireno goes to the well with Zani. They pull up the shield from the well. |

---

[185] The manuscript says that Magnifico "echoes". This stage direction appears in other plays in this collection and usually means that this character says something similar to what has recently been said.
[186] This scene was split to emphasize the entrance of the spirit.
[187] There is some sense that tied-up Zani was the frog, who is now transformed back to a human.
[188] Not clear what this means, because of too many pronouns. Is Zani working on Flori's side?
[189] This is an added plot point to make her reaction clear.

3.04	**Flori**	[Flori has the dagger and the book] Sireno asks her for Delia. Flori says she does not want to give her back to him. Sireno reveals the shield. She is stunned and falls. Sireno takes the book from her. He reads and finds out how one must burn the tree. **Sireno and Zani**[190] **exit.**
3.05	**Orfinio**	Orfinio sees the stunned sorceress and the dagger. He takes the dagger and wants to use it to kill her. Flori regains consciousness. He scratches her with the dagger.[191] She falls in love with Orfinio. She begs him to love her. Orfinio runs away from her. She follows close behind. **Orfinio and Flori exit.**
3.06	**Sireno** **Zani**	[With torches to burn the tree] Sireno and Zani give prayers to Demogorgon.
3.07	**Demogorgon** **A Centaur** **Flori**	[Flori is tied up] The Centaur is leading Flori, who he just tied up.[192] Demogorgon takes the book from Sireno and tells him to burn the tree. They burn it, **Delia comes out.** Sireno embraces her.
3.08	**Orfinio** **Flori**	Demogorgon throws the book, the dagger, the shield into the well. He forbids Flori from using the magic arts.
3.09	**Argano**	Demorgogon strikes Argano with lightning, turning him human again[193].
3.10	**Prisoners**	The prisoners come out, celebrating[194]. Sireno and Delia do a love scene and agree to marry. Flori promises delicious food to Orfinio, he realizes that he loves her, and they agree to marry. Their mission accomplished, **Demogorgon and the Centaur exit.**
3.11	**Magnifico**[195] **Laura**	Magnifico looks at the released prisoners and does not see Laura. Dancing with joy, **the prisoners exit.** He calls for her, and with an elderly gait, Laura comes out at last. Magnifico and Laura reunite. **Magnifico, Laura, Orfinio, Flori, Sireno, and Delia exit.** Zani and Argano do a quick lazzo. **Zani and Argano exit.**

[190] The manuscript doesn't say when Zani exits, but he reenters with Sireno, so he exits here.
[191] Added plot-point, seems implied from actions in the original.
[192] Added plot-point, explains how Flori is tied up, and gives Centaur something to do.
[193] In the manuscript Argano is struck by lightning and never mentioned again.
[194] The bulk of the plot points in this scene are invented for this version. In the original the play ends with no exits, and no concrete resolutions mentioned. Here we supply the obvious resolutions.
[195] In the manuscript, there is a mention of Magnifico's daughter entering here as well. She has no plot points, and is otherwise not mentioned in the play, so we left her out of this scene.

Jove & Io

This is a short play that can have wonderful spectacle if you build the right stage equipment. It is about Jove and his love of a young woman that incurs the wrath of his jealous wife Juno.

Dramatis Personae   4M-2F + a Cow

Inachus	King of Argos
Io	Daughter of Inachus
Jove	King of the gods
Juno	Wife of Jove
Argo	A giant with many eyes
Mercury	Messenger of the gods
Cow	Io in disguise

Props

Sword for Mercury
Cloud
Cow costume

Set: two places
• Outdoors
• Heaven

Special Skills and Effects

- Io transforms into a cow.
- A cloud surrounds Io and later lifts.
- Mercury transforms (into a great singer/poet)
- The actor playing Mercury must have good musical performance skills.
- A gadfly prop is needed to irritate the cow.

Performance Considerations

- We need to set up in Act I that Inachus cares a lot for his daughter.
- Argo has to be a sufficiently unsympathetic character that Mercury is not a villain for killing him.
- At the end of Act III, we need a heart-rending dialog between Jove and Juno that results in Juno overcoming her jealousy and freeing Io.

Relationship Diagram

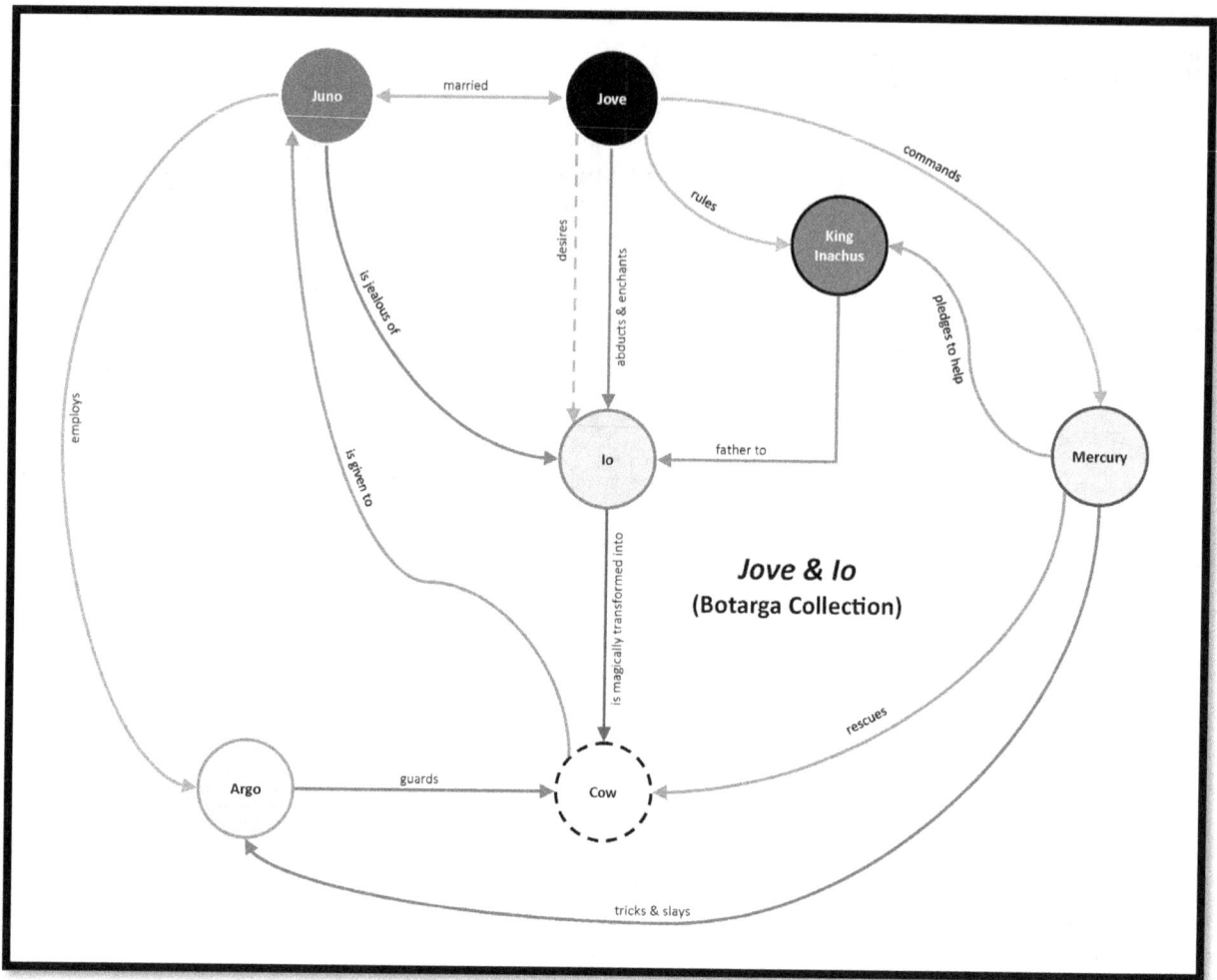

Backstory (Argomento)[196]

Io was the princess of Argos, and daughter of King Inachus and a lovely Nymph. Jove was quite taken with her, but fearing consequences from his jealous wife Juno, he made some rash choices.

Act I

1.01	Inachus Io	Io tells her father, Inachus, that she does not want to depart from him.[197] **Inachus exits**.
1.02	Jove	Jove forcefully takes Io away with him. He hears Juno and he covers Io with a cloud.

---

[196] There are no backstories in the manuscript. The one constructed here tells the minimum.
[197] There needs to be something explaining why Inachus wants to leave her behind. Did he previously make a deal with Jove, the king of the gods?

1.03	Juno	Juno asks Jove what is covered under the cloud. He says it is nothing. Finally, the cloud disappears, and Io comes out as a cow. She asks Jove to give the cow to her. Trapped, Jove obliges and gives her the cow. **Jove, Juno and the cow exit.**

Act II

2.01	Juno Argo Io	Juno gives the cow to Argo to be guarded. **Juno exits.** **Argo and the Cow exit.**
2.02	Jove Mercury	Jove orders Mercury to get the cow from Argo. **Jove exits.** Mercury says that to do this job, he needs to transform himself. **Mercury exits.**
2.03	Inachus	Inachus laments the loss of the daughter.
2.04	Io-cow	She moos and writes with the foot. Inachus recognizes her as his daughter. He grieves. They are interrupted.
2.05	Argo	Argo drives Inachus away (to the far side of the stage). Argo takes the cow and **Argo and the Cow exit.** Inachus prays to Jove.
2.06	Jove	[From the sky] Jove promises Inachus that his daughter, Io, will return. **Jove withdraws.** After a brief monologue[198], **Inachus exits.**

Act III

3.01	Mercury Argo The Cow	[Mercury is transformed] Argo praises himself for guarding the cow. Mercury praises Argo, sings, makes him fall asleep, and then cuts off his head. [...][199]. Mercury prepares to take the cow. **Mercury exits.**
3.02	Juno	Juno screams from Heaven and sends a Fury to the cow. **Juno Withdraws.**
3.03 200	Gadfly	A big stinging insect pursues the cow.
3.03	Jove Inachus	Jove covers the cow with a cloud. **The Gadfly exits.**

---

[198] This monologue isn't mentioned in the manuscript but is implied.
[199] In the manuscript this line was cut for the binding. Up to ten words might state what happens to Argo's body.
[200] Added scene to show the gadfly and cow physical comedy.

| 3.04 | Juno | Jove requests Io's restoration as a grace. Juno pulls the cloud back to herself. **Jove and Juno exit**. [201] |
| | | Io comes out of the cow; her father, Inachus, embraces her. **Io and Inachus exit**. |

---

[201] Note that in the manuscript the order of Juno's appearance, and the movement of the cloud seem out of sequence. We have corrected here for it to make sense.

The Lion

Here we have the Piramus and Thisbe play as a comedy, including what might be played as a sarcastic lion.

Dramatis Personae   7M+2F + extras

Magnifico	A merchant
Zani	Servant of Magnifico
Francese	Servant of Magnifico
Orazio	A young man
Trastulo	Servant of Orazio
Ortenzia	Daughter of Magnifico
Curzio	A high-ranking young nobleman
Capitano Gamberro	Soldier for Curzio
Isabella	A young woman
A Lion	Several scenes, no lines
The Signore	An older nobleman (Deus-ex-machina)
Porters	1 scene

Props

Wine and cheese
Ropes, a veil
Treasure chest
Big clay pot
Mud

Set: two houses, plus
• Magnifico's house
• The guard house
• Isabella's house
• A well
• The woods

Special Skills and Effects

- People fall into the well and should make a splash noise.
- Someone will want to work out how to move and look like a lion.
- People use ropes to pull others out of the well.

Performance Considerations

- The actors playing Francese & Trastulo can also play the Lion and the Signore.
- Curzio must be played to make him worthy of love at the end.
- In 3.06 the Lion makes fun of the two broken-hearted lovers. The director will need to choose how anthropomorphized the lion is before performing that scene.
- There is a sonnet-length poem that two people have to memorize.

Relationship Diagram

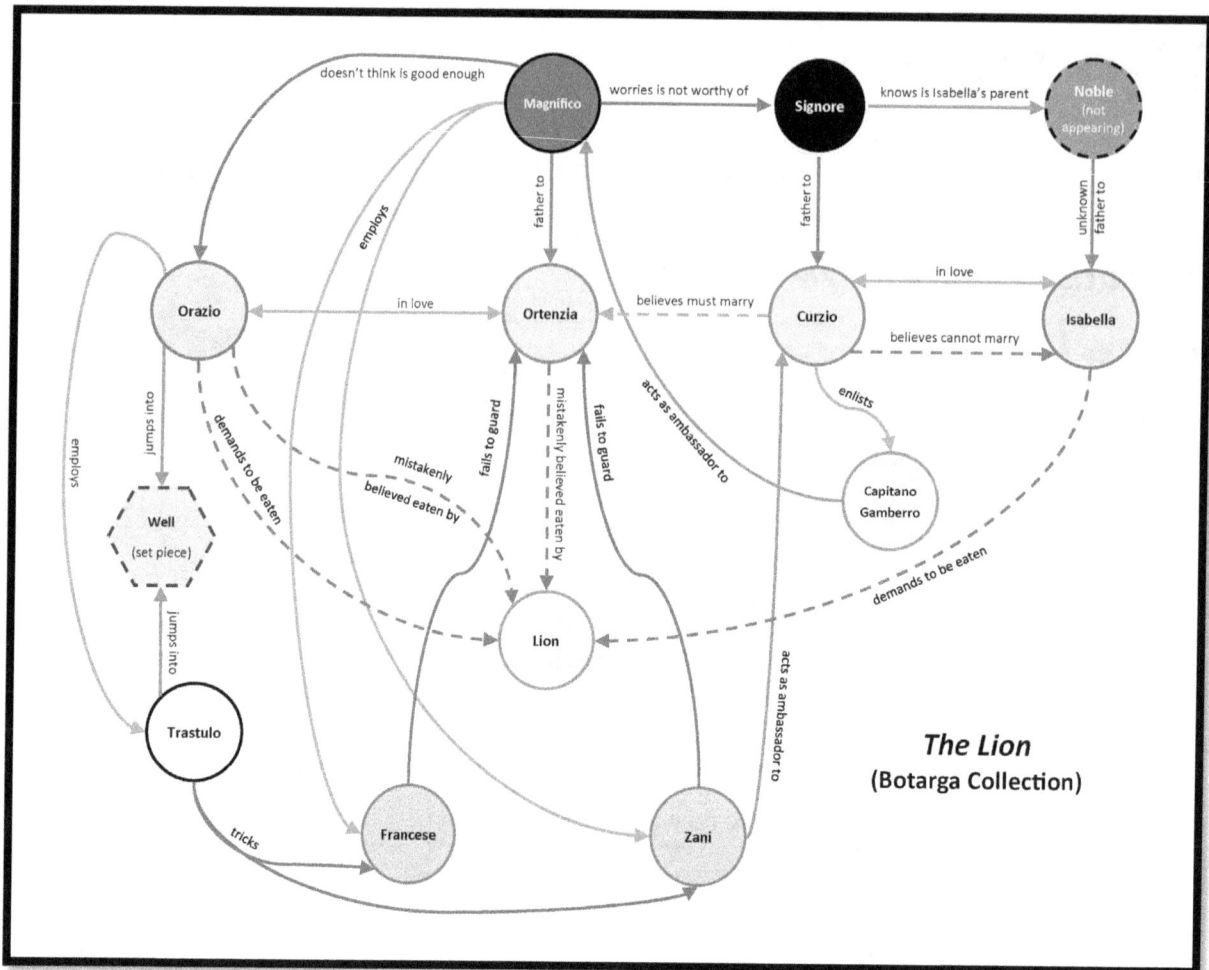

The Lion
(Botarga Collection)

Backstory (Argomento)[202]

Isabella loves the Signore's son Curzio. Unbeknownst to anyone, including her, she is the orphaned daughter of a wealthy nobleman of whose fortune the Signore has been the custodian. She has some token or birthmark that proves it. Orazio and Ortenzia love each other, but Ortenzia's father wants her to marry someone more worthy than Orazio.

---

[202] There are no backstories in the manuscript. The one constructed here tells the minimum.

Act I

1.01	**Magnifico** **Zani** **Francese**	Magnifico puts Zani and Francese on guard duty[203]. Magnifico says he came to stay in the country villa because he doesn't want to give Ortenzia to Orazio. **Zani and Francese exit into the guard house**.
1.02	**Orazio**	Orazio monologues about having followed Ortenzia and her father, Magnifico.[204] Orazio asks Magnifico for Ortenzia' hand in marriage. Magnifico replies that he doesn't want to give her to him. They argue. Magnifico tells the guards to keep Orazio away from Ortenzia. From inside, Francese, Zani agree. **Magnifico exits**. Orazio complains, including that he has only a little money.
1.03	**Trastulo**	Orazio promises Trastulo a favor if he finds a way of letting Orazio speak to Ortenzia. Trastulo has a plan and goes to get cheese and wine. **Trastulo exits**. **Orazio stands aside**.[205] At that:
1.04	**Zani**	Zani is at the door of the guard house.[206]
1.05	**Trastulo**	[With wine and cheese] Trastulo asks Zani to come out. Trastulo tells Zani that he won't have to share the cheese with Francese if he goes down the street to eat it.[207] **Zani exits**.
1.06	**Francese**	Francese is at the door of the guard house. Trastulo asks Francese to come out. Trastulo tells Francese that he won't have to share the wine with Zani if he goes down the street to drink it. **Francese exits**. Orazio and Trastulo call Ortenzia.
1.07	**Ortenzia**	Orazio and Ortenzia have a love scene.[208] Ortenzia promises to be his wife. They hear people coming. **Orazio and Trastulo exit** fleeing. **Ortenzia exits** into the house.

---

[203] The Italian says "bona guardia", which means "good guard". In context it simply seems to mean guard duty, other stage directions suggest that there must be a guard house.
[204] This monologue is implied in the original.
[205] In the Italian it says he retires, which may mean sits down, or otherwise relaxes.
[206] In the Italian it simply says that Zani is on guard.
[207] This specific ploy (in this scene and the next) isn't specified in the original, only that Zani gets the cheese and exits.
[208] This love scene is implied in the original

1.08 [209]	Zani Francese	[Francese is drunk] Zani and Francese do a lazzo about recognizing that they were played. **Zani and Francese exit** into the guard house.
1.09 [210]	Orazio	Orazio monologues about his love of Ortenzia. Hearing people coming he hides at the edge of the stage. **Orazio hides**.
1.10	Curzio Capitano Gamberro	Curzio monologues that his father, the Signore, wants him to marry a wealthy girl. He loves Isabella, but she is poor and is poorly regarded by everyone. He believes Ortenzia, daughter of Magnifico, would satisfy his father.[211] They call.
1.11	Isabella	Curzio tells Isabella that he prefers Ortenzia. After a scene of bitter dialog, in pain, **Isabella exits**. Curzio sends Gamberro to Magnifico to ask for Ortenzia. **Curzio exits**. Gamberro calls for Magnifico.
1.12	Magnifico	Gamberro asks Magnifico for Ortenzia for his master, Curzio. Magnifico, says he does not believe that the family of high-born Curzio really wants his daughter[212]. After a lazzo[213] Magnifico calls Zani.
1.13	Zani	Magnifico tells Zani that he wants him to go with Gamberro as an ambassador[214] to the Signore. To discuss details, they enter the house. **Zani, Curzio, Gamberro, and Magnifico exit** into Magnifico's house.
1.14	Orazio Trastulo	**Orazio steps forward** as Trastulo enters. Orazio, knowing he will lose Ortenzia, spirals in desperation. At the end, he throws himself into the well.[215] **Orazio exits** into the well. Trastulo, screams: "**help**", **Trastulo exits**.

---

[209] 1.08 was two scenes giving Zani and Francese separate parallel scenes. Here combined into one to give them more opportunity to invent some comedy together.

[210] This is an added scene that was implied by the final scene in the act in which Orazio has heard everything.

[211] This scene was changed to make Curzio a more sympathetic man to justify his happy ending.

[212] In the manuscript, it simply says that Magnifico doesn't believe him, clarity about what isn't believed is added here.

[213] In the original it simply says: "in the end". The lazzo is implied.

[214] The Italian is ambiguous as to intent. Based on events in Act 2, here it is assumed that Zani will be an ambassador for Magnifico to Curzio to find Curzio's intentions.

[215] This is a minor change from how it is expressed in the Italian, but is essentially the same action, just more specific.

Act II

2.01	**Magnifico** **Capitano Gamberro** **Zani**	Magnifico gives Zani the ambassadorial message. **Gamberro and Zani exit**. Magnifico monologues about his hopes for Ortenzia.[216] He is interrupted:
2.02	**Trastulo** **Porters**	[Trastulo has ropes] Trastulo says that Orazio threw himself into the well out of desperation.
2.03	**Orazio**	[Orazio has a treasure chest] Orazio shouts from the well. They pull him out with a treasure chest. Trastulo pays and dismisses the porters. **The porters exit**. Magnifico regrets not having given Ortenzia to Orazio; Magnifico makes offers. Orazio now does not want her because Magnifico has given her in marriage to Curzio. **Magnifico exits**. Orazio knocks for Ortenzia. **Trastulo stands aside** to observe.
2.04	**Ortenzia**	[At her window] They agree that she will run away, and Orazio will wait for her at the Fonte Bella by the back door. **Orazio exits, Ortenzia withdraws**. **Trastulo steps forward**, and after a monologue, Trastulo throws himself into the well to look for treasure. **Trastulo exits** into the well.
2.05	**Curzio** **Zani** **Capitano Gamberro**	Zani gives the ambassadorial message to Curzio. Curzio wants to tell Ortenzia before going to give the message to his father, the Signore.[217] **Curzio, Zani, and Gamberro exit**.
2.06	**Isabella** **Francese**[218]	Isabella sees Francese in the guardhouse, and in desperation calls him. They talk about the pain of lost love. **Francese exits** into the guardhouse. Convinced that a new life or death are the only two choices, **Isabella exits** into the woods.
2.07	**Ortenzia**	[Wearing a veil[219]] Ortenzia flees to find Orazio. **Ortenzia exits**.
2.08	**Magnifico**	Magnifico regrets again not giving his daughter to Orazio. Trastulo screams from the well.

[216] Added plot point that had been implied.
[217] In the original it isn't clear from the pronouns who is doing what. This reconstruction is consistent with actions in other scenes on these topics.
[218] Francese is added to this scene to let Isabella have a dialog about love, and to give Francese an entrance in Act 2.
[219] The veil is a disguise, or face covering.

2.09	**Trastulo**	[Trastulo, in the well, has a big clay pot full of treasure] Trastulo yells: "**Treasure!**". Magnifico becomes cheerful. They are interrupted:
2.10	**Zani**	Zani is also happy. They pull Trastulo up with his big clay pot. All three start to bitterly argue; they physically fight each other; they get dirty; Zani and Magnifico shout at Trastulo. **Trastulo exits**, running away with the treasure. *Note: this is Trastulo's final exit. He may well be yelling about being rich and nobody's servant.*
2.11	**Curzio** **Capitano Gamberro**	Curzio and Gamberro came for Ortenzia. Curzio wants to touch the hand of Magnifico; Magnifico, because his hands are dirty, hides himself. Magnifico sends Zani to call Ortenzia. **Zani exits** into the house. From inside, Zani shouts that he can't find Ortenzia. This repeats two or three times[220]. **Zani reenters.** Curzio and Gamberro grab their swords. **Zani and Magnifico exit** fleeing into the house. Gamberro says that the Signore will punish Magnifico. Curzio agrees. **Curzio and Gamberro exit.**
2.12	**Ortenzia**	Ortenzia monologues that she went to the Fonte Bella and that Orazio never came. **Zani shouts from inside.**
2.13	**Zani**	Zani grabs Ortenzia and wants to bring her with him to end Curzio's ire. They are interrupted:
2.14	**The Lion**	After a lazzo of panic, **Zani exits** escaping into the house. **Ortenzia exits** into the woods. **The lion exits** following Ortenzia.

Act III

3.01	**Orazio**	Orazio monologues a complaint about how he came to the Fonte Bella and did not find Ortenzia.
3.02	**Zani**	Zani tells Orazio that a lion came and that he thinks it devoured Ortenzia. They are interrupted:

---

[220] The Italian is ambiguous. Perhaps he calls her to come two or three times. Maybe Zani says she will come.

3.03	**The Lion**	[With Ortenzia's veil in its mouth] Orazio grieves and shouts. **The Lion exits** fleeing. Orazio follows the Lion. **Orazio exits**. Zani monologues about his fear that the lion would kill him if he followed it.
3.04	**Ortenzia**	Ortenzia laments that she could not find Orazio. Zani tells Ortenzia that the lion killed Orazio. Grieving, **Ortenzia exits**. After a sad aside, **Zani exits**.

3.05	**Orazio**
	Isabella
		Grieving that they want to die, they recite this poem:
		
		"Gentle spirit who, with such a clear trumpet,
		    you left the mortals an immortal cry
		    of virtue and honor, here is your faithful
		    husband sitting here today at your grave.
		Come, oh soul as beautiful as a dove,
		    to the murmuring of the bridegroom
		    and leave the dear nest of oblivion while I pierce
		    this dense air, which echoes in the sky.
		Here you come; and stay with me, oh noble spirit,
		    while I retell the pain of your death along with these
		shepherds.
		Receive, dear wife, these flowers,
		    sad sorrowful sign of this ominous fate,
		    for they are made of cypress, poplar, and myrtle."

3.06	**The Lion**	Orazio and Isabella beg the lion to kill them. (***Suggestion:*** *They do a lazzo of who is the saddest.*) The Lion makes fun of them, and **the lion exits**. After a monologue of desperation, **Isabella exits**.
3.07	**Capitano Gamberro** **Zani**[221] **Francese** **Curzio** **Magnifico**	Zani is surprised that Orazio is alive.[222] Orazio wants to kill or to be killed. After a lazzo of gentle combat so as not to damage Orazio, they tie up Orazio to take him to the Signore. Gamberro tells Orazio that he has business before the Signore, **All exit**.
3.08	**Ortenzia**	In a monologue, she laments Orazio's death and her own misfortune. She plans to do herself harm. She hears noises and is about to flee, but she is interrupted.[223] She sees Orazio. **Ortenzia stands aside** to observe.

[221] The manuscript just says Capitano and others. Here we specified who the others are.
[222] Added plot point, to remind us of Zani's previous state of mind.
[223] There is a bit missing from the manuscript. She is about to flee but is there for the next scene. This is our reconstruction.

3.09	**The Signore** **Magnifico** **Orazio** **Zani**[224] **Francese** **Capitano Gamberro** **Curzio**	[The Signore makes a grand entrance][225] While court is being set up,[226] The Signore discusses the plight of young lovers with Magnifico. The Signore sends Magnifico to get Isabella. **Magnifico and Francese exit**.[227] Orazio is held captive by Gamberro and the others, Orazio says he wants to die because Ortenzia was eaten by a lion. Curzio sobs, now imagining that the missing Isabella was the one eaten by a lion.[228]
3.10	Ortenzia[229]	**Ortenzia steps forward**. She tells Orazio not to die. There is a scene of romantic reunion. The signore opens his court. The signore gives Ortenzia to Orazio as a wife. Orazio and Ortenzia celebrate. Curzio complains, but the Signore tells him to be patient.
3.11	**Isabella** **Magnifico**	Isabella says that she had wanted to kill herself by fire. The Signore tells Curzio that he (The Signore) was wrong to insist that he marry Ortenzia for money.[230] The Signore tells Isabella of her inherited status.[231] After a genuine love scene, Curzio marries Isabella. In a celebratory procession, **the couples and vecchi exit**. Gamberro reveals to Zani and Francese how Orazio and Trastulo became wealthy. **Gamberro exits** following the Signore. After a short lazzo, **Zani and Francese exit** into the well.

---

[224] As in 3.07, the manuscript has the Signore, Orazio, and others entering. Here we have specified the others.

[225] This specified entrance is implied in the manuscript, but not stated explicitly.

[226] Setting up court is implied in the manuscript but not explicitly stated. The Signore is a man of very high rank, and in this and later scenes he decrees with authority.

[227] This is an added plot point.

[228] Added plot point to give Curzio another chance to seem worthy of a happy ending.

[229] 3.09 & 3.10 are one scene in the original but split here to allow Ortenzia's reentrance to involve more drama.

[230] Several of the plot points in this scene were implied but not directly stated in the original.

[231] As noted in the Backstory, you have flexibility as to how it is revealed that Isabella has inherited status.

The Three Cuckolds

This is unusual in that it has only two acts. Note that in other, later version of this play, there are no new scenes, but the acts are split to make a three-act play. This is a comedy in which three men are cuckolded, in a variation on musical chairs, and the odd man out burns down his own house.

Dramatis Personae   *4M-3F*

Magnifico	A wealthy man
Ortenzia	Magnifico's wife
Cassandro	A lemon merchant
Coralina	Cassandro's wife
Curzio	A handsome young man
Franceschina	Freelance servant
Zani	Freelance servant

Props

A wagon of lemons
A large, wheeled washtub
Firewood

Set: three houses
• Magnifico & Ortenzia's
• Cassandro & Coralina's
• Zani & Franceschina's

Special Skills and Effects:
- Simulating fire burning down Zani's house.
- The wagon of lemons must be big enough for Cassandro to hide under the lemons.
- The washtub big enough to carry Magnifico must be moveable by one person but fit through doors.

Performance Considerations:
- For this play to please the audience, they must be happy or hopeful for the success of some people, and not actually despise those being unfaithful to their spouses, unless you play it that Zani burning down his house is a rejection of world-wide immorality.

Relationship Diagram

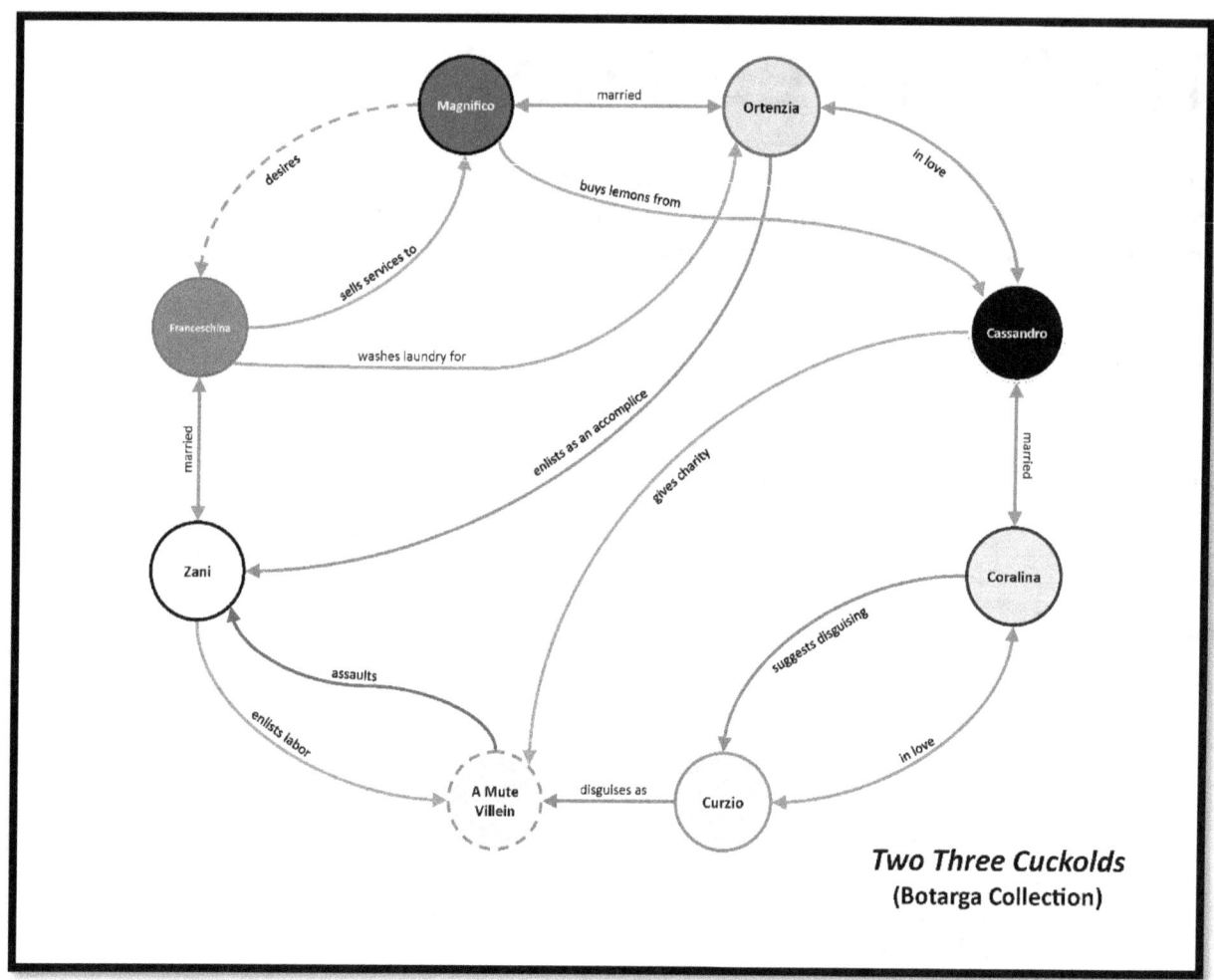

Two Three Cuckolds
(Botarga Collection)

Backstory (Argomento)

There are three couples, but, of late no one feels fulfilled by love.

Act I

1.01	**Magnifico** **Ortenzia**	They have a dialog about jealousy. Ortenzia asides that she sees Cassandro coming. She asks Magnifico for some lemons to donate to the convent.

1.02	**Cassandro**	[Pulling a wagon of lemons] Magnifico and Ortenzia ask for some lemons. He agrees to sell them some. **Magnifico exits** into his house.
		Ortenzia and Cassandro discuss their love, and whether they could arrange a tryst if he could hide in the wagon of lemons. **Cassandro exits** up the street.
		Ortenzia exits into her house.
1.03	**Curzio**	Curzio monologues about his forbidden love for Cassandro's wife Coralina. He knocks at Cassandro's door.
1.04	**Coralina**	[At her window] Coralina tells Curzio to go dress as an urban peasant. **Curzio exits** up the street.
		Coralina withdraws.
1.05	**Franceschina**	Franceschina monologues about "the pregnancy".[232] She wants to do her laundry. She calls Zani.
1.06	**Zani**	Franceschina sends Zani to get firewood. **Zani exits** up the street.
1.07	**Magnifico**	Magnifico is romantically and physically passionate with Franceschina. She demands money. He gives it. Franceschina tells him to leave now. **Magnifico hides** to observe.
		Franceschina knocks on Magnifico's door. Magnifico does a scene of panic.
1.08	**Ortenzia**	[At her window] Franceschina asks Ortenzia for her laundry and her washtub. **Ortenzia withdraws.**
		Magnifico does a scene of relief. **Ortenzia enters** with the washtub and laundry. **Ortenzia exits** into her house.
		Franceschina asides that she hears Zani coming. She tells Magnifico to hide in the washtub and he does.
1.09	**Zani**	Franceschina tells Zani to help[233] take the tub into the house. **Franceschina and Zani exit** taking the washtub into the house and immediately **Zani reenters**.

---

[232] This is the only mention of 'the pregnancy'. Many of her actions in the play are about trying to get more money, so perhaps her expectancy drives the mission to do laundry, and willingness to entertain Magnifico.

[233] In the manuscript, she tells him to do it (alone?), but here we let them both do it.

1.10	**Ortenzia**	[At her window] Ortenzia calls to Zani and asks him to go to Cassandro's shop to get the wagon of lemons. She reveals that Cassandro will be hidden under the lemons. **Ortenzia exits** into her house. **Zani exits** up the street.
1.11	**Curzio**	[Dressed like an urban peasant] Curzio approaches Coralina's house but is interrupted.
1.12	**Zani**	Zani asks the peasant (Curzio) for help with the lemons. Curzio pretends to be mute. They do a lazzo of difficult communication. As they bring the lemons into Ortenzia's house. **Curzio and Zani exit**.
1.13	**Curzio** **Zani**	Zani mistreats silent Curzio, and Curzio wants to get to his amorous business, but Zani keeps criticizing Curzio poor effort with the lemons. Then Zani beats Curzio. Curzio talks, telling Zani about the disguise and his amorous ambition.[234] **Curzio and Zani exit** separately.

Act II

2.01	**Zani**	Zani enters from the street, is very sad and Zani stands outside of his house (*looking away from his house, he must not see Magnifico's upcoming entrance.*).
2.02	**Magnifico**	[From Zani's house] Magnifico enters. Zani is in despair.
2.03	**Franceschina**	Franceschina enters from her house and does the lazzo of the quarta[235] to Zani. **Zani and Franceschina exit** into their house. Magnifico monologues praising his wife. He knocks at his door.
2.04	**Ortenzia**	Ortenzia, pretending her eye hurts, asks Magnifico to help remove the speck in her eye.[236] They try.
2.05	**Cassandro**	Cassandro enters from Magnifico's house. **Magnifico and Ortenzia exit** into their house. Cassandro goes to his house.
2.06	**Curzio** **Coralina**	They do a lazzo of Curzio being mute.[237] Cassandro gives money to Curzio. **Cassandro and Coralina exit** into their house.

---

[234] Most of the plot points in this scene are inplied in the terse manuscript.

[235] The lazzo of the quarta is not recorded in any known extant document, but based on content, it has to do with blocking someone's view by placement.

[236] This is a lazzo as 'eye that will be cured' in the manuscript. This is a way to keep Magnifico from looking up to see Cassandro leaving his house.

[237] This lazzo is so that her husband will not suspect this beggar as a potential love interest of his wife.

2.07	Zani	Curzio tells Zani about his amorous near success with Coralina. **Zani and Curzio exit** up the street.
2.08	Magnifico	[From his house] Magnifico monologues laughing about the lazzo of the quarta, and how well it worked getting passed Zani.
2.09	Cassandro	[From his house] Cassandro is laughing about the lazzo of the speck in the eye. Magnifico laughs. Magnifico tells Cassandro about the lazzo of the quarta. They both laugh. **Magnifico exits** up the street.
2.10	Zani	Cassandro tells Zani about the the eye trick. Cassandro then tells about the quarta trick. Zani tells Cassandro about the fake mute (showing that Cassandro is a cuckold). Enraged **Cassandro exits** into his house.
2.11	Magnifico	Magnifico is happy, and he mocks Zani, laughing. Zani tells Magnifico about the eye trick (showing that Magnifico is a cuckold). Magnifico is enraged and wants to kill his wife Ortenzia. **Magnifico exits** into his house.
2.12	Franceschina	Zani tells Franceschina that he wants to end their marriage. [Using the lazzo of bad acting] Franceschina pretends to cry. Zani pretends to leave. **Zani hides** to observe. Franceschina laughs.
2.13	Magnifico	Magnifico asides that he could not kill his wife. **Franceschina and Magnifico exit** into Zani's house. Zani says that he will get some firewood and set his house on fire. **Zani exits** up the street.
2.14	Cassandro	Cassandro saw Magnifico exit and asides about Ortenzia being alone. **Cassandro exits** into Ortenzia's house.
2.15	Curzio	Curzio saw Cassandro exit, and asides about his desire for Coralina. **Curzio exits** into Coralina's house.
2.16	Zani	[Carrying firewood and kindling] Zani monologues about wanting to burn down his house. He calls to Franceschina but hears amorous noises of caressing.
2.17	Franceschina	[At her window] Zani says he wants to kill her. She negotiates to spare Ortenzia's laundry. **Franceschina withdraws**. Franceschina reenters pushing Magnifico in the washtub. Zani sets fire to the house. **They all exit**.

Thefts

This is a fun, straight-up comedy with people disguising as other people mixed with the usual Commedia dell'Arte theme of young lovers trying to get together over the objections and obstacles of the older generation.

Dramatis Personae   *7M-3F*

Cassandro	A Fabric merchant with a warehouse
Curzio	Son of Cassandro, loves Ortenzia
Zani	Servant of Cassandro
Alejandro Albertucci	A Dottore
Isabella	Daughter of Alejandro
Trastulo	Servant of Alejandro
Laura	A widow
Ortenzia	Daughter of Laura
Magnifico	A merchant
Orazio	Son of Magnifico, loves Isabella

Props

A piece of damask
Chef disguise for Curzio
Ortenzia's luggage

Set: three buildings
• Magnifico's house
• Laura's house
• Alejandro's house

Special Skills and Effects

- Zani must be able to credibly disguise himself as Alejandro. A huge beard helps.

Performance Considerations

- Cassandro in 1.01 needs to be powerfully angry so that his return is a threat to many characters.
- Cassandro's warehouse needs to be offstage, but in sight of the actors as there are scenes when characters observe action there that the audience doesn't see.
- Because he gets dragged to the Justice three times, Trastulo should have a strong reaction to this, to show it as a thing he rightfully fears or values.

Relationship Diagram

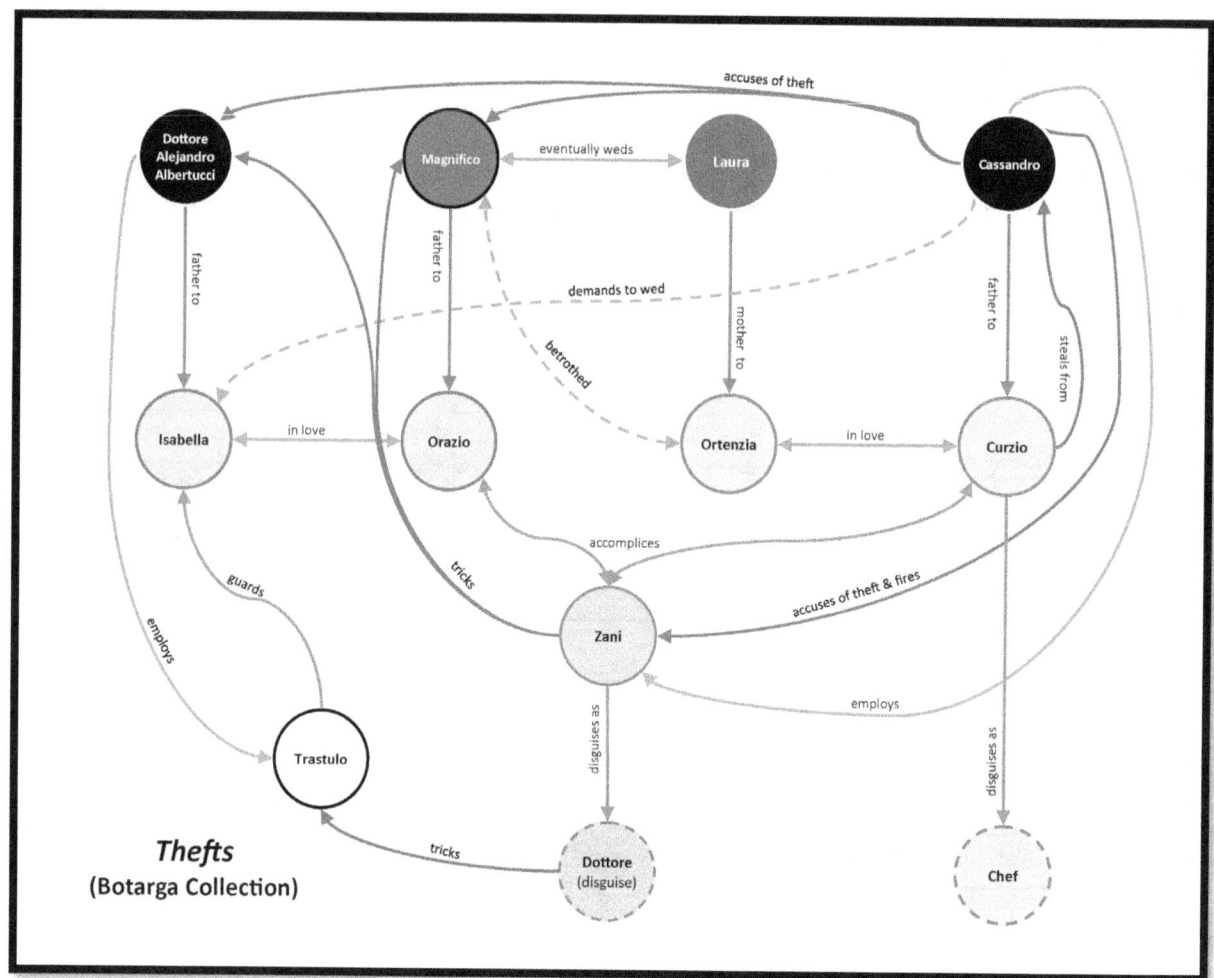

Backstory (Argomento)[238]

Dottore's daughter Isabella and Orazio love each other. Laura's daughter Ortenzia and Curzio love each other. Magnifico also wants to marry Ortenzia. The Dottore is out of town and cannot give consent for Isabella's marriage yet, and so Zani has promised to help the young lovers.

---

[238] There are no backstories in the manuscript. The one constructed here tells the minimum.

Act I

1.01	Cassandro[239] Zani	Cassandro accuses Zani of stealing from the fabric warehouse and fires Zani, no longer trusting him. **Cassandro exits.** Zani monologues that he promised Ortenzia to Curzio, and Isabella to Orazio. Zani calls out to Trastulo, who is minding Alejandro's house and protecting Isabella.
1.02	Isabella Trastulo	[Isabella at her window] Zani says he has promised Isabella to Orazio. Isabella delights at this.[240] Trastulo says no because she is the daughter of Dottore Alejandro degli Albertucci, who is traveling, and they are waiting for him. Petulant, **Isabella withdraws.** Zani makes one more appeal.[241] **Trastulo exits.** Zani complains. **Zani exits.**
1.03	Laura Magnifico	They have agreed that Magnifico will marry her daughter Ortenzia. They discuss details. Magnifico is content. They call Ortenzia.
1.04	Ortenzia	Ortenzia refuses to marry Magnifico. Laura makes her touch his hand by force.[242] Delighted, **Magnifico exits.** Horrified, Ortenzia laments.
1.05 [243]	Isabella	Isabella, Laura, and Ortenzia discuss what they yearn for, and the realities of being married. **Isabella, Ortenzia, and Laura exit.**
1.06	Zani	Zani monologues about desperation concerning his employment, and about the fate of the young lovers.[244] He is interrupted:
1.07	Ortenzia	Ortenzia calls Zani. She tells him about the new family situation (*her betrothal to Magnifico*) and that he should tell Curzio. Zani is even more desperate. **Ortenzia exits** into the house.
1.08	Orazio	Zani caresses Orazio. Zani tells Orazio that Trastulo won't let him marry Isabella until the Dottore approves it.[245]

---

[239] The transcription of the manuscript guesses that Orazio might be in this scene. It appears that Orazio isn't there, since Cassandro's exit is singular, and only Zani is left at the end.
[240] This is an added plot point to tell something obvious to the actors.
[241] Added plot point to separate Trastulo's exit from Isabella's.
[242] This act signals the betrothal, and the wedding is committed to by both sides.
[243] Added scene to give the three female characters more time to reveal their characters.
[244] The manuscript doesn't say what Zani is desperate about. We included the obvious.
[245] The manuscript doesn't specify for this scene why Orazio can't have Isabella but has been previously stated.

1.09	Curzio	Zani tells Curzio that he can't have Ortensia. Everyone despairs and they defeatedly tell each other to take care. Zani suddenly has an idea.[246] He will tell them his plan if they all go get something to eat. **Zani, Curzio, and Orazio exit.**

Act II

2.01 [247]	Cassandro Orazio Curzio	[Curzio is hiding a piece of Damask] Cassandro is furious about the thefts from the warehouse. He's depending on Curzio to protect it. **Cassandro exits.** Orazio and Curzio discuss having just stolen expensive fabric (the Damask) from Curzio's father's warehouse. They hope that Zani will succeed in arranging for them to marry the women they love. To watch out for the old men, **Orazio exits.**
2.02	Zani	[Zani dressed as Dottore Alejandro, and has an extra fake beard, a chef's hat, and an apron] Zani tells Curzio how he wants to deceive Trastulo and pretend to be Alejandro, because he knows Alejandro well enough to imitate his mannerisms, clothes[248], and beard shape. Zani asks for the Damask, and Curzio gives it to him. Zani tells Curzio to dress as the chef. **Curzio exits** to get disguised. Zani calls Trastulo.
2.03	Trastulo	Zani pretends to be Alejandro; Zani gives Trastulo the piece of Damask, praising Trastulo's long, loyal service. To trade the cloth for money,[249] **Trastulo exits** crying.
2.04	Isabella	Isabella is still grieving for being apart from Orazio. Zani[250] teases her and reveals himself (*he is disguised as her father, but lets her know he is Zani*), and explains that Trastulo is away, and Orazio can now steal her away. To pack, **Isabella exits** into the house. Zani calls Orazio.[251]

---

[246] This idea and plan are implied but not explicitly stated in the manuscript.

[247] This is an added scene to help establish the how and why of the Damask fabric. This scene is implied by text in the original first scene.

[248] In the manuscript it is "his own clothes" but the pronouns are ambiguous, and the sense of the play is that he is dressed as the Dottore.

[249] This statement of why Trastulo receives the cloth is implied but not explicitly stated in the manuscript.

[250] In the manuscript it says Ganassa teases her, but that is Zani's other stage name.

[251] These last two plot points are part of inserting Orazio and Isabella eloping, rather than just disappearing.

2.05 [252]	**Orazio** **Isabella** **Curzio**	Orazio and Isabella do a hasty love scene and Zani suggests where they should go (a cabin nearby).[253] Curzio wishes them good luck. **Orazio and Isabella exit**.
		Removing his disguise, **Zani exits** in the opposite direction.
		Curzio calls at Ortenzia's house.
2.06	**Ortenzia**	Curzio pretends to be the cook for the wedding feast and asks to be let in. Not wanting to marry Magnifico, Ortenzia tries to send him away. Curzio reveals himself. She cheers up. They hear Laura coming. **Curzio and Ortenzia exit** into the house.
2.07	**Laura**	Laura monologues about the suspicious noises from inside the house. Laura calls Ortenzia.
2.08	**Ortenzia**	Ortenzia is very cheerful[254]. Laura queries, and Ortenzia says she's been with the man she's about to marry. (*Do not reveal that she doesn't mean Magnifico.*) Laura is furious.[255] They do the lazzo of the turned bosoms[256].
2.09 [257]	**Curzio**	[Still dressed as a cook] Curzio escapes the house in a lazzo of Ortenzia keeping Laura's eyes looking away from the door. **Curzio exits**.
		Laura and Ortenzia exit into the house.
2.10	**Alejandro Albertucci** **Zani**[258]	Dottore Alejandro has come to pick up his daughter. Zani, who has heard him, tells him (lying) that Trastulo has gone to visit Cassandro.[259] **Alejandro exits**.
		Zani laughs and says that he wants to detain Magnifico. Zani calls Magnifico.

[252] This scene is added. It is the elopement of Orazio and Isabella, one of the thefts that the title of the play refers to.
[253] This nearby cabin is a detail added to support the ending we invented.
[254] "Pretends" - We believe this might mean that Laura 'sees' that Ortenzia is cheerful, hence the lazzo of the torsos.
[255] The direction about Laura's fury is implied later, when Laura accuses Magnifico of despoiling a maiden.
[256] What lazzo of the turned (or gyrating) bosoms? We suspect Isabella is distracting her mother from seeing Curzio's escape.
[257] This is an added scene to let Curzio escape the house.
[258] Zani's entrance isn't specified, but he gets a plot point here.
[259] In the manuscript, it says Trastulo has gone to visit 'him'. Cassandro makes sense here as 'him'.

| 2.11 | **Magnifico**[260] | Zani makes Magnifico believe that he (Zani) wants to help him get Ortenzia to accept him.[261] Zani sends Magnifico to the warehouse on an errand (*actors invent this errand, specifics don't affect the rest of the play*) important to his wedding to Ortenzia.[262] **Magnifico exits.**

Laughing that Magnifico will get blamed for the theft of the damask, **Zani exits.**[263] |

Act III

3.01	**Cassandro** **Alejandro Albertucci**	Having not seen each other for several years, they exchange compliments. Both discuss Laura's loneliness and Magnifico needing to remarry.[264] **Alejandro exits.**[265] Cassandro keeps talking but is interrupted.
3.02	**Trastulo**	[Trastulo has the piece of Damask] Trastulo wants to sell the cloth to Cassandro, who examines it. Cassandro asks who gave it to him, Trastulo replies that it was his master, Dottore Alejandro Albertucci. Cassandro complains about Alejandro as a thief. In his fury, he demands the hand of Trastulo's master's[266] daughter. Trastulo is torn about what the right thing to do is, but in the end concludes that Cassandro is right.[267] Trastulo agrees to give her. Cassandro tells Trastulo to go to the justice to make the legal arrangements. Cassandro will go to the warehouse. [Off stage] they see Magnifico coming out of the warehouse.[268] Cassandro's rage turns to Magnifico as the thief. Taking Trastulo as a witness, Cassandro goes toward the Justice. **Trastulo and Cassandro Exit.**
3.03	**Curzio** **Ortenzia**	They are fleeing. Curzio and Ortenzia do a love scene as he steals her away with her luggage. They are going to the same cabin Zani suggested to Isabella and Orazio.[269] **Curzio and Ortenzia exit** up the street.

---

[260] In the manuscript this is an entrance for Stefanelo, which is the other name for Magnifico.
[261] He cares, or more literally, about the cure. The original Italian is ambiguous. Here we have spelled out Zani's actions in more detail.
[262] Added this reason for going to the warehouse.
[263] This laughing is implied and inserted here to give the act a strong ending.
[264] This is an added plot point to support our ending in which Magnifico and Laura marry each other.
[265] The manuscript doesn't mention this exit, but Alejandro enters in 3.05 with no other exit.
[266] In the manuscript it uses ambiguous pronouns about 'his' daughter. All the business about fury, and accusing Alejandro of theft is implied, but not in the manuscript.
[267] This added detail helps the actor playing Trastulo, who usually tries to follow all rules, so this should be difficult for him.
[268] This seems to be implied among the pronouns and verb endings. It is the action that makes the most sense here.
[269] This is an added detail to support the ending we created.

3.04	**Zani**	Zani monologues that he is about to get into big trouble for the missing maidens and the stolen cloth. He saw Magnifico outside the warehouse and can maybe still find a way to blame Magnifico and Trastulo.[270] He is interrupted.
3.05	**Alejandro Albertucci**	Alejandro recognizes Zani; Zani makes Alejandro believe that Trastulo wants to sell Alejandro's daughter Isabella and says to not tell anyone because he (Zani) will put Trastulo in his (Alejandro's) hands to bring him to justice.
3.06	**Trastulo**	Trastulo asides that they didn't get to the justice, because Cassandro wanted to confront Magnifico himself.[271] Zani accuses Trastulo of selling Isabella to Cassandro. Trastulo acknowledges that this happened and tries to explain about the stolen cloth.[272] Going to the justice **Alejandro and Trastulo exit.** Zani laughs and enters the warehouse. **Zani exits.**
3.07	**Laura**	[From her window] Laura is yelling and calling Ortenzia. **Laura withdraws.**
3.08	**Magnifico Cassandro**	Magnifico says that he will give to Cassandro the value of the missing cloth, which he did not steal, because he (Magnifico) is an honest man wanting to keep his reputation.[273] Magnifico goes to Laura.
3.09	**Laura**	She tells Magnifico that he is a traitor and that he has ruined a maiden, her daughter Ortenzia. Cassandro goes toward the warehouse to see what is missing. They are interrupted.
3.10	**Zani**	Zani Confesses to everything: to disguising himself as Alejandro, to the theft of the damask, to framing Magnifico for the theft, and arranging for the lovers to marry.[274] At first the old people are upset. Zani makes a loud signal to the young lovers.
3.11	**Curzio Ortenzia**	Magnifico is furious at losing Ortenzia, but Cassandro is proud of his son's ingenuity. Curzio and Ortenzia say very loving things to and about each other, and that they are very happy. Cassandro and Laura, who is pleased that Magnifico didn't ruin her daughter, bless the marriage.

[270] There is more detail here than in the manuscript.
[271] This is an added plot point. No one from justice ever shows up in the play, but there are several threats to go to the justice. We've opted that no one ever reports any of this to the justice.
[272] Trastulo trying to explain is implied but not stated in the manuscript.
[273] It is very unclear from pronouns and missing text what happens here. We've inserted what seems to make sense in context.
[274] The manuscript ends on Zani's confession in scene 3.10. Here we've added the obvious resolutions.

3.12	**Alejandro Albertucci Trastulo**	Alejandro never made it to the justice because they returned when they heard the noise. (**note**: *this is the third failed trip to the justice, some lazzo can be made of that*)
3.13	**Orazio Isabella**	Orazio and Isabella do a happy-together scene. Seeing how happy his (Alejandro's) daughter is, Alejandro forgives Trastulo. Now in a better mood, Magnifico and Alejandro bless the marriage. Celebrating, **the four lovers exit.**
		Cassandro and Alejandro persuade Magnifico and Laura to also wed, and they do. To record the marriages at the justice,[275] **Trastulo and the four old people exit**.
		Zani gives a short monologue about how some thefts are good for all concerned. **Zani exits.**

---

[275] Note: this last trip to justice is only here to satisfy the rule of threes, giving Trastulo a third trip to Jusitce.

The Most Inane Lady

This is another straight-up comedy about lovers with an obstacle. In this case the obstacle is another young lover who is obsessed with one of the true lovers. She tells lies and concocts tricks to split them up to make the man of her desires available to her.

Dramatis Personae   5M-3F

Magnifico	A wealthy old man
Tofano	A wealthy old man
Isabella	Daughter of Magnifico
Curzio	Son of Tofano
Trastulo	Servant of Tofano and Curzio
Zani	A caterer
Laura	A young widow[276]
Franceschina	Wife of Zani[277]

Props

Letter
Catering supplies
Candied almonds (confetti)
Key to Laura's house

Set: two houses
• Magnifico's house
• Laura's house

Special Skills and Effects

- The lazzo of Confetti might require some sticky "food" to be thrown about, and then cleaned up between acts.
- Magnifico's house needs working shutters on its window(s).

Performance Considerations

- Zani and Franceschina know there is a wedding planned, but for whom, Curzio and Trastulo do not know. Isabella doesn't know for whom.
- Tofano and Magnifico should start off as two men interested in Laura so as to help them accept her calumny more seriously, and possibly to set up a happy ending.
- Franceschina and Trastulo have very little stage time. There is room in this play for them to fill some of the plot holes.
- We did not include an ending with pairs of characters exiting at the end. This is an easy play to construct such an ending, possibly pairing Laura with Magnifico or Tofano.

---

[276] The manuscript doesn't say she is a widow, but she has a house and agency, so it is implied.
[277] The relationship isn't obvious, but she knows of the wedding and has the confetti (sweet treats).

Relationship Diagram

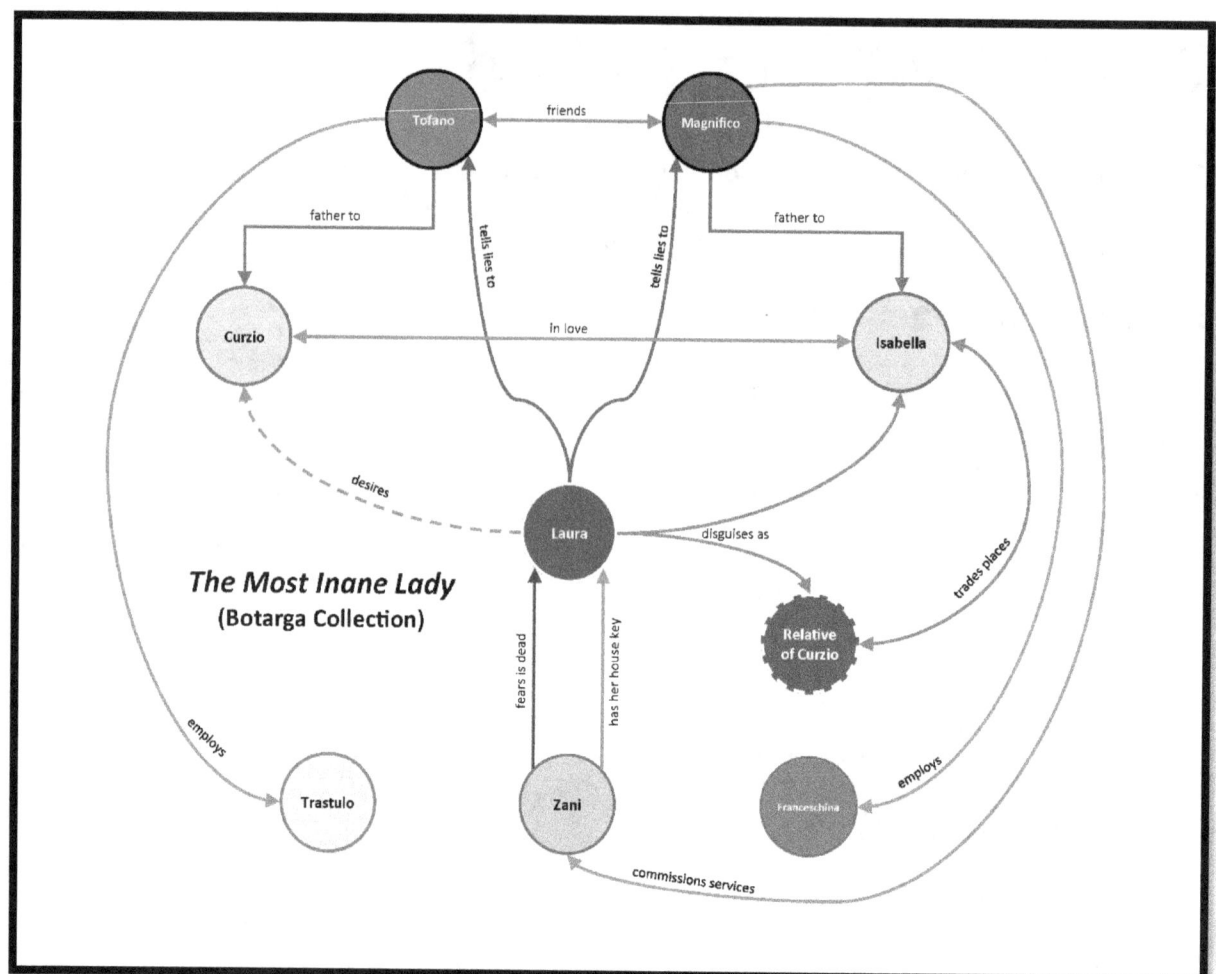

Backstory (Argomento)[278]

Magnifico and Tofano have been friends for a long time. Their children Isabella and Curzio respectively have developed a deep affection for each other. The old men arranged the marriage between them. The young widow next door to Magnifico has also developed a powerful unrequited love for Curzio and wants to disrupt the wedding.

---

[278] There are no backstories in the manuscript. The one constructed here answers the questions of how the characters knew each other, traveled at the same time, and yet didn't recognize each other until the play starts. It is possible to answer these questions with some other backstory if you are motivated to do so.

Act I

1.01	**Magnifico** **Tofano**	They talk of wanting to marry Tofano's son, Curzio, with Magnifico's daughter Isabela. They agree not to say anything to their children[279]. **Tofano exits** up the street.
1.02	**Isabella**	Magnifico tells Isabella that she should prepare to be a bride, and he does not tell her with whom. **Magnifico and Isabella** exit into the house.
1.03	**Curzio** **Trastulo**	[Curzio has a letter] Curzio goes on at length about his secret love for Isabella and his secret plans to run away with her.[280] Curzio gives Trastulo a letter to Isabella. **Curzio exits** up the street. **Trastulo exits** into the house.
1.04	**Zani** **Franceschina**[281]	Zani and Franceschina used to be servants for Laura's late husband Vechio[282], but are now caterers.[283] They are excited for their first big client. To get treats, **Franceschina exits**. To make a list of things he needs to do, **Zani stands aside.**
1.05 [284]	**Isabella**	[At her window] Isabella looks for Curzio to warn him that she is getting married soon. She doesn't see him. With Sadness, **Isabella withdraws**.
1.06	**Laura**	Laura monologues saying that she is in love with Curzio. She lists his qualities that would make him a great next husband for her.[285] She despairs, fearing that he is going to marry someone else. She sees Zani, who tells his former mistress that he is catering for Curzio's wedding. She faints. Zani, thinking her dead, runs around the stage and panics[286]. **Zani exits** fleeing.[287]

---

279 We are confident that Ganassa and Botarga did not steal this idea from "The Fantastics".
280 This monologue is an added plot point. It is implied by later actions and reactions.
281 Franceschina is added to this scene to establish their relationship, and to give an opportunity to give backstory.
282 This backstory about Zani and Laura's household is invented to show that Laura is a widow (implied in the manuscript), and that he has knowledge of her modos operandi. The name Vechio is invented for this version.
283 Vignarolo could mean winemaker or grocer.
284 Added scene to help establish Isabella's character.
285 This lazzo of the list of qualities is not in the manuscript but is inserted to benefit actors building the case that she desires him.
286 This word is missing in the manuscript. It is a reflexive verb. 'He panics himself' is our guess.
287 The manuscript is missing one word that is certainly this necessary exit.

1.07	Trastulo	[Trastulo has a letter] Trastulo states his pleasure that he has a love letter from Curzio to Isabella[288]. Laura grabs it and tears it up. **Laura exits** into her house. Desperate, **Trastulo exits** up the street.
1.08	Franceschina Zani	[Zani at the window] Zani screams to Franceschina about Laura being dead. She does a lazzo of getting him to lower his voice.[289] To see if Zani is right about Laura[290], **Franceschina exits** into the house. **Zani withdraws.**
1.09	Trastulo	Trastulo is crying (*because of the torn letter*).
1.10	Zani	Zani is crying (*because he believes Laura is dead*).
1.11	Franceschina	Franceschina does the lazzo of confetti. (*Confetti in this case is a basket of candied almonds distributed at weddings*). **Everyone exits.**

Act II

2.01	Magnifico	Magnifico cheerfully monologues about the new family ties.
2.02	Zani	Magnifico scolds Zani for bringing no food or drink from the house. Zani wants to explain, but also to please[291]. Magnifico makes him go back. **Zani exits** into the house.
2.03	Laura	[Laura has a key] Laura gives a long dishonest, but heart-felt, diatribe against Curzio and Tofano. To undo the betrothal, **Magnifico exits**. Just then:
2.04	Tofano	Laura gives a long dishonest, but heart-felt, diatribe against Isabella and Magnifico. To undo the betrothal, **Tofano exits**. Just then:
2.05	Curzio	Laura is sobbing. Curzio tries to console her[292]. Just then:

---

[288] This speech by Trastulo is implied as the reason that Laura is irritated by the letter.

[289] "Makes him get lower" is a direct translation. Among the things it could mean: 1- Lazzo of F getting Z to lean out of the window more to tell it more clearly, 2- She wants him to come outside, 3- His voice was high and squealy speaking of the dead woman. Other options are possible.

[290] The manuscript simply says "to see if it is true". Here we assumed that "it" means Laura's dead condition.

[291] This plot point is added. It seems to have been implied and is added here to aid actors.

[292] "La simula", technically means "simulates her". This could be a stage direction that he was mocking her. Here we left it simply that he didn't know what she had just said to Tofano and was being humane.

2.06	Isabella	[Isabella at her window] Isabella misunderstands Curzio's intent and scolds Curzio.[293] Laura makes a long stream of rude insults against Isabella. With polite silence, **Isabella withdraws**. Curzio asides about his anger at Laura. To show how he feels, Curzio tells Laura that he will elope with Isabella tonight. **Curzio exits** up the street. **Laura stands aside** to observe.
2.07	Zani	Zani arrives and realizes he forgot the cheese. He is stomping back into the house when:
2.08	Isabella	Isabella tells Zani that she needs to talk to Curzio right away[294] and she sends him to look for Curzio. Zani asides that something is wrong.[295] **Zani hides** to observe.[296]
2.09 [297]	Trastulo	Trastulo is sobbing and tells Isabella of Curzio's plan to run away with her tonight, and of the letter that was torn up. Isabella expresses joy and enthusiasm about Curzio's love. **Trastulo exits** up the street.
2.10		Laura asides that she has heard everything and has a plan. The plan is that she will switch places with Isabella, and keep it dark, so Curzio won't know who he has eloped with until it is too late. She puts on a veil[298].
2.11	Laura	**Laura steps forward**. [Using the lazzo of bad acting] Laura says good things to Isabella. Laura says that she is a relative of Curzio. She tells Isabella that Curzio is not what he seems and that Curzio plans to do harm to Isabella, but that she (Laura) can save her.[299] They exchange veils and change houses to save Isabella. Laura hands the house key to Isabella[300] as Isabella lets Laura into Isabella's house. **Laura exits** into Isabella's house. **Isabella exits** into Laura's house. Zani quickly monologues that he must find Curzio and fix this. **Zani exits** up the street.[301]

---

[293] This plot point is implied but not spelled out in the manuscript.
[294] This reason for Isabella sending Zani to find Curzio was added for clarity.
[295] This is an added plot point to justify Zani staying to watch.
[296] In the manuscript, Zani exits here.
[297] This scene is added. Its existence is mildly implied as a setup to Isabella agreeing to Laura's trick.
[298] This plan and plot point is implied by Isabella not recognizing her as the woman who insulted her three scenes ago.
[299] There is a missing part of the manuscript detailing Laura's plan. This choice mirrors something done in the play Ramiro.
[300] The manuscript mentions the key in Act 3. It's use here is implied by the changing houses.
[301] Added plot point to explain Zani's actions and what he knows.

| 2.12 | **Laura**[302] | [At the window] Laura asides that it needs to be dark for her trick to work. She closes the shutters. **Laura withdraws**. |
| 2.13 | **Franceschina**[303] **Tofano** **Magnifico** | [Franceschina has cheese] Franceschina is bringing cheese for the wedding. She sees the old men arguing, and asides a fear that she and Zani might not get paid if the wedding is off. **Franceschina exits**.

The old men continue to argue, echoing Laura's earlier talking points.[304] It gets heated, and they undo the betrothal. **Both exit**. |

Act III

3.01	**Zani** **Franceschina**	Franceschina tells Zani that they might not get paid if the wedding is cancelled[305]. Zani says that he has not found Curzio.
3.02	**Curzio**	Zani tells Curzio about Laura's tricks, the cancelled wedding, and of Isabella being in Laura's house.[306] Curzio embraces[307] him.
3.03	**Isabella**	[In Laura's window, with a key] Isabella calls Curzio. She drops the key for him. Using the key, **Curzio exits** into the house. **Isabella withdraws**. Zani asides that he will give them privacy. To find Tofano and explain things, **Franceschina exits** up the street.
3.04	**Magnifico**	Zani prevents Magnifico from entering his own house. Eventually **Magnifico exits** into his house. Zani yells into the house saying that Laura was lying about Curzio and Tofano.
3.05 [308]	**Magnifico**	Magnifico asks why all of his windows are closed. (*They are closed to keep Laura in the dark to help mistaken identity.*) Zani promises to reveal more, **Magnifico and Zani exit** into Magnifico's house.
3.06 [309]	**Franceschina** **Tofano** **Trastulo**	Franceschina says that Laura lied, and Isabella is innocent of Laura's accusations and insinuations. We hear yelling from inside Magnifico's house.

[302] This added scene is implied in the original, but not explicitly written.
[303] Franceschina added to this scene to let her know the wedding is off.
[304] This stage direction is implied, but explicitly in the manuscript.
[305] Added plot point to show that Zani knows that the lovers' hopes have been thwarted.
[306] The manuscript is merely says that Zani tells him about Isabella. Here more detail is supplied.
[307] In the manuscript, the verb used translates to "caresses".
[308] Original 3.04 split to make Magnifico's re-entrance more obvious.
[309] This scene was added to lay groundwork for the happy ending.

3.07	**Laura** **Magnifico**[310] **Zani**	Laura runs out of Magnifico's house, with Magnifico and Zani chasing her. **Laura, Magnifico, Tofano, Franceschina, Trastulo, and Zani exit** up the street.
		Laura returns and monologues about her grief. She calls at her door.
3.08	**Curzio** **Isabella**	Curzio and Isabella receive Laura. (*This should be a long emotional scene that resolves everything.*)
3.09	**Magnifico** **Tofano**[311] **Zani**	Zani explains to the old men what happened. Everybody makes peace and Isabella and Curzio are married. **All exit**.

---

[310] Magnifico is added to this scene as we build to the conclusion.
[311] Tofano is added to this scene to complete the story for everyone.

Ambassadors

This is a tale of long-lost love and young love in the same story. A young woman is promised to marry a dead man, but the dead man's half-brother will also be able to fulfill the deal. Unbeknownst to all, that's exactly who she falls in love with. Meanwhile some roving scoundrels are creating chaos.

Dramatis Personae   6M-3F

The Signore[312]	A nobleman
Capitano Gamberro	Assistant to the Signore
Magnifico	A fake Cycladean ambassador
Zani	A fake Cycladean ambassador
Isabella	A midwife, sister of the Capitano
Laura	Mother of Curzio
Trastulo	An innkeeper
Ortenzia	A young woman
Curzio	A young man, son of Laura

Props

2 fancy matching rings
A stick to beat Magnifico & Zani

Set: three buildings
• Isabella's house
• The Tavern
• Laura's house

Special Skills and Effects

- The two rings should be very similar, and it would be good if they connected in a way that showed them as two parts of one larger thing.

Performance Considerations

- The conman patter, and quick wits of Magnifico and Zani require a little practice. They are the comic core of this play. Note that they are playing scoundrels in this play, which is uncommon for these characters.
- For this play to work, the audience needs a lot of sympathy for Laura, and she should play with some good reason why she doesn't just present herself to the Signore. She must have some worry that gets erased in the end.
- It would help if the Innkeeper had some backstory concerns. The play doesn't give him much.

---

[312] "The Signore" ranks as a King or Prince.

Relationship Diagram

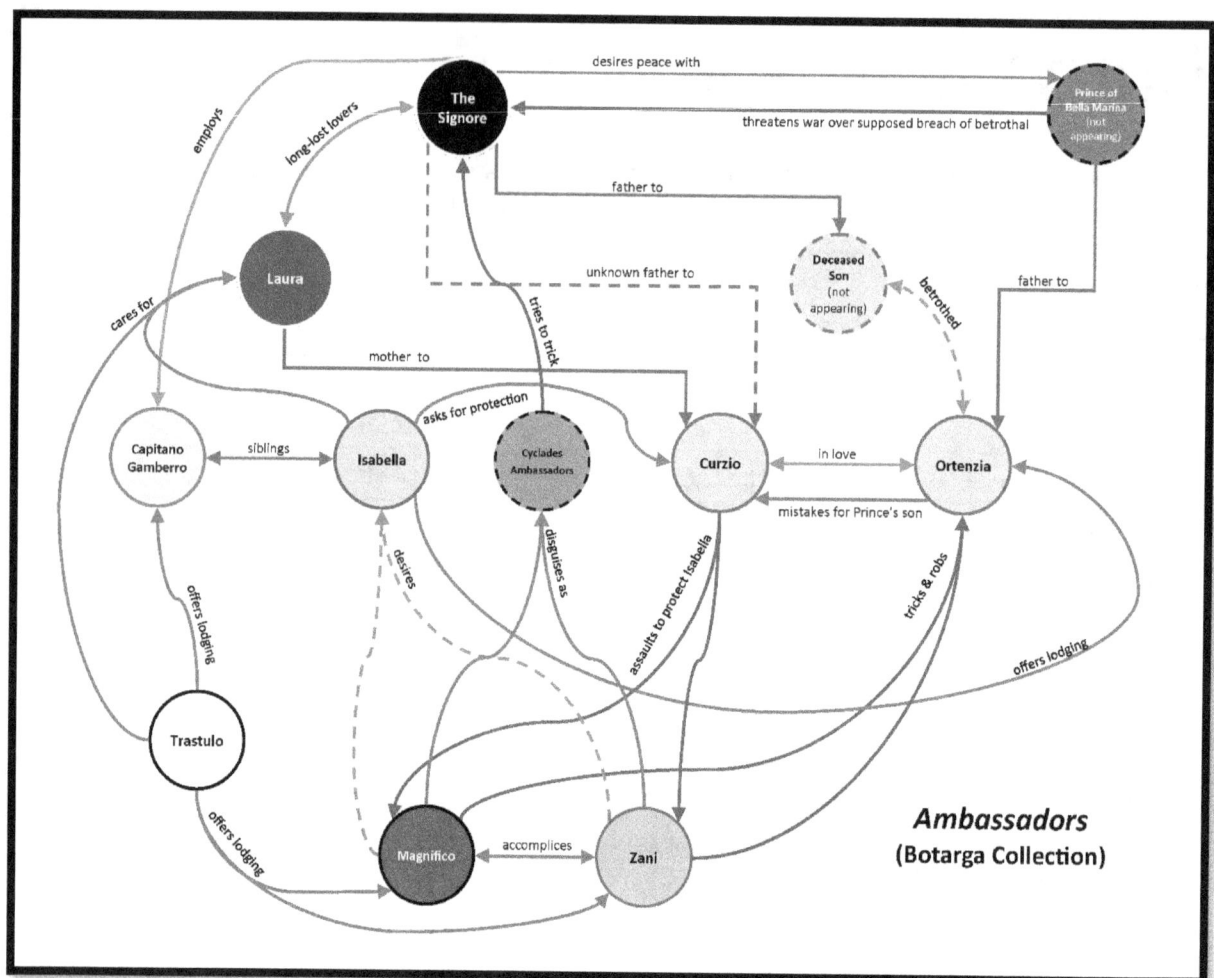

Backstory (Argomento)³¹³

Years ago, The Signore, a widower with a young son, had a romantic night with a woman he promised to marry, but the threat of war pulled him away after the first night. He gave her a special ring as a symbol of his promise. Sometime later, to avoid future conflict, he promised his young son from his first wife, as a husband to the young daughter of the Prince of Bella Marina. Recently the young son was killed in the wars. Now upset, and looking for a way to end these wars, he summoned ambassadors from many fiefs and princedoms to meet in a palace a few nights away from here, to which he is travelling. Meanwhile, the daughter of the Prince of Bella Marina has set off on her own to this gathering, hopefully to find her promised husband and bring an end to these damaging battles. Magnifico and Zani are conmen, who recently stole the clothes from the ambassadors of the Cyclades. Recently, these conmen also stole the ring from the Princess of Bella Marina while Curzio was walking with her.

---

³¹³ There are no backstories in the manuscript. The one constructed here tells the minimum.

Act I

1.01	**The Signore** **Capitano Gamberro**	The Signore talks about not wanting to get married because of a woman he'd promised to marry, years ago. She went hunting with him in a forest and he killed a wild boar. That night, he took her honor and gave her a ring as a sign of his promise to marry her. On later occasion, he promised his son by his first wife to be the husband of the daughter of the Prince of Bella Marina. He was not able to keep his word because that son[314] died. The Prince of Bella Marina, not believing him, wants to wage war. The Signore awaits ambassadors of all his allies.
1.02 [315]	**Trastulo**	Trastulo greets the visitors outside the inn. The Signore commands Gamberro to make the arrangements in the inn[316]. **All exit** into the inn.
1.03	**Magnifico** **Zani**	They have a dialog about their travels revealing that the Cyclades is the land of cowardice. (*Note: they are conmen, not ambassadors, but the audience doesn't need to learn that until later*) They look for a tavern. They are interrupted:
1.04	**Isabella** **Laura**	[Laura is at her door][317] Isabella is on her way to her house coming from a childbirth. Magnifico and Zani greet her. Each man asides about suddenly loving Isabella. **Isabella exits** into her house. Laura directs Magnifico and Zani to the tavern. They call at the door.
1.05	**Trastulo**	Trastulo greets and receives Magnifico & Zani. **Magnifico and Trastulo exit** into the Tavern. **Laura exits** into her house.[318] Zani goes to talk with Isabella. He calls her.

[314] Probably the son has died, in the manuscript we get the pronoun 'he'.
[315] The first scene from the original is split here to give Trastulo a later entrance and give him a plot point of greeting.
[316] In the original, The Prince orders the Capitano to receive them inside. Here we take that to mean that he is to make the arrangements in the Inn for The Prince's stately suite.
[317] The manuscript says nothing about where Laura is, but she may not have been with Isabella at the birth.
[318] In the original, it isn't clear whether Laura exits into the Inn with them. Here we chose no, for story consistency.

1.06	Isabella	[At her window] Isabella doesn't want Zani's attention. He refuses to take no for an answer.[319] Isabella tells Zani he must dress as a woman to be able to visit her discreetly.[320] **Zani exits** up the street. **Isabella withdraws.**[321]
1.07	Ortenzia Curzio	Curzio had just met Ortenzia and had been walking with her for the last few miles leading into town. Ortenzia and Curzio have a romantic dialog. She lets slip that she thinks he is the son of the Signore. Curzio reveals that he is not a prince, but that, due to the resemblance he has with the Signore of this realm, her mistake is understandable.[322] Ortenzia laments about tricks and deception, and how she was tricked, and her ring was stolen. Curzio prepares to leave.
1.08	Trastulo	Protecting the Signore's privacy, Trastulo says and does things to drive Curzio away. He is interrupted:
1.09	Laura	Trastulo drives both Curzio & Ortenzia away (edge of the stage). Laura goes toward Isabella's house. **Trastulo exits** into the Inn.
1.10	Capitano Gamberro	Gamberro tells them that there is no room for Ortenzia in the Inn, but he has an idea. Gamberro calls for Isabella.
1.11	Isabella	Isabella receives them and Ortenzia is glad about that. **Gamberro exits into the Inn.** **Laura and Curzio exit** into Laura's house. **Ortenzia exits** into Isabella's house.[323] Isabella gives a short monologue but is interrupted.
1.12	Magnifico	Magnifico tells Isabella about his love for her. She refuses him, but he is persistent.[324] She tells him to dress as a woman[325] to be able to visit discretely. **Magnifico exits** up the street. Isabella calls Curzio.

---

[319] Added plot point to help justify Curzio's assault of Magnifico and Zani.

[320] In the manuscript "Gives him the order of the woman". This order is to dress as a woman. Here we also supplied a why he must do this.

[321] This exit is implied, but not explicitly stated in the manuscript.

[322] Some plot points about their romantic interests were implied, but here added explicitly.

[323] In the original, it looks like all four exit into Isabella's house, but there is no story reason for that.

[324] Similar to the added plot point in 1.05.

[325] Again, she gives the order of a woman, just as she did with Zani.

1.13	Curzio	[Curzio is at his window] Isabella asks Curzio to protect her by using a stick to beat the two men who have been bothering her.[326] They will be the ones who are dressed as women. **Isabella exits into her house.** **Curzio withdraws and enters** carrying a stick. Just then:
1.14	Zani	[Dressed as a woman] Zani asides about how he imagines the loving affection of Isabella.
1.15	Magnifico	[Dressed as a woman] Magnifico asides about how he'll express his desires for Isabella. Curzio beats them and chases them. **All exit** up the street.

Act II

2.01	Curzio Ortenzia	Curzio and Ortenzia discuss how naïve they were to let those men get her ring (*Note: actors should plan some story about how the conmen tricked them*).[327] Curzio comforts Ortenzia by saying he believes that he has seen the people who stole the ring from her. **Ortenzia exits into Isabella's house.**
2.02	Laura	Laura gives Curzio her ring, to go and sell it to the Signore, and no one else.[328] Laura calls Gamberro.
2.03	Capitano Gamberro	After a short discussion Gamberro agrees to lead Curzio to the Signore[329] to sell his jewelry. **Gamberro and Curzio exit** into the inn.
2.04	Magnifico	[Magnifico is dressed as an ambassador and has a ring] Magnifico praises Isabella and gives Laura a ring to give to Isabella for him. Laura asides that it looks like it pairs with the ring she just gave to Curzio. She accepts it and **Laura exits** into the house.
2.05	Zani	[Zani is dressed as an ambassador] He greets Magnifico. They are interrupted.
2.06	The Signore Capitano Gamberro	In a lazzo, Zani and Magnifico deliver a fake ambassadorial message from the Cyclades. The Signore takes them to eat with him. **The Signore, Zani, and Magnifico exit.** Gamberro goes to Isabella's house and calls for her.

---

[326] This and the next two scenes have been reworded to make it clear that Curzio is protecting Isabella from annoying men, not beating men because they dress as women.

[327] This is an added plot point which is implied by other scenes and seems best to be in this scene.

[328] In the original, she only tells him to sell it. Selling it to The Prince is implied by where he goes to sell it.

[329] In the original there is a word that translates to Palace, which we took to mean, the royal presence.

2.07 330	Isabella	[At her window] Gamberro and his sister Isabella talk about how long he will be in town, their beloved dead parents, etc. He reminds her that he will always protect her. **Gamberro exits** into the inn.
2.08 331	Trastulo	Trastulo monologues about the mixed blessing of having royalty take over the inn for a day. Trastulo and Isabella talk about their protective feelings for Laura, and her difficult life as a single mother.332 **Trastulo exits** into the inn. **Isabella withdraws**.
2.09	Ortenzia Laura	[Laura has Ortenzia's ring] They talk about the ring and whoever gave it to her. Laura tells her it was Magnifico, the ambassador. Ortenzia tells her to take it to the Signore. Ortenzia cheers up. **Ortenzia exits** into Isabella's house.
2.10	Curzio	Laura shows him the ring; she says she wants him to take it to The Signore. He doesn't want to because he didn't stop the conmen from tricking Ortenzia. Laura says it will all work out. **Laura and Curzio exit** into their house.
2.11	Magnifico Capitano Gamberro Zani	Gamberro, believing Magnifico and Zani to be ambassadors, wants to introduce them to Isabella. Gamberro calls for Isabella.
2.12	Isabella Ortenzia	Magnifico and Zani reveal in asides that they recognize their former victim Ortenzia and must avoid her identifying them. In a lazzo of fake protocol, Magnifico and Zani refuse to go into Isabella's house.333 Isabella and Ortenzia want to know about Gamberro's guests. **Magnifico and Zani exit** quickly up the street. **Gamberro, Isabella, and Ortenzia exit** into Isabella's house.

Act III

3.01	Magnifico Zani	They are ready to run away. Hearing others coming **Magnifico and Zani exit**.
3.02	The Signore Capitano Gamberro Trastulo334	[Gamberro has Laura's ring] The Signore asks Gamberro who gave him that ring. He says that it was Curzio. The Signore says that Curzio must come into his presence. Gamberro calls for him.

---

330 This is an added scene to reveal some backstory about Isabella and Gamberro
331 This is an added scene to give Trastulo some stage time in Act 2.
332 This plot point is an added detail.
333 The call for this lazzo is implied, but not explicitly stated in the original.
334 In the original, it says 'servants'. For the sake of a performance troupe, we limited it to Trastulo, and removed unnamed servants.

3.03	**Curzio**	The stern stately presence and questioning frightens Curzio, and he runs away. **Curzio exits.**
		To capture him, **Gamberro and Trastulo exit.**
3.04	**Ortenzia**	She reveals to the Signore that she is the daughter of the Prince of Bella Marina as would be proved by her ring. She asks for Curzio to be pardoned and that the ambassadors be punished as the thieves that tricked her out of the ring.[335]
3.05[336]	**Capitano Gamberro Curzio**	Curzio is held by Gamberro.
3.06	**Zani Magnifico**	Magnifico and Zani seek the Signore but are identified by Ortenzia.[337] They attempt to flee. Gamberro seizes them.[338] The Signore has them taken and put in jail. The Signore calls Curzio and asks him who he is and who gave him the ring. Curzio says it was his mother.[339]
3.07	**Trastulo Isabella[340]**	Trastulo says that Curzio is the son of woman who is hiding in that house for Heaven's sake[341]. They call her.
3.08	**Laura**	[Laura has Ortenzia's ring] Laura shows the ring to The Signore and tells them what happened. The Signore recognizes Curzio as a son. The Signore fulfills his promise to the Prince of Bella Marina, as Curzio marries Ortenzia.[342] The Signore marries Laura and frees the prisoners. All celebrate.
		Romantically, **The Signore and Laura exit** into the Inn.[343]
		Enthusiastically, **Curzio and Ortenzia exit** into Laura's house.
		Discussing family, **Isabella and Gamberro exit** into Isabella's house.
		Talking about food, **Trastulo, Magnifico, and Zani exit** up the street.

[335] Several plot points were added here to make it obvious what the connections are.
[336] Added scene, needed to bring Curzio back.
[337] This added plot point is implied.
[338] This seizure is an added plot point.
[339] Another implied plot point.
[340] In the original Isabella doesn't appear in Act 3. She enters here to be present for the finale.
[341] For God's sake is just an expletive.
[342] Added implied plot point.
[343] All of the exits are added by for this modern version.

The Inn

This is another straight-up comedy about infidelity and drunken old undeserving husbands. Tricks and pangs of conscience also come to bear.

Dramatis Personae   5M-2F

Zani	Servant of Magnifico
Curzio	Son of Magnifico
Magnifico	A wealthy merchant
Ortenzia	Wife of Magnifico
Orazio	A young nobleman
Trastulo	Runs the tavern
Franceschina	Wife of Trastulo

Props

A carafe of wine
A stick for beating
Tavern sign

Set: two buildings
• Magnifico's house
• A tavern

Special Skills and Effects

- Magnifico, Trastulo and Zani need to be able to act drunk.
- There are several beating scenes.

Performance Considerations

- Moving the tavern sign from house to house confuses the drunk people and makes them feel lost and do rude things.
- Orazio and Ortenzia have no doubt about their intensions. This is in big contrast to Franceschina and Curzio who never get to consummate things until after the play. This tension is important to making the audience care about the outcome. Similarly, there needs to be a constant supply of demonstration as to why Magnifico (and Trastulo) are poor husbands.

Special Note

The three plays: The Three Cuckolds, The Tavern, and The Tunnel (Grota) are plays with drinking and marital misbehavior but are weak in the matter of characters developing or learning life lessons during the play. That makes them comic, but less dramatic than the other seventeen plays in this collection, or any of the plays in the Flaminio Scala collection. In this play, there is some room for development in the characters of Franceschina and Curzio who seem to desire each other, but do not get to consummate their relationship until after the play ends.

Issues

There is a lot of beating people up. Perhaps that is only to remind them to drink less wine. Drunkenness and cuckoldry seem to be the main sources of humor here.

Relationship Diagram

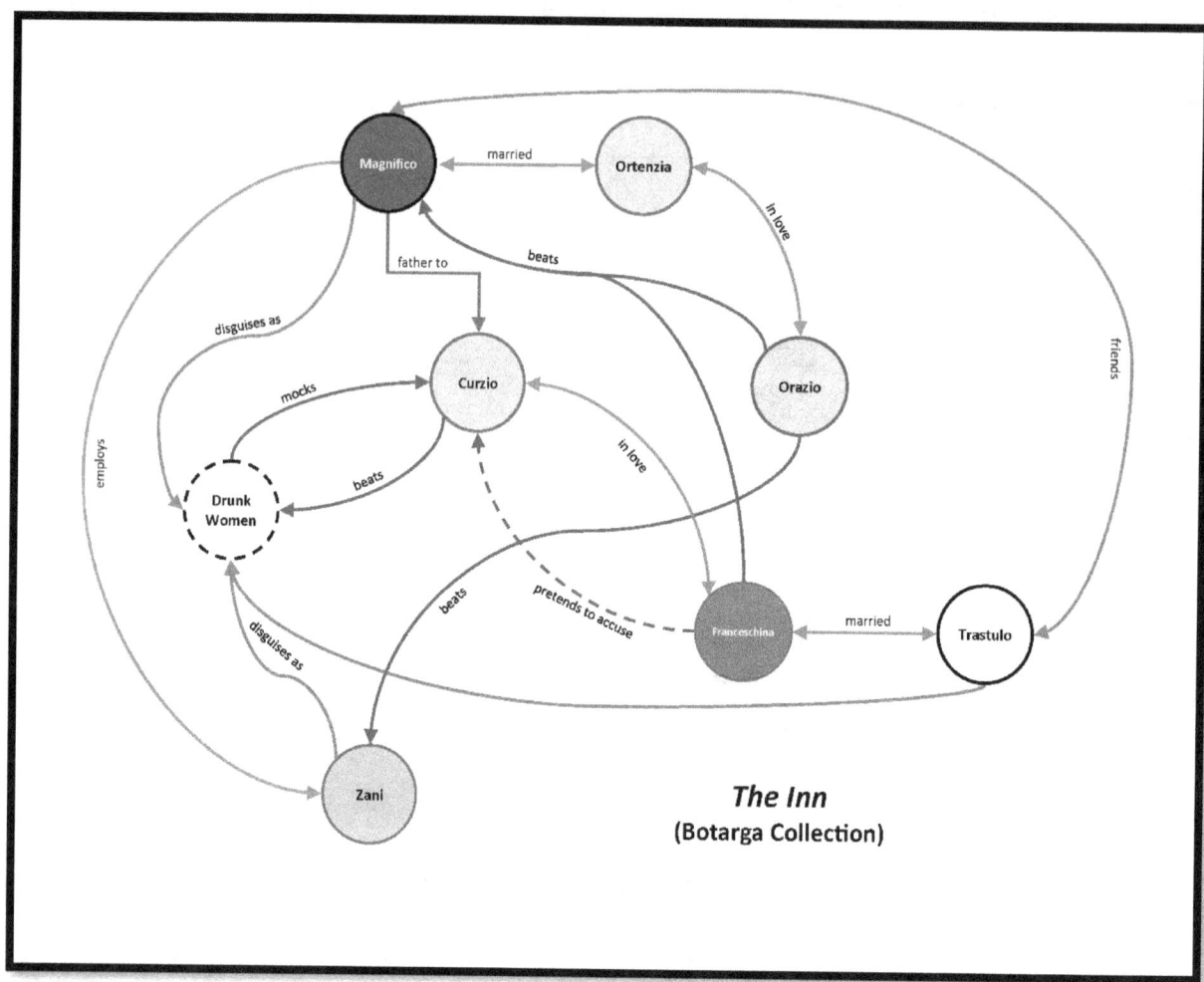

The Inn
(Botarga Collection)

Backstory (Argomento)[344]

Magnifico is an old wealthy merchant and lives next to a tavern. He has a beautiful young pregnant wife and a son, Curzio, from a previous marriage. Magnifico's old friend Trastulo runs a tavern with his young wife Franceschina.

---

[344] There are no backstories in the manuscript. The one constructed here tells the minimum.

Act I

1.01	**Zani** **Curzio** **Magnifico**	Magnifico criticizes Zani for poorly managing the house. Zani argues back. Magnifico sends Curzio to get groceries. Irritated, **Curzio exits**. Magnifico talks about his pregnant wife, Ortenzia. They call her.
1.02	**Ortenzia**	Ortenzia says that she wants red wine. Magnifico promises that she will get some wine, but, because he has to go to a banquet, he will have Zani send her the wine. Magnifico doubts Zani's ancestry and asks Zani about who he is the son of and what is his name.[345] **Magnifico exits**. Just then:
1.03	**Orazio**	Orazio monologues about his love of Ortenzia. He sees her. She tells Zani to bring a carafe of wine. **Zani exits**. **Orazio and Ortenzia exit** into the house.
1.04	**Trastulo** **Franceschina**	Franceschina shouts about Trastulo's bad management of the inn, she sends him out to buy wine. **Trastulo exits**.
1.05	**Curzio**	Curzio sees Franceschina. They have a friendly chat, and **Curzio and Franceschina exit** into the tavern.
1.06	**Zani**	[With wine] Zani calls at Magnifico's door. At that:
1.07	**Orazio**	[Disguised as Zani] Zani and Orazio both have wine. They do a lazzo of the shadows[346]. They march around. It ends with Orazio beating Zani until he gives Orazio his wine. **Orazio exits** into the house. Zani starts crying. **Zani exits**.
1.08	**Curzio** **Franceschina**	Franceschina wants Curzio to leave for love[347] of her husband (Trastulo). Disappointed, **Curzio exits**.[348] Having an idea, Franceschina takes down the sign and **Franceschina exits** into the tavern.
1.09	**Ortenzia** **Orazio**	Orazio is afraid of getting caught and wants to go. Ortenzia has an idea, and they put up the sign of the Tavern on Magnifico's house, so Magnifico won't come into the house. **Ortenzia and Orazio exit** into the house.

[345] This is a very unusual plot point for these plays. It may be in indicator for a lazzo. It may also be foreshadowing about the real father of his wife's unborn baby.

[346] This is a lazzo. Probably of imitated movement.

[347] Love, fear, worry that she's never previously been unfaithful, something else?

[348] The original is a little fuzzy about this plot point, but it seems clear that Curzio leaves at this time, even if it isn't explicitly stated in the manuscript.

1.10	**Magnifico**	Magnifico does a lazzo of being drunk. He wants to go home.
1.11	**Orazio**	Orazio beats Magnifico. Magnifico laughs for having gone to the tavern. **Orazio exits** into the house. Magnifico goes to the tavern singing.
1.12	**Franceschina**	Franceschina beats Magnifico. He staggers, in pain. **Magnifico exits**.
1.13	**Trastulo**	Trastulo is drunk. Franceschina criticizes and beats him. In pain, **Trastulo exits**. **Franceschina exits** into the tavern.

Act II

2.01	**Ortenzia** **Orazio**	Ortenzia and Orazio take off the sign of the Tavern. **They exit** into the house.
2.02	**Curzio** **Franceschina**	Franceschina signals to Curzio. **Curzio enters**. Curzio and Franceschina put up the sign of the Tavern. **Curzio exits** up the street. **Franceschina exit** into the tavern.
2.03	**Magnifico** **Zani** **Trastulo**	They are all crying[349] for being lost.
2.04	**Ortenzia**	Ortenzia criticizes Magnifico for going around drunk. Everyone laughs. They also mock Zani for his drunken behavior. **Ortenzia exits**.
2.05	**Franceschina**	She does the same with Trastulo. To buy more wine[350], **Magnifico, Zani, and Trastulo exit** to the piazza.
2.06 [351]	**Ortenzia**	[At her window] Isabella and Franceschina discuss their young men, their drunken husbands and Zani. Hearing someone coming **Ortenzia withdraws**.
2.06	**Curzio**	Curzio expresses his love to Franceschina. She gives him sweet words. He wants to kiss her. They are interrupted.

---

[349] Plural, all three are lost.
[350] Literally 'to spend more money'.
[351] This is an added scene to give the women more time for exposition and character development.

| 2.07 | **Magnifico** **Zani** **Trastulo** | **Curzio exits** with haste. Trastulo accuses Franceschina of disloyalty.[352] She [lying] tells them how Curzio wanted to force her. She sends them to dress as women[353] to the house to catch the Lothario[354]. **Franceschina, Magnifico, Trastulo, and Zani exit**. |

Act III

3.01	**Orazio**[355] **Ortenzia**	Orazio complains about all the interruptions with Ortenzia. He takes her into the house to enjoy one another. **Orazio and Ortenzia exit** into the house.
3.02	**Curzio** **Franceschina**[356]	[Franceschina at her window] Franceschina is afraid of an unruly mob hurting her or damaging the tavern. She asks Curzio to protect her.[357] **Franceschina withdraws**. Hearing people coming, **Curzio stands aside** to observe.
3.03	**Magnifico** **Zani** **Trastulo**[358]	[Still drunk[359] and dressed as women[360]] They do a lazzo of exaggerated women's behavior[361]. Curzio steps forward. They mock Curzio and try to lure him. Now furious, Curzio beats them up and **Curzio exits** up the street. Realizing that they are out of coins,[362] Magnifico, Zani, and Trastulo decide to go to the mint[363]. (*Note: they do not leave*)
3.04	**Ortenzia** **Orazio**	Ortenzia orders Orazio to beat up the three loud drunks.[364] Orazio goes to do the beating.

---

[352] This plot point is implied in the original.

[353] A torn page left out something critical. We have inserted something that is implied by later actions.

[354] Another torn page omission, this is a best guess as to intent.

[355] In the manuscript this is Curzio. We think that Botarga got the young male lovers reversed in Act 3. We've made this change to keep the men constant to their loves, and to keep Curzio from having a fling with his stepmother.

[356] Franceschina does not appear in the original version of this scene.

[357] This is an added plot point to make Curzio's attack on the three drunk men (including his father) more justified for someone who gets a happy ending.

[358] Note: in the original Trastulo and Franceschina do not appear in Act 3. We've added them in as naturally as we can.

[359] Added note to advise the actors.

[360] Zani is dressed as a woman.

[361] Originally "They mock a piece".

[362] This justification for why they are going to the mint is added.

[363] To get more coins for buying wine.

[364] The original says: 'beat up her husband'. Here we have softened the 'beat the cuckold' aspect of the joke.

| 3.05 | **Franceschina** **Curzio** | Orazio beats the drunken men.[365] Magnifico and Trastulo plead for the beatings to stop. Franceschina and Ortenzia ridicule them as worthless husbands. The husbands agree to let the wives find satisfaction where they may if they (the husbands) can continue drinking to excess. The wives agree. Everyone is happy. **All exit**. |

[365] The rest of this scene is our invention, drawn from affirmations of drunkenness and less faithfulness in marriages as seen in some earlier plays.

The Tunnel

This is small-cast simple comedy about infidelity, drunken old unworthy husbands, tricks, and a soldier recruiting for the war effort.

Dramatis Personae   4M-2F

Zani	Servant of Magnifico
Curzio	A young man
Magnifico	A wealthy merchant
Ortenzia	Wife of Magnifico
Capitano Gamberro	A soldier
Franceschina	Gamberro's woman

Props

A veil

Set: two houses, plus...
• Magnifico's house
• Curzio's house
• Tunnel entrance

Special Skills and Effects

- There needs to be a tunnel entrance.
- Magnifico and Zani have drunk scenes.
- Gamberro's house could be a fourth house of the set.

Performance Considerations

- There is an ambiguity about Fabio (who doesn't appear in the play). Was he Ortenzia's previous lover (explaining part of the jealous scene in 1.01), or was he Franceschina's secret paramour, or an invention of Franceschina's to get invited in to gossip? There are other possibilities, but they all affect the end of the play, and probably need to be agreed upon before the play starts.

Relationship Diagram

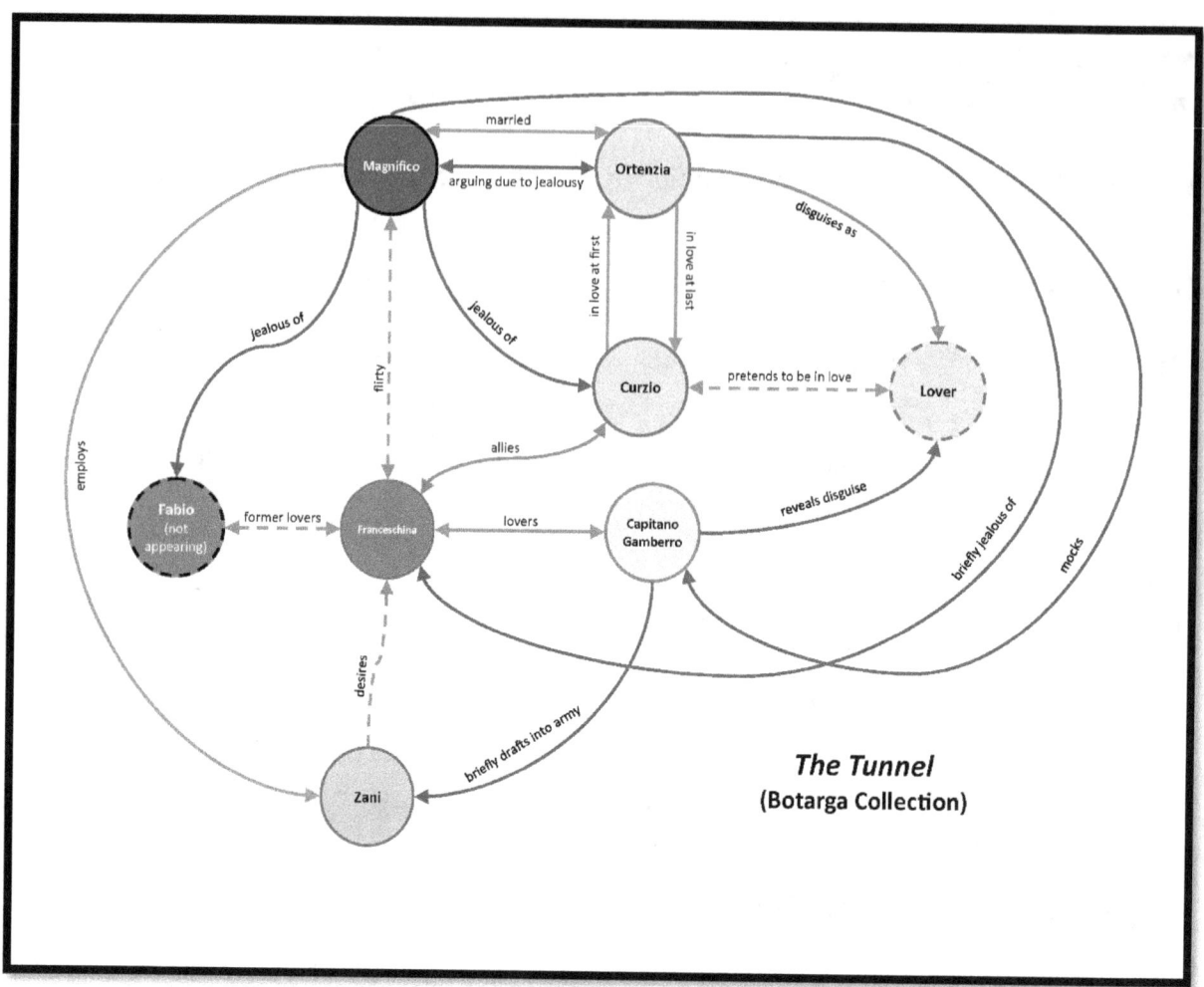

The Tunnel
(Botarga Collection)

Backstory (Argomento)[366]

Magnifico had a beautiful, and much younger unsatisfied wife named Ortenzia. He suspected her of yearning for other men, just as he yearned for more compliant women. A young new neighbor named Curzio moved in next door. Ortenzia was also friends with Franceschina, the beautiful woman of the bold Capitano. At the start of this play Magnifico has been invited to a banquet honoring the Prince (who does not appear in this play).

---

[366] There are no backstories in the manuscript. The one constructed here tells the minimum.

Act I

1.01	Magnifico Ortenzia Zani	Magnifico wants to take his wife Ortenzia to the banquet, but he and Ortenzia are fighting because of jealousy. **Ortenzia exits** into the house. Magnifico and Zani discuss their desire for Franceschina, woman of the Soldier. They go to the piazza to see if she is there. **Magnifico and Zani exit**.
1.02	**Curzio**	Curzio monologues about his love for Ortenzia. He crosses the stage.
1.03	**Ortenzia**	[At her window] Curzio wants Ortenzia to love him. She tests him and rejects him. **Curzio exits** up the street. **Ortenzia withdraws**.
1.04	**Franceschina Capitano Gamberro**	Gamberro tells Franceschina that he wants to go off to war. Just then:
1.05	**Magnifico Zani**	Gamberro talks Magnifico into giving him Zani as a soldier for the war.[367] Zani is unhappy about the idea, but **Zani and Gamberro exit** up the street. Magnifico, using all his charm, asks Franceschina to go to a banquet with him, she agrees. They are interrupted:
1.06	**Zani**	Who has escaped from Gamberro, bumps into Magnifico. They go to the banquet. **Zani, Magnifico, and Franceschina exit** up the street.

Act II

2.01	**Curzio**	Curzio complains about Ortenzia rejecting his love. He is interrupted:
2.02	**Franceschina**	Franceschina comforts him saying that she will make it so Ortenzia can be with him. She sends him home and **Curzio exits**. Franceschina goes to Ortenzia's window and calls her.

---

[367] This plot point is implied in the original.

2.03	**Ortenzia**	Franceschina deceives her by saying that Fabio[368], her (Franceschina's) lover, has come. They discuss secret lovers.[369] Ortenzia lets her in. **Ortenzia and Franceschina exit** into Ortenzia's house.
2.04	**Magnifico** **Zani**	Magnifico and Zani are drunk. They have come from the banquet. After a drunken lazzo, **Magnifico and Zani exit** up the street.
2.05	**Ortenzia**	Ortenzia monologues about being in a better mood, having heard Franceschina's plan. (*The audience doesn't yet know the plan.*)
2.06	**Curzio** **Franceschina**	Curzio is laughing with Franceschina about the lazzo of Fabio.
2.07	**Franceschina**	Ortenzia thinks Curzio has moved on and becomes upset. Franceschina tells Curzio about the tunnel (into Curzio's house), then they go to get fish (go to the fishmonger)[370]. Delighted, **Curzio and Ortenzia exit** into the tunnel.[371]
		Franceschina monologues about love.[372] **Franceschina exits** into her house.[373]
2.08	**Magnifico** **Zani**	Magnifico and Zani are no longer drunk. They see that Curzio has a woman in his house.[374] Magnifico is angry, thinking she is Ortenzia. They call Curzio.
2.09	**Ortenzia** **Curzio**	[Curzio at his window] Ortenzia passes through the tunnel and secretly goes to her door and greets Magnifico. Magnifico is satisfied that Curzio is with some other woman. Ortenzia in a tricky move looks like she goes into Magnifico's house, but **Ortenzia exits** into the tunnel.
		Magnifico invites Curzio and his woman to the banquet. **Curzio withdraws**.
		Magnifico and Zani knock for Franceschina.

---

368 It is ambiguous whose lover Fabio is, but it is only a lie, there is no Fabio. The actors can put in as much backstory as they like in this lazzo.
369 This plot point is added to help the two women build their characters.
370 This is a lazzo in which Franceschina compares intimate relations with buying fresh fish.
371 This exit is implied.
372 This monologue is added to give the lovers time for love.
373 This exit is implied.
374 These two plot points are implied in the original.

| 2.10 | Franceschina | [From inside] Ortenzia and Curzio make the noises of playing.[375] Franceschina discusses love with Magnifico.[376] Eventually, **Magnifico, Zani, and Franceschina exit** separately. |

Act III

3.01	Franceschina Magnifico Zani	Magnifico tells Franceschina to get Curzio and his woman. Franceschina goes to Curzio's house and calls him.
3.02 [377]	Curzio Ortenzia	[Ortenzia is wearing a veil] Magnifico receives them. Zani, greats the 'new' lady with ceremonious pleasantries. They prepare to go.
3.03	Capitano Gamberro	Gamberro returns from the war, they tease him[378]. Magnifico mocks Gamberro for returning early, and for leaving his woman unguarded. Gamberro says that he came back to get Zani, but that he will not be mocked by a cuckold. Gamberro removes Ortenzia's veil. Magnifico wants to kill the wife. In a long scene of ups and downs and fractured logic, they appease him.[379] Gamberro convinces Zani that going to war is more dignified than this. **Gamberro and Zani exit** up the street. Coming to terms with the situation, Magnifico renews his invitation to take Curzio and his new woman to the banquet. **Magnifico, Franceschina, Curzio, and Ortenzia exit** up the street.

---

375 The manuscript uses the word '*trastulo*' which is the name of a character in many of these plays, but here simply means playing, or a child's toy.

376 This is an added plot point to give the three on stage something to do while reacting to the noises of love from inside.

377 The first scene was split to allow for the implied entrances.

378 Are they teasing Magnifico.

379 Many of these plot points were implied, but not explicitly stated. We invented everything that happens after this to give resolution and exits at the end of the play. Depending on how you want to stage it, feel free to end when Magnifico is appeased, and finish with a dance or something.

Fighting for Love

Intermezzo: Adonis

This is a pastoral comedy about a poor shepherd who loves the sister of his friend, a wealthier shepherd with a powerful and protective magical father. They are compelled to fight each other for the lover to prove himself worthy. The intermezzo is the story of Adonis.

Dramatis Personae   5M-1F + many Extras

Sireno	A young shepherd
Orfinio	A young shepherd, son of Mago
Flori	A young woman, sister of Orfinio
Magnifico	A wealthy old man
Zani	Servant of Magnifico
Pastorella	A young shepherdess (one scene)
Mago	A great magician
Serpent	A fierce giant snake (one scene)
Lucina Juno	Goddess of childbirth (one scene)
Many Shepherds	extras
Spirits	Mostly controlled by Mago
Shadow of Acrisius	More powerful than Mago

Props

Flour
A fire prop
Fake eyes for Zani
Baskets of food
Horns (off stage)
Spirit costumes
Shadow of Acrisius effect

Set: one Tomb
• The tomb
• The underground entrance

Intermezzo Cast

Nurse	The royal nurse
Mira	Princess of Cypress
Cinara	King of Cypress
Messenger	(one scene)
Two Cypriots	(one scene)
Adonis	Handsome ill-born son of Cinara
Venus	Goddess of love
Mars	God of War
Wild Boar	A dangerous animal

Tree that opens releasing a baby.
A boar costume
A stage that can open
A flower

Set: open space
• The underworld entrance

Special Skills and Effects

- Flames
- Wild Boar
- Earth opens to take Adonis, and then a flower springs up
- Mars communicating from above
- Tree things, including giving birth to Adonis
- Serpent
- Shadow of Acrisius

Performance Considerations

- This play is a vehicle for spectacle, which means to do it well, you'll need clever set design and special effects.
- Flori does a lazzo of gouging Zani's eyes out, and he is blind for the next scene, but apparently recovers. It could be done as a spell instead of actual clawing of the eyes.
- There is a scene with an undescribed lazzo that involves flour at the end of Act I. This could require some cleanup. The lazzo of the Fountain/Natural Spring, and the Lazzo of the Scorpion are also going to require invention for any performance.
- It isn't clear from the scenario whether Orfinio wants Sireno to marry Flori but knows that fighting Orfinio is the only way that Mago would allow it (possibly meaning that he loses on purpose), or whether Orfinio, in addition to Mago, is against the idea. Pick the answer that gives you the best drama.

Issues

- Adonis is the son of an incestuous relationship between a father and his daughter, which is very dramatic. If you'd like to avoid such matters, the pastoral can stand by itself.

Relationship Diagrams

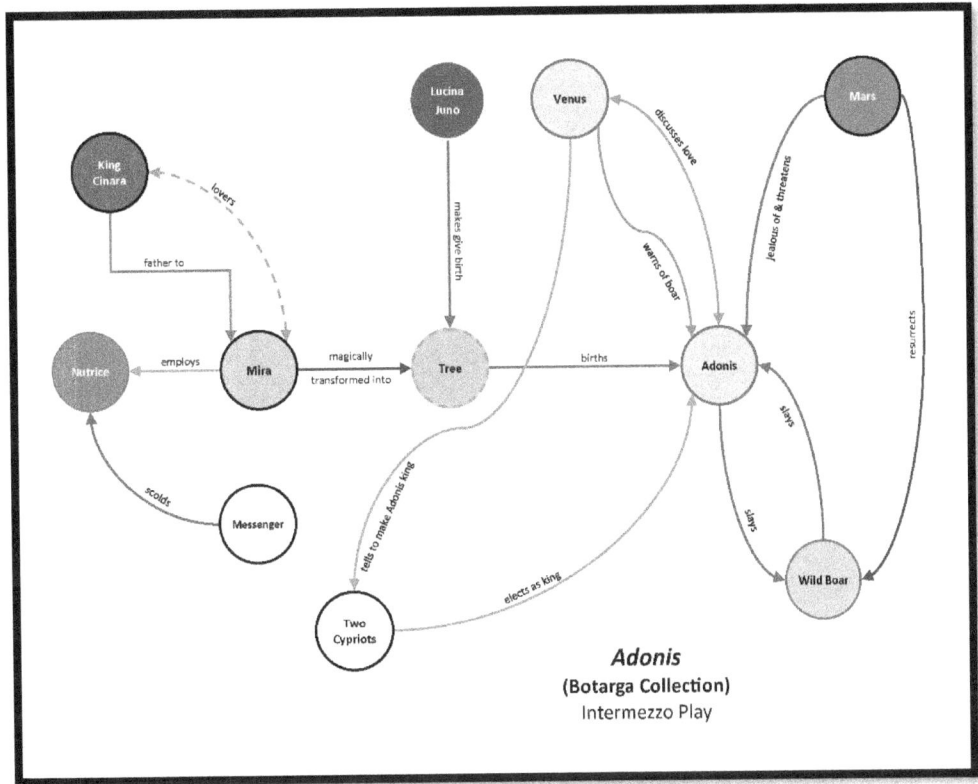

Adonis
(Botarga Collection)
Intermezzo Play

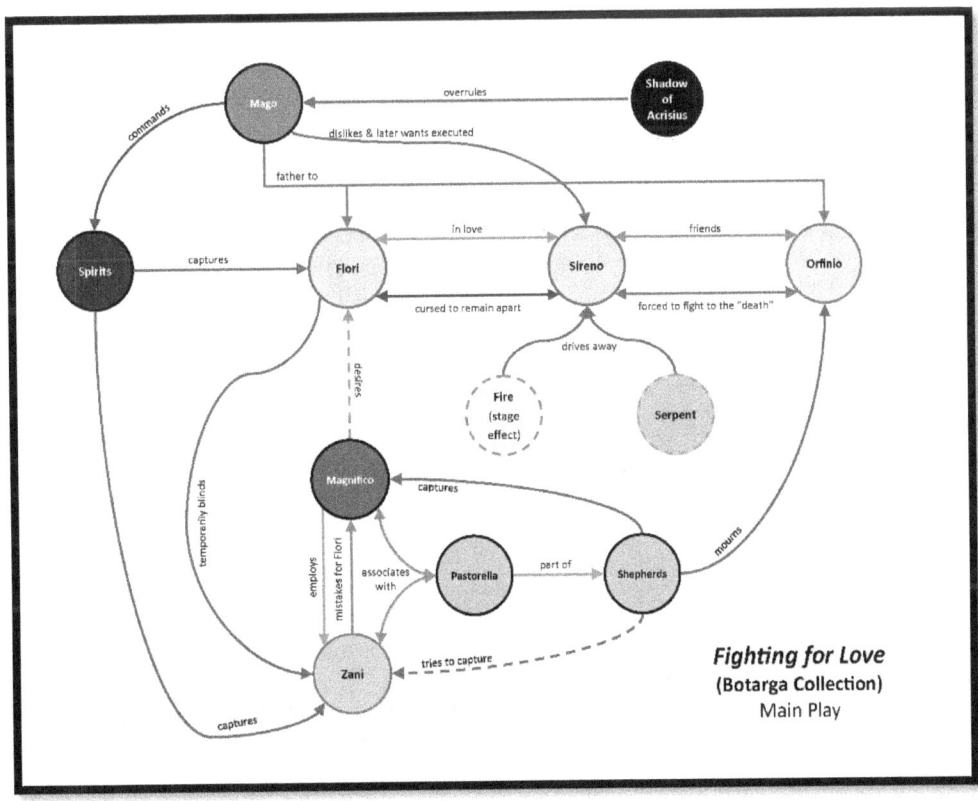

Fighting for Love
(Botarga Collection)
Main Play

Backstory (Argomento)[380]

In the Pastoral part of this work, Sireno loves Flori, but Mago forbids their love.

First Intermezzo

A.01	**Nurse**	Nurse monologues about Mira's love with her (Mira's) father, and that the nurse had joined them together by night, and that she (Mira) is pregnant and due to deliver soon.
A.02	**Mira**	Mira begs the Nurse to join her with her father again, before the delivery. She will meet him in the usual place. **Mira exits.**
A.03	**Cinara**	Wants to go and enjoy with someone[381] who he has never seen and who has brought the bait that is ignited with spit.[382] Nurse guides him. **Cinara exits.**
A.04	**Messenger**	He scolds Nurse for not guarding Mira. **Nurse and the messenger exit** separately.
A.05	**Mira**	Mira is excited and eager to be discovered.
A.06 [383]	**Cinara**	Cinara followed her. Mira converts to tree. **Cinara exits** in panic.[384]
A.07	**Lucina Juno**	Mira's limbs groan. Lucina[385] makes her give birth as the tree splits open and Adonis is born. **All exit.**

Act I

1.01	**Sireno**	Sireno talks of being in love with Flori, sister of his friend Orfinio, and that he cannot have her because Prince Mago separates them with enchantments. He goes to sleep.
1.02	**Orfinio**	Orfinio brags about being the richest and strongest shepherd in Arcadia. He sees Sireno, who reveals to him that he (Sireno) is in love with his (Orfinio's) sister. Orfinio says that if he (Sireno) wants her, he will have to fight him (Orfinio). They go to Prince Mago to ask for her. **Sireno and Orfinio exit.**
1.03	**Flori**	Flori complains that though she loves and is loved in return, she cannot have her love because of the enchantments.

---

380 There are no backstories in the manuscript. The one constructed here tells the minimum.
381 Feminine, so it is a woman he wants to enjoy.
382 This may be crudely erotic to indicate that Cinara is an imperfect man.
383 Scene split to separate Juno's entrance.
384 Literally, Cinara "throws himself from the precipice". But this is an idiom for leaving in a panic. He doesn't reappear, so you could potentially play it that he gives a speech and then kills himself for drama's sake.
385 Lucina was another name for Juno/Hera, who was among other things the goddess of childbirth.

1.04	**Sireno**	Sireno sees Flori and asks for a kiss from her. Fires rise. Sorrowful, they part. **Sireno and Flori exit separately**.
1.05	**Magnifico** **Zani**	They speak of love and hunger. They want to get Flori to love Magnifico.
1.06	**Flori**	The old men sing. She makes the lazzo of a fountain. **Flori exits**.
1.07	**Pastorella**[386]	[with flour] They do a lazzo. **All exit**.

Second Intermezzo

B.01	**Two Cypriots**	They do not know who they should elect as king of Cyprus and they want to pray to Venus.
B.02	**Adonis**	Adonis says he is the son of Cinara. At that moment:
B.03	**Venus**	Venus tells them that they must take Adonis as king. **The Cypriots exit**. Venus tells Adonis to beware of the wild boar. They talk about their loves.
B.04	**Mars**	Mars is jealous[387] and threatens them. Venus comforts Adonis.[388] **All exit**.

Act II

2.01	**Magnifico**	He does an echo[389]. **Magnifico exits**.
2.02	**Mago** **Orfinio** **Sireno**	They beg Mago. Mago asides that he's sure that Orfinio will win a fight and kill Sireno, especially if Mago provides the weapons.[390] Mago agrees and will provide the deadly weapons. **Mago and Orfinio exit**.
2.03	**Flori**	Flori takes his right hand and wants to fight.
2.04	**Serpent**	The fearsome serpent makes Sireno run away. **Sireno and the serpent exit** separately.
2.05	**Zani**	Zani tries to get Flori to marry Magnifico. Flori is furious.[391] Flori does a lazzo of tearing Zani's eyes out.[392] **Flori exits**.

---

386 Pastorella is a young shepherdess.
387 The manuscript doesn't mention the jealousy, but it is a key part of the story.
388 Venus comforts Adonis is a guess filling in some missing words.
389 "Fa l'eco" is a stage instruction to echo something recently said. Context suggests that Magnifico echoes something Mars said.
390 This plot point is implied but not explicitly in the manuscript.
391 This is implied but not explicitly in the manuscript.
392 How do you want to stage this? Clearly Zani can see again by the next act.

2.06	Magnifico	Blind Zani mistakes Magnifico for Flori. Fearful, **Magnifico exits**. Following, **Zani exits**.
2.07	A Shepherd	With many things to eat, he places them at the tomb. **The shepherd exits**.
2.08	Magnifico	Magnifico starts eating the food. At that:
2.09	Zani	[Perhaps able to see again] Zani also eats. They hear war-horns. For safety, **Magnifico and Zani exit** into the tomb.
2.10	Mago Flori Sireno Orfinio Many Shepherds	At the tomb, Mago offers weapons to Sireno and Orfinio.[393] They choose. They fight[394]. Sireno wins. Orfinio appears dead. Prince Mago grieves.
2.11 [395]	Spirits	The spirits take Flori away. **Flori and the spirits exit**. Mago decrees that whoever gives him Sireno's head will have Flori. Desperate, **Sireno exits**. They place Orfinio in the tomb. **Mago, Orfinio, and the shepherds exit** into the tomb. [From the tomb] There is noise and commotion.
2.12	Mago Zani Magnifico Many Shepherds	They find Zani and Magnifico. Mago and the Shepherds grab Zani and Magnifico. Zani does the lazzo of the scorpion. Zani escapes. **Zani exits**. **All exit**.

Third Intermezzo

C.01	Adonis Wild Boar	[The boar is dead] Adonis monologues praising himself in this hunt.
C.02	Mars	Mars, from above raises the pig. **Mars exits**.
C.03	Wild Boar	The wild boar kills Adonis. **The Wild Boar exits**.
C.04	Venus	Venus is in pain. She gestures and the dry land swallow the corpse of Adonis.[396] A flower rises. **Venus exits**.

Act III

| 3.01 | Sireno | Sireno monologues about his grief. |

---

[393] This plot point was implied.
[394] Fano a la Iota literally means "they fight at first".
[395] Scene split to allow Zani and magnifico to enter after being discovered.
[396] This plot point is not in the manuscript but is implied from its sources.

3.02	Flori	[From within the Earth] Flori calls Sireno. They do a scene of increasingly tragic love.[397] Flori screams, then falls silent.[398] Sireno sets off with a heavy heart to give his head to Mago to free Flori. **Sireno exits**.
3.03	Zani	Zani echoes Sireno's speech about (Zani) giving Sireno's head to Mago.
3.04	Spirits	The Spirits takes Zani underground. **Zani and the spirits exit** into the tomb.
3.05	Mago	Mago, in his fury, wants to to kill Sireno.
3.06	Sireno	Sireno, without removing it, hands Mago his (Sireno's) head. At that:
3.07	Shadow of Acrisius	Acrisius declares that the decree is over, and that Flori must be released given to Sireno; also, that Orfinio was only half dead. They open the tomb. **Acrisius exits**.
3.08	Orfinio	Orfinio says: "**I live**". They all rejoice. Mago commands the spirits to bring up Flori and Zani, **the spirits exit**. They also set Magnifico free.
3.09	Flori Zani Magnifico	Sireno and Flori marry. Everyone celebrates. **All exit**.

---

[397] Literally this translates to "They make the climbs." But in context
[398] Added plot point to make the sequence clear.

Two Crazy People

This is comedy about lovers who were separated by circumstance and who each went crazy during a decade-long desperate search. They find each other and are at peace.

Dramatis Personae   6M-3F + Extras

Magnifico	A wealthy man
Isabella	Magnifico's daughter
Franceschina	Isabella's servant
Zani	Magnifico's servant
Tofano	An old man
Orazio	A young man
Giacomo[399]	Orazio's servant
Crazyman/Curzio	Magnifico's lost son
Crazywoman/Ort.	Tofano's lost daughter Ortenzia
Spirits	They ask the audience for money

Props

Isabella's luggage
Playing cards

Set: two houses
• Magnifico's house
• Tofano's house

Special Skills and Effects

- Giant luggage gag.
- Crazy-people babbling.

Performance Considerations

- The players playing Curzio and Ortenzia will need to practice stage-madness.
- Tofano must be a sympathetic character while also demonstrating to the audience what an awful husband he would be for Isabella.

---

[399] This character is nameless in the manuscript.

Relationship Diagram

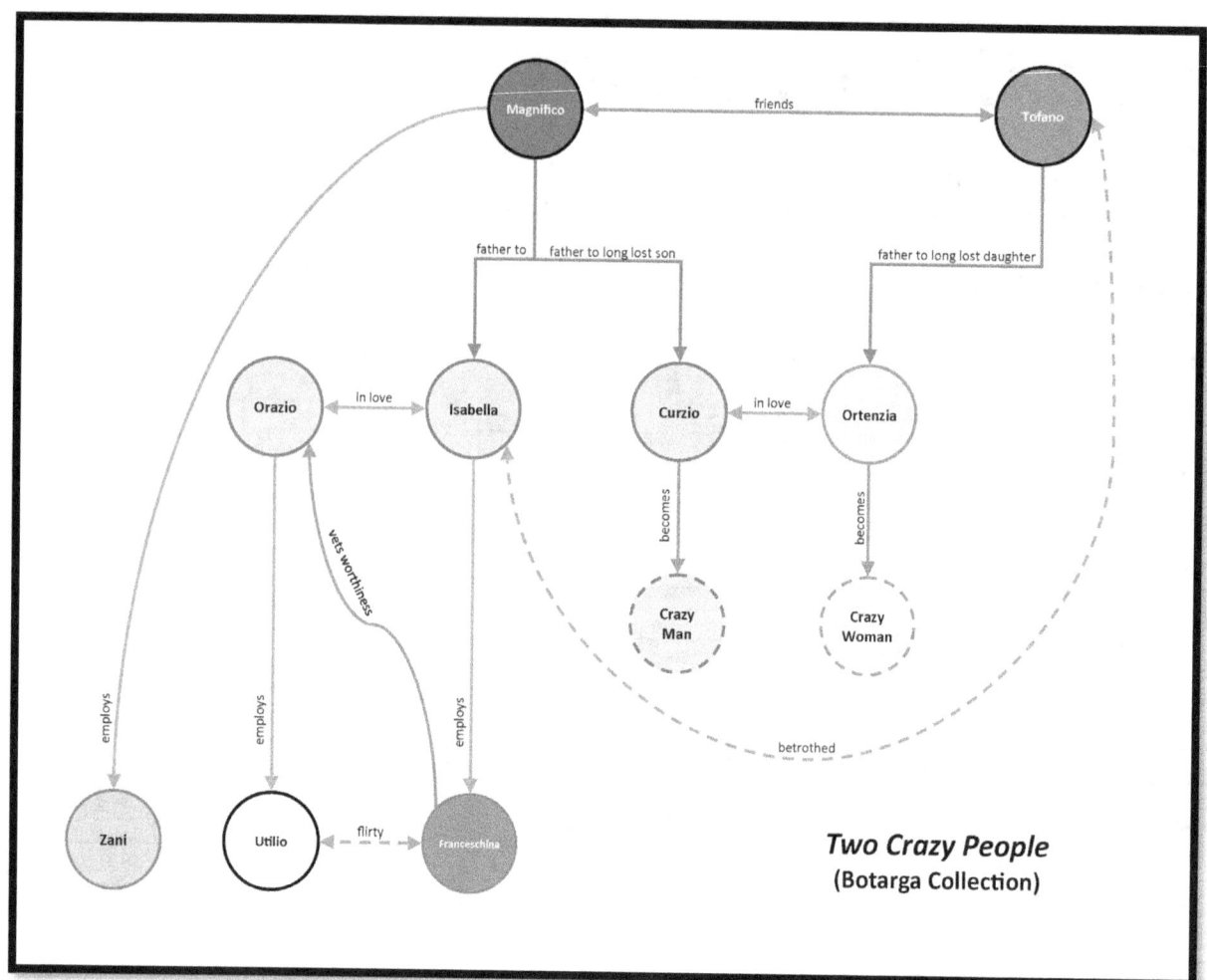

Two Crazy People
(Botarga Collection)

Backstory (Argomento)

Years ago, Magnifico's son Curzio was lost travelling. Curzio loved Tofano's daughter Ortenzia. When she heard that he was lost, she went to look for her love, and herself became lost. During their long frustrating search, both young lovers went crazy. Just before the start of this play, Magnifico's younger daughter fell in love with a young man named Orazio, but Magnifico wanted her to marry his old friend Tofano.

During this play, the crazy lovers returned separately, and were not immediately recognized.

Act I

1.01	**Magnifico** **Zani**	Magnifico monologues about his lost son Curzio. He tells Zani that he wants to marry his young daughter Isabella to Magnifico's old friend Tofano.

1.02	**Tofano**	Magnifico and Tofano do a lazzo about old men marrying young women. Tofano laments his lost daughter Ortenzia. Magnifico calls Isabella.
1.03	Isabella	Magnifico makes Tofano touch Isabella's hand (*beginning the period of betrothal*). Upset, **Isabella exits** into her house.
		Magnifico and Tofano agree they need to draw up a marriage contract. To find a notary, **Magnifico, Tofano, and Zani exit** up the street.
1.04	**Orazio** **Giacomo**	Orazio tells Giacomo about Isabella, and how much he (Orazio) loves her. After discussing options, Giacomo suggests that they ask Isabella's servant Franceschina for help. Giacomo calls Franceschina.
1.05	Franceschina	They discuss Orazio's hopes, and Franceschina agrees to talk to Isabella alone. **Orazio and Giacomo exit** up the street.
		Franceschina knocks at Isabella's door.
1.06	Isabella	After a discussion, Isabella agrees to meet Orazio. **Isabella and Franceschina exit** into Isabella's house.
1.07	**Crazyman/Curzio**	Curzio (*Using names is optional*) monologues his history as described in the backstory.
1.08	**Magnifico**	They do a lazzo of Magnifico not understanding or respecting the crazy person (*Possibly foreshadowing the card-playing in 1.12*).
		Magnifico exits into his house.
		Crazyman exits up the street.
1.09	**Orazio** **Giacomo** **Franceschina**	Orazio knocks at the door, and **Franceschina enters** from inside.
		Franceschina wants proof that Orazio loves Isabella. Orazio makes an impassioned statement of love. Franceschina is almost convinced but says they cannot come in. **Orazio and Giacomo exit** up the street.
		Franceschina exit into the house.
1.10	**Crazywoman/Ort.**	Crazywoman (Ortenzia) monologues her story as described in the backstory. She hears people coming and prepares to greet the strangers.
1.11	**Magnifico** **Zani**	The three of them do a lazzo of difficult communication. **Crazywoman exits** up the street.

| 1.12 | Crazyman/Curzio | Crazyman, Zani, and Magnifico talk. They agree to play Primero (*a card game similar to Poker*). They play until Crazyman gets upset. **Crazyman exits** up the street. **Magnifico and Zani exit** into Magnifico's house. |
| 1.13 | Spirits | {*Optional scene. The spirits come out of the houses and beg for money from the audience. The Spirits exit.*} |

Act II

2.01 [400]	Tofano Crazywoman/Ort.	Tofano meets the Crazywoman (*his daughter Ortenzia, whom he does not recognize*) and starts to talk to her. Crazywoman talks about diverse tangential topics, and Tofano tries to reply. **Crazywoman exits**.
2.02	Isabella Magnifico	[At her window, Magnifico hides to observe] Tofano woos badly. Isabella rejects Tofano's advances. **Tofano exits** up the street.
2.03	Zani	**Magnifico steps forward**. Magnifico tells Zani his suspicions about Isabella's activities. Zani asks Isabella, and she confesses (lying) that Orazio has become her lover. Furious, Magnifico drives his daughter away. [Using the lazzo of Bad Acting] Isabella acts distraught and says she will drown herself. Looking like she is going to the waterfront, **Isabella hides**. Magnifico and Zani worry that they've done something terrible in chasing Magnifico's only remaining child away. To go rescue her, **Zani exits** up the street. While Magnifico is watching Zani, Isabella sneaks into her house unseen. **Isabella exits** into her house. Magnifico knocks at his house.
2.04	Isabella	[At her window] Isabella scolds Magnifico and chases him away from the house. **Magnifico exits** up the street. Storming off, **Isabella withdraws**.
2.05 [401]	Orazio Giacomo	Orazio and Giacomo want to get Isabella. They signal at her window.
2.06	Franceschina	Franceschina, again, wants proof of Orazio's love for Isabella and tests him. This time she is convinced, and Franceschina calls Isabella.

[400] Scene added to give Tofano and Ortenzia more time to establish characters, and once again show Tofano's unworthiness as a husband to Isabella. This extends into the early plot-points of 2.02.
[401] Scenes 2.05, 2.06, and 2.07 were added to further the plot line of Isabella's romance as a parallel to the crazy-people story. It also gives Franceschina a chance to complete the rule-of-three for tests of Isabella's would-be lover.

2.07	Isabella	[At her window] Isabella and Orazio begin a love scene. Franceschina and Giacomo have a parallel love scene. Orazio and Isabella finish their love scene agreeing to elope and avoid unpleasantness with Tofano. Isabella tells him to come back in the evening, and she'll be ready to go with him. She calls Franceschina into the house to help pack. **Franceschina exits** into the house. **Isabella withdraws.** With great hope, **Orazio and Giacomo exit** up the street.
2.08	Crazyman/Curzio Crazywoman/Ort.	The two crazy people meet. In a lazzo they start off crazy, but recognize each other, and realize their years of searching are over. Knowing they must make plans, they run off together. **Curzio and Ortenzia exit** up the street.

Act III

3.01	Isabella Zani Franceschina	[Zani hides to observe, Isabella and Franceschina are at their window] Franceschina gives wedding night advice to innocent Isabella. Zani quietly reacts to the advice.
3.02	Orazio Giacomo	Isabella and Franceschina throw the luggage from the window to Orazio and Giacomo. **Isabella withdraws and enters. Isabella, Orazio, Franceschina[402], and Giacomo exit** up the street.
3.03	Magnifico Tofano	**Zani steps forward** and tells Magnifico and Tofano that Isabella has escaped with Orazio. The old men are agitated. To go find Isabella, Zani will search one way, and the vecchi the other. Before they can leave, they are interrupted.
3.04	Curzio	[No longer crazy] Curzio asks the old men about Magnifico. The old men and Zani recognize him as Magnifico's long-lost son Curzio. Curzio tells Tofano that he has seen Ortenzia today and will bring her back to him. **Curzio exits** up the street.
3.05	Orazio Isabella Giacomo Franceschina[403]	[Giacomo is carrying luggage] The luggage is too bulky to carry to the next town. Orazio and Isabella ask Magnifico if they can marry. Tofano releases Magnifico from his promise, and Magnifico agrees that Isabella and Orazio may wed. Franceschina asks Giacomo if he wants to try being married, and he agrees.[404]

---

[402] The manuscript doesn't mention Franceschina exiting, but she has no plot points until the lovers come back.

[403] This entrance is implied but doesn't appear in the manuscript.

[404] We added this plot point to make a triple wedding.

| 3.06 | **Ortenzia**
Curzio | Ortenzia and Curzio ask their fathers if they may marry, and the old men agree. Everyone celebrates in a dance. **Isabella and Orazio exit** into Magnifico's house.

For some fun, **Giacomo and Franceschina exit** up the street.

To get some wine and food for continued celebrations, **Zani, Tofano, and Magnifico exit** up the street.

Continuing to dance and sing, **Ortenzia and Curzio exit** into Tofano's house. |

Jewels of Chastity

Intermezzo: Perseus & Medusa

This is an entwined pair of plays. Jewels of Chastity is a pastoral comedy about two young shepherds that fall in love with two nymphs, but the Nymphs have Jewels of Chastity that make them disinterested in romance. Through tricks, the shepherds steal the jewels, and then they become disinterested in romance. Eventually love prevails. The other play is the story of Perseus and Medusa, in which Medusa gets her start by not wanting to be loved by Neptune, who then causes her transformation and serpentine coiffeur.

Dramatis Personae   *5M-2F + many Extras*   *Props*

Orfinio	Sireno's Friend, loves Flori		2 Jewels
Sireno	Orfinio's friend, loves Delia		Spell book
Pan	1 scene		Water of Forgetfulness
Cupid	1 scene		Sphinx costume
Zani	Servant of Magnifico		Macaroni
Magnifico	An older man		Lamb for the sacrifice
Flori	A nymph		
Delia	A nymph		
Mago	A magician		
The Sphinx			
Spirit			**Set: one 'house'**
Priest of Diana			• Mago's Hut
Diana	Goddess of Chastity		• Open Space

Intermezzo Cast

Neptune/Horse	God of the Sea		Wings, sword, shield
Forco	Ancient Deity, Father of Medusa		Helm of Pluto
Minerva	Goddess of Wisdom		Bag with Medusa's head
A Fury	When wisdom alone won't work		The sisters' eye
Medusa	Divine priestess of Minerva		
Polydette	King of Serifos, loves Danae		

Servants of Polydette	
Perseus	Son of Danae and Jupiter
Mercury	Messenger of the Gods
Estenese	Sister of Medusa
Euriale	Sister of Medusa
Pegasus	A flying horse

Sets: each act is different
• Olympus
• Palace of Polydette
• Cave of Medusa

Special Skills and Effects

- Serpentine hair
- Gods ascending (pully system?)
- Horse with wings
- Decapitation
- Pan & Cupid wrestling match
- Spirits
- A Sphinx

Performance Considerations

- Note that the jewels Flori and Delia possess seem to represent their virginity or at least chastity, which strangely in this universe you can take and give back. In this play, whoever has one of the jewels wants to stay chaste. That includes the male shepherds.
- 1.03 Why is Magnifico in need of being freed?
- The sets for the intermezzi could be very elaborate if you have the budget.

Relationship Diagrams

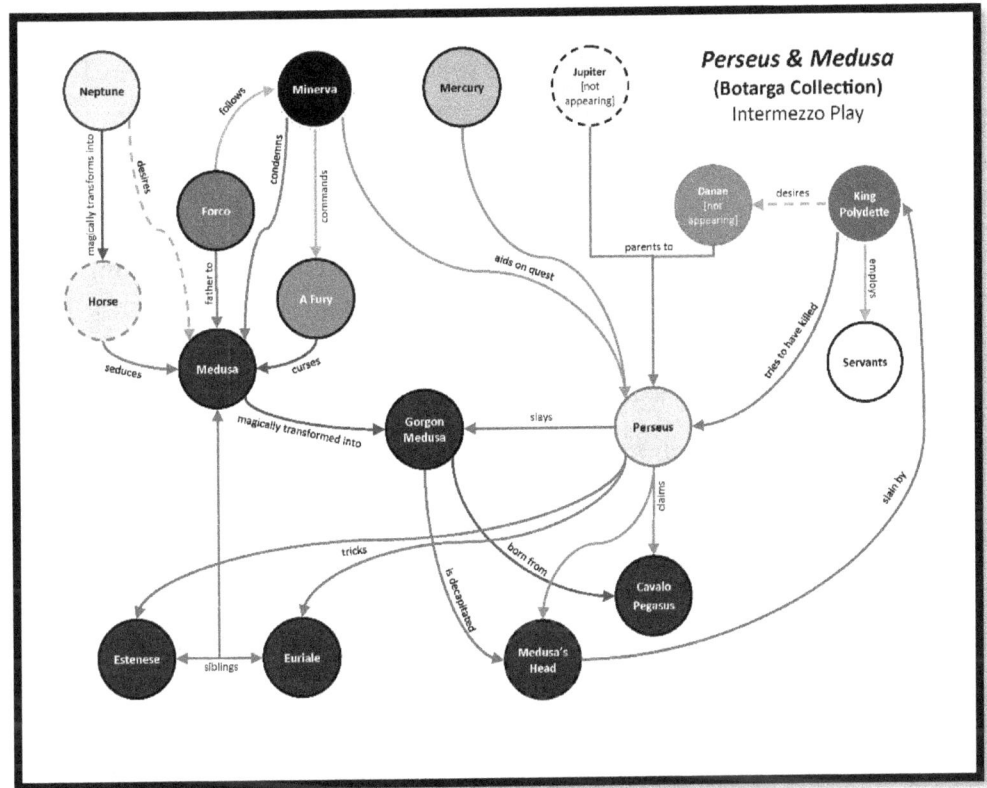

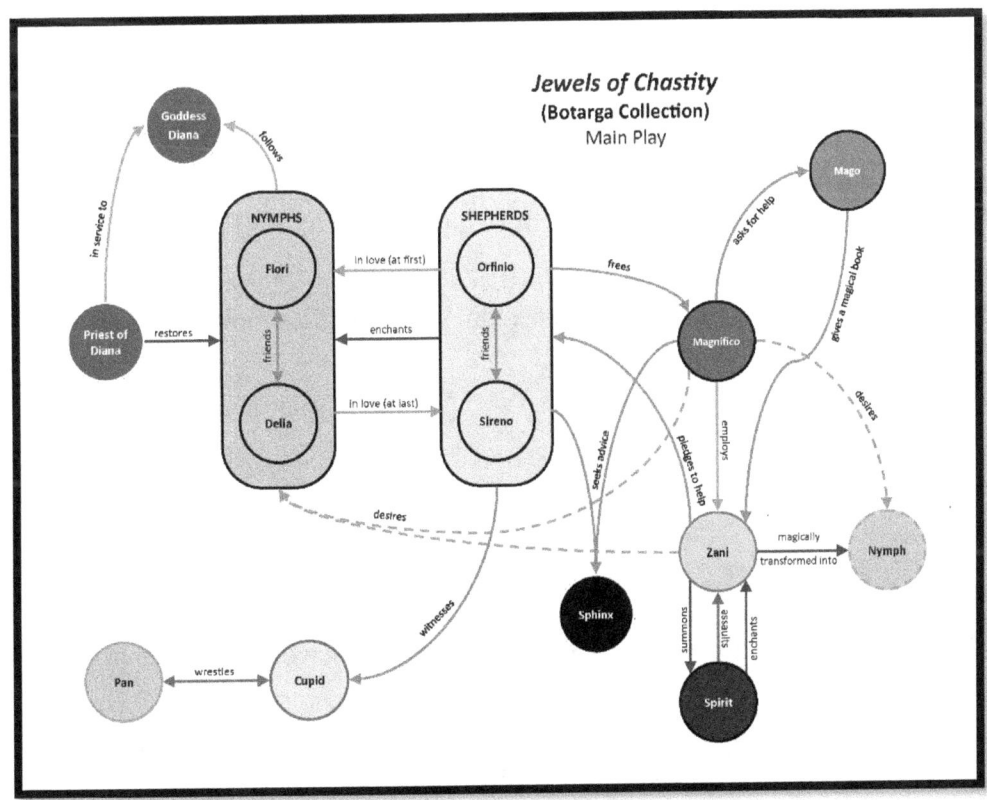

Backstory (Argomento)

Two shepherds are in love with chaste nymphs. Magnifico has gotten stuck in a predicament and needs help that Zani cannot give.

First Intermedio

A.01	**Neptune**	Neptune monologues that he is in love with Medusa, He goes to be transformed into a horse to kidnap her. **Neptune exits**.
A.02	**Forco** **Medusa**	Forco says that Medusa shouldn't get far from him, because he has foreseen her damage through the prophetic spirit. **Forco exits**. Medusa is about to exit but hears a horse. At that:
A.03	**Neptune as a Horse**	The horse persuades her. She climbs onto the horse. The horse takes her away. **Neptune and Medusa exit**.
A.04	**Minerva**	Minerva says that Medusa has violated her temple's rules. She calls a fury.
A.05	**Fury**	She orders the fury to turn Medusa's head into snakes. To do this off stage, **The fury exits**, then **Minerva exits** ascending.
A.06	**Forco**	Forco monologues about his deep sadness for his daughter's situation and frustration that she didn't stay close.
A.07	**Medusa**	With a serpentine mane, she is furious. **Forco and Medusa exit**.

Act I

1.01	**Orfinio**[405] **Sireno**	Sireno praises "Love"[406], Orfinio blames Love. They are both in love, Sireno with Delia, the other with Flori.
1.02	**Pan** **Cupid**	As a parallel allegory Pan and Cupid wrestle. Pan loses (falls).[407] Sireno narrates about the strength of love. **Pan and Cupid exit**.

---

[405] Curcio (Curzio) is in the manuscript, but almost certainly should have been written by Botarga as Orfinio.

[406] Love personified.

[407] This appears to be a tableau representing Sireno and Orfinio's argument. Pan and Cupid do not return to this play. I suggest an elaborately choreographed fight, and having Pan get up and Pan and Cupid bowing just prior to exit.

1.03	**Zani**	He gets between the shepherds. He promises help with the nymphs, if they help set Magnifico free[408], Sireno goes to free Magnifico. To get Magnifico, **Sireno exits**.
1.04	**Magnifico** **Sireno**[409]	Zani explains to Magnifico about his promise. Magnifico agrees to help. Zani and Magnifico will help Orfinio and Sireno clean and dress themselves for the nymphs. **All exit**.
1.05	**Flori**	With two jewels from Diana, looking for Delia, praising Delia's chastity as being as pure as her own.
1.06	**Delia**	Flori gives her one jewel[410] on behalf of Diana.
1.07	**Orfinio** **Sireno**	Orfinio and Sireno beg the nymphs to requite their love. The nymphs shoo the lovesick shepherds away. Sad, **Sireno and Orfino exit**.
1.08	**Magnifico** **Zani**	Magnifico and Zani fall in love with the nymphs. They (nymphs) do the lazzo of burbe[411]. **Flori and Delia exit**.[412] At that:
1.09 413	**Mago**	[Mago with his spell book] Magnifico asides that he knows Mago. Magnifico asks for help. Mago invites Magnifico enter into his hut. Magnifico leaves Zani to help Mago. **Magnifico exits** into the hut. Mago asks Zani to hold the book and orders him not to open it. **Mago exits**.
1.10	**Spirits**	Zani opens the book. Evil spirits come out. He orders them to bring macaroni. They beat him. **All exit**.

Second Intermedio

| B.01 | **Polydette**
Servant(s) | Polydette monologues about how Perseus is blocking Polydette's romantic pursuit of Danae (*Mother of Perseus, and not appearing in this play*) and of wanting to send Perseus to death. Polydette calls Perseus. |

---

[408] Why is Magnifico needing to be free? Not sure, but it must be something just a little too hard for Zani to do, like stuck in a ditch, or surrounded by sheep, or something else. He clearly is not imprisoned by Mago. Actors should invent something that works in a pastoral environment.

[409] Sireno's entrance is omitted in the manuscript, but strongly implied.

[410] The manuscript is ambiguous about the number of jewels, except that Delia receives only one of the two or more, but in context, they get one each.

[411] "burbe", possibly meaning being gruff or angry: see adjective burbero. The nymphs say and do angry things uncharacteristic of sweet young ladies.

[412] This exit may be implied by whatever the lazzo of the burbe is. Clearly they aren't in the next scene.

[413] This scene split to give the spirits an explicit entrance.

B.02	**Perseus**	Polydette sends him on a mission to get the head of Medusa. **Polydette and servants exit.**
		At that:
B.03	**Mercury**	[With wings and a sword] Mercury gives him the wings and the sword and then **Mercury exits**.
B.04	**Minerva**	[With a shield] Minerva gives him the shield and tells him to look for the helmet of Pluto. **Minerva and Perseus exit** separately.

Act II

2.01	**Magnifico** **Mago**	Mago tells Magnifico to have Orfinio and Sireno go to the Sphinx. Mago cannot find Zani nor the book. The lost book will cost Zani dearly. To find Zani, **Mago exits.**
2.02	**Sireno** **Orfinio**	Magnifico tells them about the sphinx, and about the riddles[414]. **Magnifico, Sireno, and Orfinio exit** to get in order.
2.03	**Zani**	[With the book] Zani says that he wants to turn into a nymph to be with the nymphs. **Zani exits.**

---

[414] "dubii" means doubts. Could be that they are the riddles, or the water of forgetfulness, or just about doubts about who loves who.

2.04	**Magnifico** **Orfinio** **Sireno** **Sphinx**	They ask the Sphinx for help with the nymphs. The Sphinx proposes riddles, and they resolve them: *Tell me, wise spirit, in what season* *The feather of the angel, that is so light,* *Keeps the men of the Earth either with a sad face* *Or a happy face?*[415] *I was surrounded by my enemies* *From below and from above* *My house went out through the windows* *And I remained in jail, unfortunate.* *When will that day be, wise spirit,* *That the skin of an animal, hitting hard,* *Will invite anybody to kill themselves,* *Making with its sound a big commotion?* *When, tell me, being warned,* *He who is desperate, without mercy,* *Let him suck the blood of those that have deceived him,* *And killed his father?* The Sphinx gives them a vial of the water of sleepiness.[416] **The Sphinx exits**. In order to go find the nymphs, **All exit**.
2.05	**Flori**	[Carrying her jewel] Flori monologues about having lost Delia. At that:
2.06	**Delia**	[Carrying her jewel] Delia asides about having lost Flori. They see and greet each other enthusiastically.
2.07	**Sireno** **Orfinio**	[With water of sleepiness] The shepherds sprinkle water on nymphs. The nymphs fall asleep. The shepherds take the jewels rather than kiss the nymphs. **Sireno and Orfinio exit**.
2.08	**Zani**	[Made to look like a nymph, carrying the book] Zani sees the nymphs. He sits between them; he monologues about wanting to kiss them.
2.09	**Spirit**	The spirit takes the book from Zani. **The spirit exits**. Zani is frightened. **Zani exits**.

[415] Answers: Winter, Pistachios, The day the war drums are sounded, The alcoholic son of an alcoholic. Feel free to sub in your own riddles.

[416] This is called "l'aqua de l'oblio" but only forget having the jewels of chastity, they just fall asleep, so for this version we call it water of sleepiness.

| 2.10 | **Delia** **Flori** | The nymphs wake up. They agree that they desire the young shepherds. Flori loves Orfinio, and Delia loves Sireno. Excited, they go to look for the shepherds. **Delia and Flori exit.** |
| 2.11 [417] | **Sireno** **Orfinio** | The young shepherds in a lazzo of escalation realize that they aren't interested in silly love. **Sireno and Orfinio exit.** |

Third Intermedio

C.01	**Estenese**[418] **Euriale**	[They have one eye, and the Helmet of Pluto] They agree to pass the eye.
C.02	**Perseus**	Perseus takes the eye from them. He makes them promise to give him the enchanted Helmet (of Pluto). They give it to him and get the eye back. **Estenese and Euriale exit.** He puts on the helmet. At that:
C.03	**Medusa**	Medusa screams. Perseus, using the shield as a mirror cuts Medusa's head off. Perseus puts the head in a bag and keeps it.
C.04	**Pegasus**	Pegasus rises up. Perseus mounts Pegasus. The spring of water rises up[419].
C.05	**Polydette**	Polydette returns from his hunt, and Perseus shows him the head. Polydette turns to stone. **All exit.**

Act III

3.01	**Sireno**	Sireno brags about his flock.
3.02	**Delia**	Delia begs Sireno to love her. He shoos her away. **Sireno exits.** **Delia exits** following him.
3.03	**Flori**	Flori wants Orfinio to love her.
3.04	**Orfinio**	Flori begs for his love. He shoos her away. **Orfinio exits.** **Flori exits** following him.
3.05	**Magnifico** **Zani**	Magnifico thinks Zani is a nymph and he falls in love. Zani reveals that he is Zani, and not a nymph. They go to Mago to lift the spell. **Magnifico and Zani exit.**

---

[417] An entire short scene was cut during the binding process. We've inserted a scene that makes dramatic sense.

[418] In traditional mythology the pair of women sharing one eye is someone else, but in this play, it is Medusa's sisters, to cut back on the number of scenes needed for Perseus' eventual victory.

[419] This rise of the fountain may be a call for a change of scenery.

3.06	**Sireno** **Orfinio** **Flori** **Delia**	[The shepherds have the jewels] The shepherds continue to shoo away the nymphs. The nymphs say they want to kill themselves. At that:
3.07	**Priest of Diana**	The priest takes away the jewels from the shepherds and returns them to the Nymphs who are transformed into young women. The lovers are in love again. The priest orders the sacrifice.
3.08	**Magnifico** **Zani**	Magnifico lights the fire, and Sireno and Orfinio provide lambs for the sacrifice.
3.09	**Diana**	Diana gives license for these nymphs to marry these shepherds. They celebrate. **All exit**.

Prince Tireno

Intermezzo: The Choice of Paris

This is the most tragic play in the collection. The primary play has a female villain, who creates havoc in the court of the prince who jilted her in favor of a young beauty of lesser royal rank. The intermezzi are a play about the young Trojan named Paris who must make a choice between three goddesses, and ultimately the jealous losers allow him to cause the Trojan War and Fall of Troy.

Dramatis Personae   5M-2F + many Extras   Props

King	King Marganorre		Judge disguise for Contessa
Magnifico	Runs palace operations		A coffin
Capitano[420]	Friend of Prince Tireno		Fake blood
Contessa	Prince Tireno's former lover		
Subdulo[421]	Servant of the Contessa		
Orazio	A young man		
Ortenzia	Daughter of Magnifico		
Prince Tireno	Son of the king		
Zani	Servant of Magnifico		
Priest			**Set: inside the palace**
The Palace Guards			• Magnifico's house

Intermezzo Cast

Priam	King of Troy	Golden apple
Hecuba	Queen of Troy	
Oracle		
Servant & child		
Shepherd		
Paris	Abandoned prince, raised by shepherd	

---

[420] In the comedies, we have given the Capitano a name (Gamberro), but in this tragedy, we have left his as just 'the Capitano'.
[421] The nameless servant of the Contessa, and the nameless porter in Act 1 are combined and given a name.

Mercury	Messenger of the gods		Sets: Each act is different
Juno	Queen of the gods		• Entrance of Troy
Pallas Athena	Goddess of wisdom		• The city
Venus	Goddess of love		• The forest

Special Skills and Effects

- There is a lot of death and violence in this play. Fake blood will be needed.

Performance Considerations

- The Capitano does not appear in Act III.
- At the end there are several dead characters on stage.
- Note: the main play is borrowed, with name-changes, from an episode in the "Orlando Furioso".

Relationship Diagrams

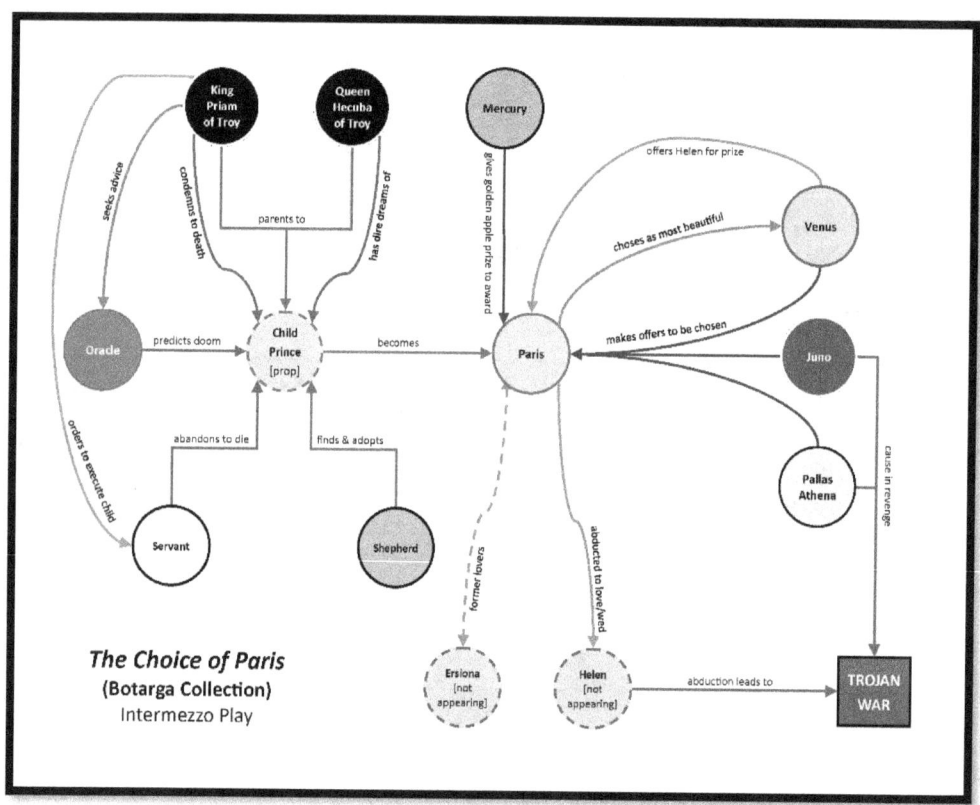

The Choice of Paris
(Botarga Collection)
Intermezzo Play

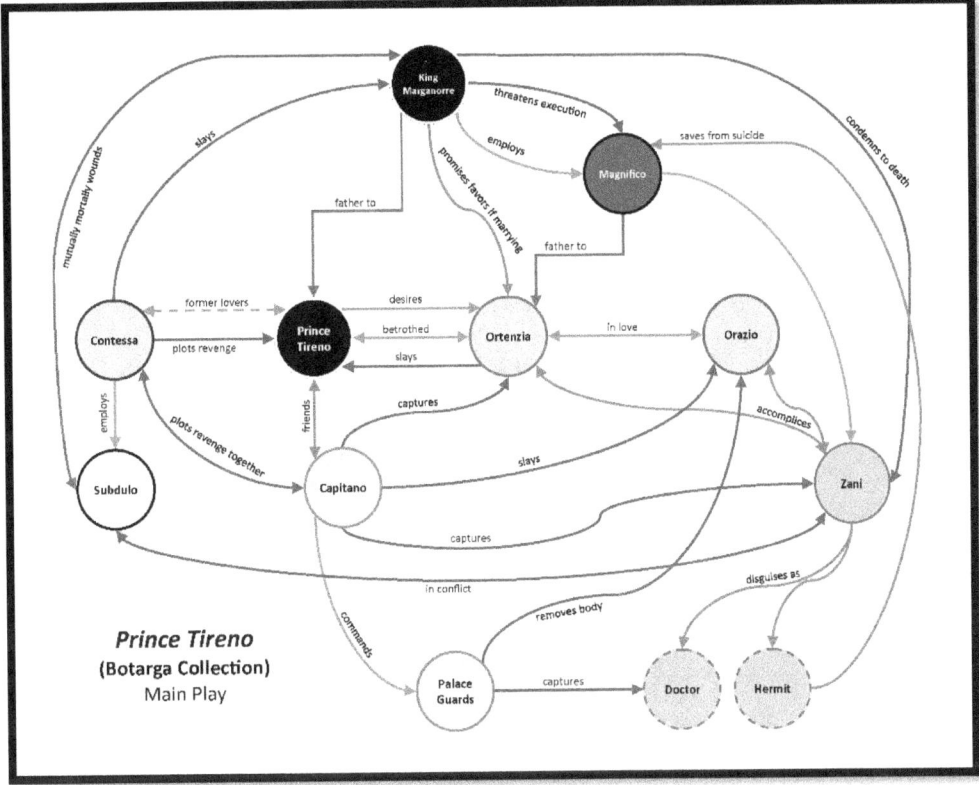

Prince Tireno
(Botarga Collection)
Main Play

Backstory (Argomento)

In the primary play, Prince Tireno has had some kind of relationship with the Contessa. Perhaps it was only that he was promised to her, or perhaps they'd been a couple already. Prince Tireno sees Ortenzia, who has just come of age, and he has lost all other desires. Everyone else wants to cure his secret illness, but the Contessa is furious.

The Intermezzi play is the familiar tale of the golden apple (or pomegranate) for the fairest, leading Venus to win it by offering Paris the young wife of Menelaus.

First Intermedio

A.01 [422]	**Priam** **Hecuba** **Servant with child**[423]	Hecuba tells Priam the dream that her baby would become a torch that burns down Troy.[424] They go to the Oracle.
A.02	**Oracle**	The Oracle says: "**He weeps, Oh Priam, because your joy is extinct; there will be a flame that will burn down Troy.**" **Hecuba exits** grieving. **The Oracle exits**. Priam orders that the child be brought to death. **Priam exits**. The servant says that he will abandon the child here in the woods. The servant puts the baby down. **The servant exits**.
A.03	**Shepherd**	The shepherd finds the baby and takes the child with him. **Both exit**.

Act I

1.01	**King** **Magnifico** **Capitano**	The three men talk about the infirmity of Prince Tireno. (*He is lovesick, but his parents only think he's sick*) The King orders Magnifico to prepare a banquet. **The King and Capitano exit**.[425]
1.02	**Contessa**	Contessa asks for an audience. Refused, she does a gesture of the sword[426]. **Contessa exits**.
1.03	**Zani**	Magnifico talks to Zani about the banquet.
1.04	**Subdulo**	Subdulo does something that provokes Zani.[427] Zani strikes Subdulo. To tell the King, **Subdulo exits**. To appease Subdulo, **Magnifico exits**, following. **Zani exits** following Magnifico.
1.05	**Orazio**	Orazio monologues about his love for Ortenzia and he believes that the prince is also in love with her. Orazio goes to Ortenzia's door and calls her.
1.06	**Ortenzia**	Ortenzia promises not to wrong Orazio. **Orazio and Ortenzia exit**.

---

[422] Split scene to give Oracle a separate entrance.
[423] Servant is male, so is the child.
[424] The original doesn't specify the dream, but it was well known.
[425] This exit is implied.
[426] This might be the dagger across the throat gesture.
[427] This plot point is implied and added here to make it more explicit.

1.07	**Tireno** **Capitano**	They talk about the prince's love of Ortenzia. Prince Tireno goes to Ortenzia's door.[428]
1.08	**Ortenzia**	Prince Tireno begs Ortenzia to marry him.[429] She refuses him. Tireno is sorrowful. **Tireno and the Capitano exit.**
1.09	**Magnifico**	Magnifico tells Ortenzia to go to the banquet. She refuses. At that:
1.10	**King** **Capitano** **Subdulo**	The King sentences Zani to death. Ortenzia begs the King that Zani merely be whipped. **The King, the Capitano, and Subdulo exit** for the banquet. **Ortenzia and Magnifico exit.**
1.11	**Zani** **The Palace Guards**	[Zani is disguised[430] as a doctor]. The guards[431] find him out, they take him. **All exit.**

Second Intermedio

B.01	**Paris**	Paris goes to sleep.
B.02	**Mercury**	Paris wakes. Mercury gives him the golden apple[432] labeled "For the Fairest" and tells him to judge who is fairest today.[433] **Mercury exits.**[434]
B.03	**Juno** **Pallas Athena** **Venus**	The goddesses make their offers.[435] With the three goddesses, Paris will go to Ida's forest to hold the contest and give the judgement. The goddesses make their offers (Juno, a kingdom; Pallas-Athena, wisdom; Venus, the love of the most beautiful woman).[436] To hear his choice, **all exit** into the forest.

Act II

2.01	**King** **Magnifico** **Capitano**	Magnifico says that his daughter (Ortenzia) is the cause of Tireno's malaise. Capitano confirms that Tireno wants her for his wife. The King accepts this. **All exit.**
2.02	**Subdulo**[437]	Subdulo asides that he has heard everything. He calls Contessa.

---

[428] To Ortenzia's house
[429] This plot point moved from the previous scene to here, after Ortenzia appears.
[430] "da" in these plays usually means that it is a disguise.
[431] Note: Sbiri is Italian slang for police.
[432] Golden apple (or pomegranate) according to legend.
[433] This second half of the sentence is our invention to help actors unfamiliar with the story.
[434] This exit is implied.
[435] In the original, it was assumed the actors knew the story.
[436] In the original, it was assumed the actors knew the story. The offers (bribes) were Juno: a kingdom, Pallas Athena: wisdom, or Venus: the love of the most beautiful woman (Helen, wife of Menelaus).
[437] Bailo is a male servant (or bailiff).

2.03	**Contessa**	Contessa wants to take revenge. **Contessa and Subdulo exit.**
2.04	**Magnifico** **Ortenzia**	Magnifico and Ortenzia argue about marriage. At that:
2.05	**Zani**	Zani says that he will advise her.[438] **Magnifico exits.**
2.06	**Orazio**	They all need to flee. Zani, to a boat. **The lovers exit** into the house. **Zani exits.**
2.07	**Contessa** **Capitano**[439]	She asides that she has heard everything. She tells the Capitano to tell the prince. Capitano delights in this mission of revenge.[440] **Contessa and Capitano exit** separately.
2.08	**Orazio** **Zani**[441]	Zani from the boat, Orazio comes from the house[442], sad and worried. They have Ortenzia's baggage for their escape. At that:
2.09	**Capitano**	Capitano kills Orazio. **Zani exits** fleeing. **Capitano exits** in chase.
2.10	**Ortenzia**	Ortenzia weeps over Orazio's dying body. At that:
2.11	**Capitano**	Having locked up Zani, Capitano takes Ortenzia by force to the palace. He calls to the guards to have Orazio[443] and Zani removed. **Ortenzia and Capitano exit.**
2.12 [444]	**The Palace Guards**	They lift Orazio's body and take it away. **All exit.**

Third Intermedio

C.01	**Paris**	Paris monologues that he wants the love of beautiful Helen as revenge on his former love Ersiona[445]. At that:
C.02	**Venus**	Venus encourages him. In exchange for the apple, he can have Helen. **Venus and Paris exit** together. Noises from offstage. Paris steals Helen.
C.03 [446]	**Pallas Athena** **Juno**	Irritated, the two goddesses plan to bring on the Trojan War.

---

[438] How did Zani escape the police? He probably needs to tell them here.
[439] This entrance is implied.
[440] This plot point was added for clarity for the actors.
[441] This entrance is implied.
[442] The original was ambiguous about whether they were coming or going to Ortenzia's.
[443] This is merely giving the order. End of the act, so some porters will come drag the body away.
[444] This scene is implied and is needed to clear the stage.
[445] Probably Enona, a nymph that Paris formerly loved.
[446] Dramatically, a scene needs to be added here to show the consequence of Paris stealing Helen, and the completion of Hecuba's vision.

Act III

3.01	**Magnifico**	[There is a coffin on stage] Magnifico monologues about Orazio's death.
3.02	**King** **Tireno**	The King complains to Magnifico about his (Magnifico's) unworthy devotion. Tireno, laments that Ortenzia does not want him. The King threatens Magnifico with death unless Ortenzia marries Tireno. Magnifico consents. **Tireno exits** for Ortenzia. **Magnifico exits.**
3.03	**Ortenzia** **Tireno**	Ortenzia pretends to accept. She asks for three favors: to give the funeral for her husband Orazio in her own way and for Zani to remain in her service. The King and Tireno agree. She commands that she be obeyed.[447] **The King and Tireno exit** to the temple. She has the coffin taken out. She cries.
3.04 [448]	**Palace Guards**	The guards remove the coffin. With the coffin, **the guards exit.**
3.04	**King** **Tireno** **Priest**	They prepare to perform the wedding. The wedding ceremony commences. She drinks and makes Tireno drink. They exchange sweet words. **They fall dead.** The King is enraged. Intending to kill all the women, he enters the palace. **The King exits.**
3.05	**Magnifico**	Finds his daughter dead. He wants to kill himself.
3.06	**Zani**	[Dressed as a hermit] Stops him. Magnifico goes with Zani. **Magnifico and Zani exit.**
3.07	**King** **Subdulo**[449]	The King and Subdulo have mortally wounded each other and **fall to the ground.**
3.08	**Contessa**	[Disguised as a judge] Contessa reveals herself and scolds the King. He, desperate, threatens her. She delivers the coup de grace **Contessa exits.**

---

[447] She asks for three favors, and then only names two. The actors can add a third or include the obey part as number three.
[448] Scene added to let the Palace Guards move the coffin.
[449] Subdulo is added to this scene to tie up his loose end.

The Deadly Sword

This is a darker comedy about a Prince with a troubled past that finally catches up to him in a better way than he feared.

Dramatis Personae   *7M-3F*

Niccolo[450]	Smart old man, and a justice
Curzio	A young man of worth
Prince	A nobleman
Magnifico	A wealthy merchant
Capitano Gamberro[451]	Head of the Prince's guard
Ortenzia	A young lady, daughter of Magnifico
Franceschina	A servant class woman
Coralina[452]	Zani's wife
Zani	Haberdasher and shopkeeper
Trastulo	A servant

Props

Jewel in a box, and the key
Fleeces
Announcements
Announcement w/ writing
Chains for the prisoners

Set: house & shop
• Magnifico's house
• Zani's shop

Special Skills and Effects

- It helps to have some kind of lighting effect around the prince to represent his terrible dream that can disappear at the end.
- The scene in which the Capitano is lining up the necks should take some practice.
- The box, and jewel inside it should be very eye-catching.

Performance Considerations

- Coralina might be a cook, to allow some sex & food jokes.
- Ortenzia needs to reject and later accept Curzio in a way that doesn't suggest that she is a gold-digger. Some acknowledgements in 1.03, 1.09, or 2.03 that she likes him, but that her father limits her romantic options could help.

---

450 In this play, this character is not named, but is called variously, the Philosopher, the Magician, and the Justice. Here we have given him the name Niccolo which had been the names of several Fifteenth Century Italian philosophers and scientists.
451 In the manuscript this character is a nameless capitano. Here we've given him the same invented name used in other plays the nameless capitano has appeared in.
452 In this play, this character is identified simply as 'The Wife', but here we have supplied a name from one of the wives in "The Three Cuckolds".

- We invented the return of Coralina with Franceschina to let the actors have more stage time and provide comic relief. We suspect that in the original the same actor played the Prince and Coralina, which could also be played for comic effect if the two characters have comparable or opposite nightmares.
- The cascade of blame in Act III needs to be high drama and fast. Each character Zani, Ortenzia, and Trastulo need to believe that their life is on the line over possession of the box, with little dawdling as you progress through the scenes.

Note

The manuscript version of this play is sparse in its descriptions of some actions and motivations. Here we have borrowed and adapted a few from versions of this play that appear decades later in other collections (with different character names) that still fit the descriptions in the original. In the later versions of the play there is more magic involved, which this play doesn't use.

Relationship Diagram

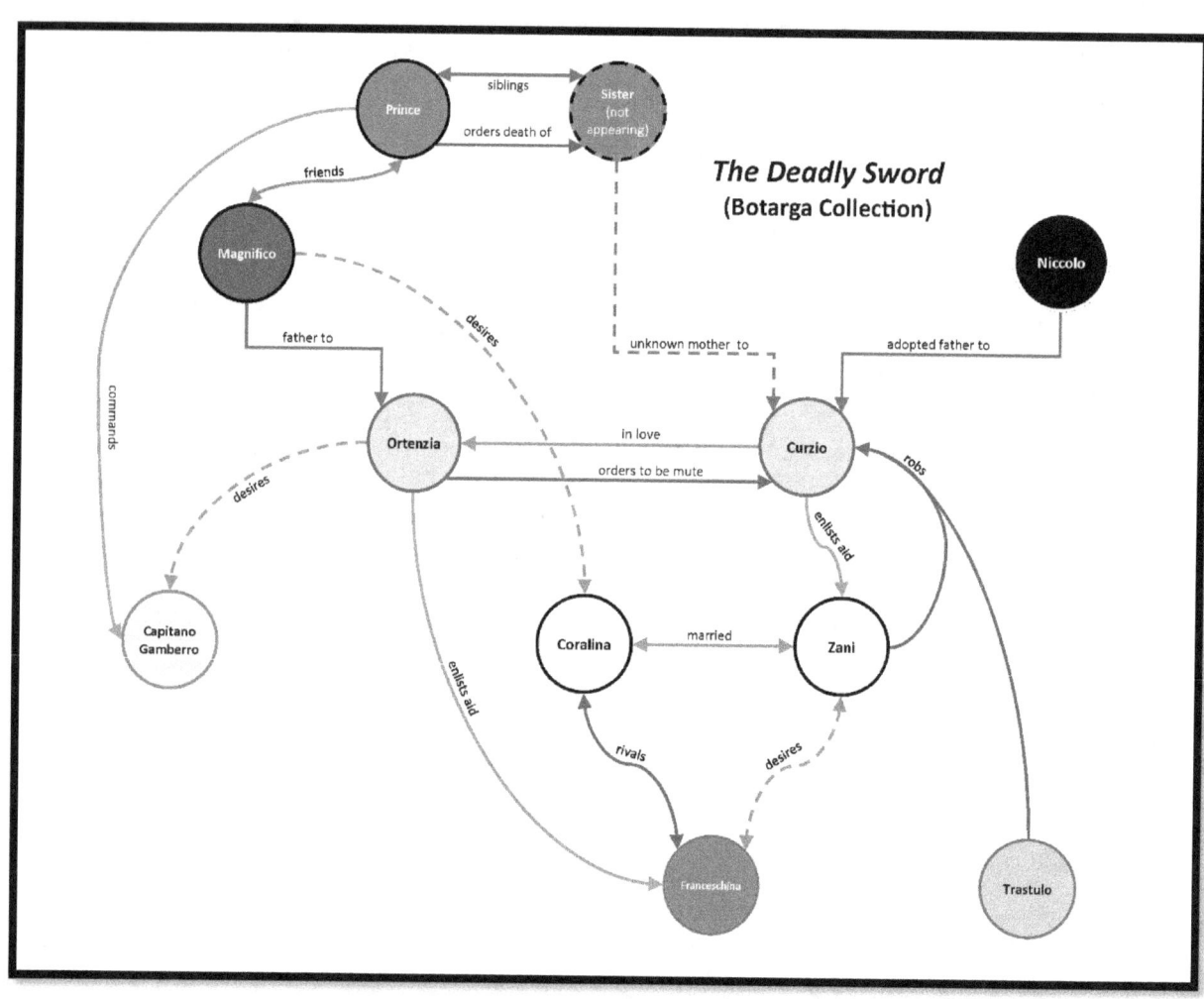

Backstory (Argomento)[453]

The Prince has no heir, but his sister had a fatherless baby. Secretly, the Prince had called for the killing of his pregnant sister shortly before she was due to deliver. Unknown to the Prince, the baby was saved, and this nephew is Curzio, who was raised as a son by a philosopher shepherd named Niccolo. Since that day, the Prince has had a recurring dream in which his guilt manifests itself as a man swinging a sword that kills him.

Zani runs a shop, which is also a place where love can be found as a short-term rental.

Act I

1.01	**Niccolo** **Curzio**	[Niccolo has a jewel] Niccolo scolds Curzio about his love of Ortenzia, who is socially too high above a mere shepherd's son[454], but also that he is not Curzio's father. Niccolo gives Curzio a locked[455] fancy box with a jewel (necklace).[456] **Niccolo exits.**
		Curzio grieves. **Curzio exits.**
1.02	**Prince** **Magnifico** **Capitano Gamberro**	[The Prince has a stack of announcements] The Prince tells of the sword that haunts him; that he has been to the oracle; who told him of "**the son of death**". He sends Gamberro to deliver the announcements offering a reward to whoever can free him of his dream. **Gamberro exits.**
		The Prince tells Magnifico of his (the Prince's) guilt in having his sister killed, and her unborn baby would have been the only heir.[457] **The Prince and Magnifico exit.**
1.03	**Ortenzia** **Franceschina**	Ortenzia talks of loving the Capitano. She sends Franceschina to find him. **Ortenzia exits** into the building.
		Franceschina exits.
1.04	**Zani** **Coralina**	Zani and his wife Coralina are screaming at each other. They resolve their differences. **Coralina exits** into their house.
		At that:
1.05 458	**Trastulo**	Trastulo wants to comfort his friend and invites Zani to breakfast. Zani says he has to set up the shop but will join him soon. **Trastulo exits.**

---

453 There are no backstories in the manuscript. The one constructed here tells the minimum.
454 This seems like the reason for the scolding but isn't spelled out in the manuscript.
455 Here we make the box locked to let the Prince unlock it adding further proof of its authenticity in Act 3.
456 In the manuscript it is just the jewel, but in Act 2, it is the box being trafficked.
457 The manuscript doesn't tell what the secret is, but here we spell it out for the actors.
458 This scene is added to show a cooperative friendship between Zani and Trastulo.

1.06	Franceschina	Zani and Franceschina have an amorous exchange. Zani leaves Franceschina to run the shop. To get breakfast, **Zani exits.** **Franceschina exits** into the shop and **appears at the window.**[459]
1.07	Coralina	Coralina has heard everything, kicks Franceschina out and takes her place[460] in the shop. **Franceschina exits.** **Coralina exits** into the shop.
1.08	Curzio	[Curzio has some fleeces] Curzio asides that he wants to speak to Ortenzia.
1.09	Zani	Curzio begs Zani to help him woo Ortenzia with the fleeces. Curzio gives the fleeces to Zani. Zani makes Curzio promise to give him and his friend Trastulo something valuable if he gets to talk to her.[461] **Curzio exits.** Zani walks to Ortenzia's window and calls her.
1.10	Ortenzia	Zani gives Ortenzia the fleeces from Curzio and convinces her to be nice to Curzio, promising her something nicer later.[462] **She exits** into her house.
1.11	Magnifico	Magnifico asks Zani for good things. Zani, in order to please his customer, sends Magnifico into the shop to select what he wants. **Magnifico exits** into the shop.
1.12	Trastulo	Trastulo also asks for good things and gets the same offer. **Trastulo exits** into the shop.
1.13	Magnifico Trastulo	Magnifico has decided he wants the woman in the shop, for his own entertainment. Trastulo is upset, knowing the woman is Zani's wife.[463]
1.14	Coralina	Coralina comes out. They play mean tricks and jokes.[464] **All exit.**

---

[459] This exit and appearance at the window is implied.
[460] Taking her place is missing text from manuscript, but this is required from later in the play.
[461] This plot point appears in later versions of this play and explains Zani's later rude treatment of Curzio.
[462] This plot point is implied, but not in the manuscript.
[463] This reappearance of Trastulo is implied. His reaction is something we speculate is also implied.
[464] The jokes are probably on Zani who had appeared unfaithful, and now, if Magnifico gets to play with Coralina, will be a cuckold.

Act II

2.01	**Curzio**	Curzio monologues that he wants to talk to Ortenzia. At that:
2.02	**Zani**	Zani sees Curzio and **hides to watch**; Curzio knocks at Ortenzia's window.
2.03	**Ortenzia**	Curzio asks her for a kiss. To make an impossible task, she offers it after he he stays silent for a year, and that he cannot defend himself and speak only to himself.[465] **Ortenzia exits** into her house.
2.04	**Trastulo**	Trastulo and Zani demand the promised nice things, but Curzio won't talk to them. They get angry. To satisfy the promise, Trastulo takes the boxed jewel. Zani takes Curzio's clothes.[466] Trastulo announces that he's going to earn a kiss from Ortenzia. **Zani and Trastulo exit** separately. Curzio is silently upset.[467]
2.05	**Franceschina**	Franceschina sees Curzio and is sad for him; she calls Ortenzia.
2.06	**Ortenzia**	She screams at nearly naked[468] Curzio and threatens Curzio.
2.07 [469]	**Trastulo**	Trastulo gives the box to Ortenzia hoping for a kiss, which he is denied. Ortenzia takes the box. **Trastulo and Franceschina exit**.[470]
2.08	**Capitano Gamberro**	Ortenzia begs Gamberro for his love. Gamberro says that she should love Curzio. **Gamberro exits**. Desperate, **Ortenzia exits** into her house. Curzio silently monologues that he wants to kill himself. [471]

---

[465] Note to actors, Ortenzia probably shouldn't be mean about this, but ask it to protect her reputation. It could be a lazzo that starts merely as 'don't tell anyone' and escalates to the final awful result.

[466] The details of this plot point are taken from later versions of the play. In the manuscript the justification of this theft is left to the actors to invent.

[467] Added plot point to help actors.

[468] We've added this nearly naked phrase to explain her reaction.

[469] This scene is invented to fill in missing actions implied later. There is a scene/line missing in the manuscript here.

[470] This exit is implied. She is not on stage after this.

[471] Word has many meanings, but we are going with wants to kill himself.

2.09	Niccolo[472]	[Niccolo has an announcement with extra writing on it] Niccolo prevents Curzio's self-harm. Niccolo gives the announcement to Curzio and tells him to give it to the Prince. He also tells him not to speak, until he sees him again. **Niccolo exits.**
		Curzio mimes his grief. **Curzio exits.**
		At that:
2.10	Zani	Zani wants the box that Trastulo got from Curzio. He knocks at Ortenzia's window.
2.11	Ortenzia	Zani, lying about the box, talks Ortenzia into giving the box to him. At that:
2.11	Magnifico	Magnifico sees the box, recognizes the royal seal, and demands it in the name of the Prince. Zani gives the box, and **Magnifico exits.**
		Ortenzia and Zani do a lazzo. **All exit.**

Act III

3.01	Prince Magnifico	[Magnifico has the box] The Prince laments that no one appears who can free him (the Prince) from the dream of the sword. At that:
3.02	Curzio	[Curzio has a copy of the announcement with additional writing] Curzio hands the note, and the Prince reads it. The Prince will be free when Curzio speaks to him. The Prince recognizes Curzio as the man in the dream with the sword.[473] In a panic, the Prince orders Curzio to the prison to have his head cut off. To find Gamberro, **the Prince exits.**
		Magnifico shows the box and demands that Curzio speak. Curzio gestures to Ortenzia's window.[474]
		Magnifico walks to Ortenzia's window and calls her.
3.03	Ortenzia	[From her window] Magnifico asks what will make Curzio speak. Ortenzia tells Curzio to give up and talk. Curzio won't give up. **Ortenzia exits.**
		At that:
3.04	Prince Capitano Gamberro[475]	The Prince, with Gamberro demands that Curzio speak. Magnifico says that the first person who had the box can make Curzio speak.

---

[472] This is listed as Magician in the manuscript but is most likely the same character as Philosopher.
[473] This plot point is implied, but not in the manuscript.
[474] Yet another implied plot point.
[475] Capitano or Curzio? It makes sense that this should be Capitano.

3.05	**Zani** **Coralina**[476] **Franceschina**	The women do the innocent bystander lazzo with Zani in the middle getting their fury.[477] The Prince recognizes his sister's box and necklace. He demands from Magnifico to know where he got it. Magnifico identifies Zani. To make Curzio speak, Gamberro seizes Zani. Coralina and Franceschina, now friends who will run the shop together, **exit for lunch**. Zani can't make Curzio speak. The Prince is furious. Zani says he got the box from Ortenzia. They call Ortenzia.
3.06	**Ortenzia**	To make Curzio speak, Gamberro seizes Ortenzia. Ortenzia can't make Curzio speak. The Prince's fear and fury rise. She says she got the box from Trastulo. They call Trastulo.
3.07	**Trastulo**[478]	To make Curzio speak, Gamberro seizes Trastulo. Trastulo stole[479] the box from Curzio. Trastulo can't make Curzio speak. The Prince wants all of their heads cut off. Gamberro is lining up all three necks for one cut. The three captives scream for help. At that:
3.08	**Niccolo**	Niccolo tells his story that Curzio is the nephew and only heir of the Prince. The Prince takes a key from a chain around his neck and unlocks the box, revealing his sister's necklace.[480] Ortenzia frees Curzio from his promise of silence and kisses him. Curzio speaks and frees the Prince from his dream. Ortenzia and Curzio get married.[481] All celebrate. **All exit**.

---

[476] This entrance and lazzo for Coralina and Franceschina is not in the manuscript. We've added it to complete their storyline.

[477] "Innocent bystander" is a lazzo in which two angry people alternate beating up a third who is trying the stop the fight.

[478] We switched the Trastulo/Ortenzia scenes to match the sequence of possession of the box.

[479] It is up to the actor how much Trastulo wants to hide his crime of theft here, or how much Curzio wants to call him out.

[480] Added plot point to support the authenticity of the box.

[481] The release from the promise of silence and the marriage are our additions to the resolution.

Emperor Maumet

This is the one play from the second collection of this notebook (*zibaldone*). It is unusual compared to the others for several reasons: first, it is more sparsely expressed than the others, second, more of it is missing from degradation of the corner of the versal page, and third, it has a play within a play. That inner play was presented by a character representing the cynical philosopher Diogenes, whose work can be amusing. We think of him as the George Carlin of his day[482].

Dramatis Personae   4M-0F + many Extras

Props

Maumet	Emperor/Sultan
Mustafa[483]	Secretary to the sultan
Guiacet	Younger brother of Maumet
Diogenes[484]	Itinerant philosopher, Gaiacet's tutor
Other Courtiers	
Guards	
Players	For the play within the play

Several donkey ears
A flat iron
Plumb bob

Set: two rooms
• The throne room
• The social room

Special Skills and Effects

- Depending on how the inner play is performed you might need players with some miming skills.

Performance Considerations

- This is an unusual play, and there are many ways that the play within the play in Act III can be played. Is it mumming (Silent and narrated)? Is it like the Pyramus and Thisbe play from MSND with over-the-top ridiculous acting? It could also potentially be played with serious acting, but that will require your actors to make more choices about the play's meaning.

---

[482] This comparison of Diogenes to George Carlin was first introduced to us by friend and collaborator on this work, and this play especially, TC Clare.

[483] In the manuscript, this character is simply 'Secretary', here we took a name from the court of Mehmed I (on whom this story might be based) and gave this diabolical character a name.

[484] Historically, Diogenes and Mehmet I were millennia apart, but appear together in this play.

Relationship Diagram

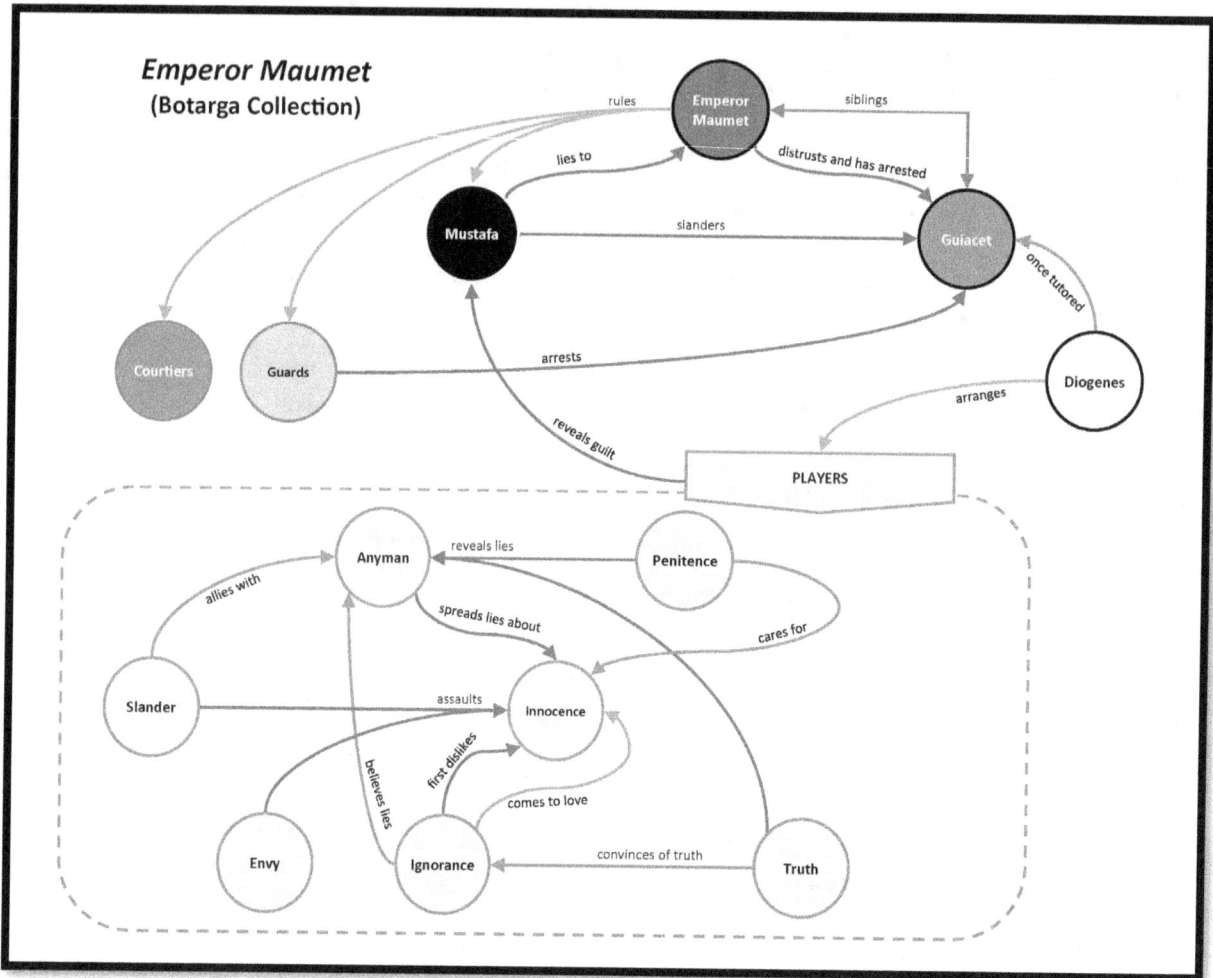

Backstory (Argomento)[485]

Emperor Maumet heard from a courtier that his brother Guiacet had said disloyal things.

Act I

1.01 [486]	**Diogenes**	Diogenes entertains the court in a monologue about life and the cynical ethics of power. Hearing Maumet, **Diogenes steps to the side** to observe.
1.02	**Maumet Mustafa**	Maumet rages that he has heard that his little brother has been disloyal. Mustafa amplifies the accusations and drives Maumet to action. Mustafa asides that he wants to destroy Gaiacet, whom Maumet loves. Maumet summons Gaiacet.

---

[485] There are no backstories in the manuscript. The one constructed here tells the minimum.
[486] This is an inserted scene to establish Diogenes' character.

1.03	**Gaiacet** **Courtiers**	Diogenes observes. Gaiacet shows his love to his brother, which Maumet takes as a façade. Mustafa begs Maumet to make no exception in the law for his family. Maumet summons the guards.
1.04	**Guards**	Maumet condemns Gaiacet to prison. **Gaiacet and the Guards exit.** Mustafa urges that Gaiacet be put to death. Diogenes advocates for his life to be spared. Diogenes tells Mustafa that he is incapable of naming the day and hour of his own death; is that why he wants to specify such for Gaiacet? Mustafa is angry. **All exit** to the prison.

Act II

2.01	**Maumet** **Mustafa**	Maumet gives the deceit-inspired judgement. The sentence is to condemn Gaiacet. Mustafa complements Maumet for this action.[487] At that:
2.02 488	**Diogenes**	Diogenes advocates for a delay. Maumet summons Gaiacet. At that
2.03	**Gaiacet** **Guards**	On the next Moon, Gaiacet will be killed. At that:
2.04		Diogenes laughs that Gaiacet's fate is placed on such a fickle orb. Diogenes offers to show them a story in the next room. Maumet agrees, Mustafa is dubious. **All exit.**

Act III

3.01	**Diogenes** **Maumet** **Gaiacet** **Mustafa**	Diogenes introduces the play. (*Diogeenes could act as Greek chorus to this fable with the players mumming.[489], or the players could play it out either sincerely or over-the-top*) All others step back and watch from the sides.
3.02	**Anyman**	[With Donkey ears in his hands] These donkey ears are lying tongues which this man has been distributing.
3.03	**Slander**	[With a pressing iron] Slander pretends not to notice the ears while supporting and augmenting the lies.
3.04	**Ignorance**	Ignorance hears the lies about the accused (Innocence) and takes them as probably true. Ignorance asks for more details.

---

[487] This is an added plot point to emphasize Mustafa as the bad guy.

[488] As you can see from the transcription of the original, much of the text of Act II has needed to be reinvented. We think this is a plausible reinvention making use of the few words still extant in the manuscript.

[489] We've tried this both ways successfully. For the Greek chorus, it helps to have the right player. The active players approach is usually livelier.

3.05		Slander tries to smooth the story for Ignorance. The man gives one of the ears to Ignorance.
3.06	**Innocence**	Innocence (a youth) lifts his hands to heaven and begs for help. Slander beats him with the pressing iron.
3.07	**Envy**	Sharp-eyed Envy also wants the satisfaction of beating Innocence, and pokes him. Slander, not to be outdone, gets in the middle of the fray. The man gives an ear to Envy.
3.08	**Penitence**	[Dressed as Dionysius of Naxos] Penitence compares the youth to Ariadne, whose innocence inspired Dionysius to save her, even when a king had forsaken her. The man tries to give an ear to Penitence, but Penitence refuses.
3.09	**Truth**	[With a plumb bob] The man tries to give an ear to Truth, but Truth refuses. Truth reveals the lies.
3.10		Innocence snatches the donkey ears, rendering Slander and Envy mute.
3.11		Ignorance sides with Truth and loves Innocence. The spectacle ends. Innocence gives the donkey ears to Diogenes. **The morality-play actors exit**. Diogenes gives the Donkey ears to Mustafa. Bowing, **Diogenes exits**.
3.12 [490]	**Maumet**	Maumet steps forward and summons Gaiacet and Mustafa.
3.13	**Gaiacet** **Mustafa** **Guards**	Maumet, calling him Slander, sentences Mustafa to prison. **Mustafa and the Guards exit**. Maumet embraces his brother. **Maumet and Gaiacet exit**.

---

[490] 3.12 & 3.13 are invented to wrap up the outer play.

Literal Versions

Our primary goal was to recover these plays for those intent to put them on stage and act them. These playable 'Performer' versions of the plays are for actors and have a lot of modifications textually from the original. **Drama historians take note:** it was a necessary middle step to transcribe and translate the plays as they appear in the manuscript. We have included these accurate translations, the 'Literal Versions', for those with more scholarly pursuits in mind and who need to see it as it was originally expressed.

Silvia's Trick[491] - Literal

Play #1, RMB II-1586-0066.jpg, C-23 (Comedy / History)

First Intermezzo

Tarquino, Sesto, Arunto, Tito, and Bruto

Sends Tito, Arunto to Apollo's Oracle; Bruto, acting crazy, goes after them. He talks to Sesto about having murdered all of his relatives, excluding Lucio Julio Brutto, his relative, who being mad has saved him. He tells about his enemies, the people of Rome, who want revenge on him by looting Ardea. He makes Sesto a capitano and enters.

Tito, Arunto, Bruto

While kneeling, they ask the Oracle of Apollo what was meant by the serpent who appeared in the royal court. The Oracle replies: At the entrance of the fierce serpent, Rome will be seen in great pleasure and, presently, laughter turns into pain, and the game into tears and death. They interpret the death of the king; they ask whoever will succeed their father as king. Tito offers a necklace, a jewel[492], Bruto, a chest. The Oracle replies: Who of you first kisses the mother will succeed the father. Brutus kisses the earth. Priest is in awe and opens the chest; he finds cloth of royal purple and gold. He praises Brutus's invention. Everyone leaves.

Act I

Curcio, Oracio

Arguing that Oracio should not marry Silvia, of low social rank. He that yes, and that he is Signore of himself. At that:

Magnifico, Servant of Oracio

He praises him and exhorts him to this. Curcio contradicts him and he leaves. Oracio orders Magnifico to have the house prepared, and to tell Zani how much he wants his daughter Silvia to be his wife. He leaves. At that:

Servants

Magnifico orders them to go to the house and he goes to the field to find Zani. They all enter.

Zani, Trastulo

Of the wedding and that he wants to give Silvia to him. They call her.

Silvia

Silvia refuses. Zani yells and shoos her into the house. They all enter.

---

[491] Neither the play nor the intermezzo was named in the manuscript. Here we provide plausible names for identification purposes.
[492] Arunto is implied.

Curcio

Upset about Oracio's desire, blames Love and women. At that:

Franceschina

How Isabella is in love with Curcio; she begs him. He dismisses her and leaves.

Zani, Trastulo

Of the wedding. At that:

Magnifico

Asks him about Silvia for Oracio. They argue.

Servant

Arrives; they close themselves in the house.

Oracio

Knocks the door to the ground. Silvia calms him down and Oracio orders Zani to accept the situation and they will find another wife for Trastulo. All happy, they go to the town.

Second Intermezzo

Sesto and Colatino

From Ardea, they have come to Colacio to see what their wives are doing having been at a banquet, and that they have found Sesto's wife is celebrating and having fun. They go toward Colatino's house.

Servant

Tells him that Lugrecia has been melancholy because of his absence. They approach the house.

Lugrecia

Complains and goes out with chores. Sesto falls in love with her. They send Lugrecia inside. Sends Colatino to invite the King to the banquet, giving up. Colatino leaves.

Sesto

Remains in love with Lugrecia. At that: Pleasure passes, he says, enjoy, foolish, sweet times of love, that whoever tastes pleasure cannot always wait. He becomes excited. At that: Repentance is, he says, short will be the pleasure short will be the contentment, because after the pleasure there is repentance. He gets strong feelings and is again excited. He enters.

Act II

Isabella and Franceschina

So that she tell her lover that she has become a nun and send Tofano to her through the back door. She enters.

Curcio

Franceschina tells that to him. He laughs and shoos her away. She leaves. He stays. At that:

Magnifico

Gives the news to Curcio about the wedding that is about to happen. Curcio, angry, leaves to disturb it. Magnifico orders the chairs to be arranged. At that:

Oracio, Silvia, Zani

They sit. [493] They wear beautiful clothes. They bring food to eat. Zani [...][494]

Curcio with the Justice

Leads Oracio to prison on behalf of the Signore. Silvia and Zani grieve. Oracio consoles them and puts Silvia, his wife, in the care of Curcio, his brother, and goes away. Silvia goes into anguish[495]. Magnifico enters for water. Curcio falls in love with her, embraces her to kiss her. She, coming back to and thinking him to be Oracio, embraces him and says loving words to him. At that:

Magnifico

Sees the situation. He goes to tell Oracio.

Curcio

Reveals his love to Silvia. She shoos him away, fleeing into the house. He, behind.

Trastulo

Goes to search for a wife.

Franceschina

She does to him the lazzo of the tabard[496].

Third Intermezzo

Sesto

Having forced Lugrecia, he returns to the camp.

Lugrecia

Grieving, she has sent for her father, husband, and relatives. At that:

Lugrecio, father of Lugrecia, Colatino, Bruto and others

She tells them the fact. She kills herself. Bruto tears off his madman's guise and swears on Lugrecia's blood to avenge her. They carry her all over Rome. They enter, taking up arms.

Tarquino

Marvels at the noise.

Bruto, Colatino

The Romans kill him. They make Bruto pro-council.

Act III

Curcio

Who could not have Silvia, who locked herself in a room, despairs.

Tofano, Isabella

Dressed as a slave, he gives her to him to guard. He introduces her and Tofano leaves. They enter. At that:

Oracio

From jail, happy to be released.

---

[493] This is a probably Spanishism. 'Si sentano'.

[494] This line of the manuscript was destroyed by the binding. Zani does something.

[495] 'Va in angoscia' literally is goes into anguish, but it seems to be an idiom for fainting from stress, and Silvia has fainted.

[496] Tabarino is either a tabard, or an over-large cape, or possibly the name of a Commedia character known in Naples 100 years later. Note: this couple does not reappear in the play.

Magnifico

Tells him that Silvia is in love with Curcio; Oracio is saddened. Curcio, withdrawn, hears everything. He goes out and, with a dagger in his hand, threatens Silvia and warns her that he has searched for love, and he goes to the side. Oracio calls her. Silvia welcomes him. He shoos away, threatens her, and calls for Magnifico.

Servant

Gives it to him and orders him to kill her in the woods. Enters with Magnifico. The servant, to kill her.

Zani

Cheering the freedom of Oracio.

Magnifico

Gives him the news about his daughter, Oracio had her killed as an adulteress. At that:

Servant

With a naked dagger, confirms that to him. Zani goes into a rage. Magnifico flees. Zani, behind. Servant narrates that wanting to kill Silvia, she disappeared, and he does not know how. He leaves.

Silvia, Diana as Judge

For her chastity she saved her life and placed her in the court of a judge to prove her innocence. She sits.[497] Diana leaves.

Curcio, Oracio

They rejoice at the death of Silvia. At that:

Zani

Desperate, he accuses them to the judge. Oracio confesses. The judge scolds him; Curcio is scared. Curcio, contaminated, reveals himself to Oracio. He wants to kill him. Silvia reveals herself, embraces Oracio and Curcio marries Isabella.

---

[497] This might translate to "she sits" or "She is grateful" depending on whether it is a Spanishism or a Venetianism.

The Wheat - Literal

Play #2, RMB II-1586-0073.jpg, C-24 (Comedy / History)

Act I

Magnifico, Trastulo, Zani

Argue about who is more loyal. Magnifico makes peace between them. Trastulo enters the house. Zani begs Magnifico on behalf of Curcio. Magnifico threatens him. Zani leaves.

Oracio

Magnifico welcomes Oracio. Oracio begs him on behalf of Curcio. Magnifico does not want Curcio in the house. They go for books.

Zani

Zani says that he saw Curcio.

Curcio

Exits. He complains to Zani. He ordered a capitano to kill Oracio, and he must give wheat to the capitano.

Capitano

Capitano bullies Zani. Zani promises it to him. Capitano, Zani leave. Curcio stays.

Magnifico

He humbles himself to him. Magnifico kicks him away. He leaves. Magnifico also.

Ortensia, daughter of Magnifico

About her love of Oracio.

Oracio

She reveals her love to him. They make the figure; she says she is not his sister. Oracio enters with her to see that.

Zani

Says he wants to trick Trastulo to get the keys to the wheat, calls him.

Trastulo

Trastulo says that Magnifico would put Zani in prison. They agree to steal the wheat. They enter.

First Intermezzo

Vechio

Complaining about his bad son.

Messenger

He orders the penalty of fire by the King; that Vechio's son must leave.

Son, with two rascals

Threatens the father. They do the trial of the pieces of wood. It ends. They pass by some little ones. They beat the children.

Act II

Oracio, Ortencia

That he wants to leave for Napoli to visit his father. Ortensia is sad.

Capitano

Capitano about to kill him, hears that he has to leave; he rejoices. Ortensia enters. Oracio leaves. Capitano also, says that he will give the impression that he has killed him.

Curcio

Gives to him the illusion that he killed Oracio. He leaves. Curcio stays. At that:

Zani

That he goes there at the hour of two, that he will give him three sacks of wheat. He gives him the gesture of the wink[498]. At that:

Trastulo

From his window, he hears everything and enters. Curcio leaves. Zani into the house.

Magnifico

Is going to his home.

Trastulo

Trastulo complains about him and reveals everything. Magnifico sends him into the house and calls Zani.

Zani

That he will not go home at night. Calls Ortensia.

Ortensia

Orders her to go to bed early. Zani pretends that it is dark, enters with Ortensia.

Magnifico

Disguised, gives the gesture.

Zani

He gives him the wheat.

Second Intermezzo

Epaminondas, Pelopida with a son

Epaminondas scolds him of his vices and of the sad children that he has. At that:

Another son of Pelopida, with a small son by the hand

Dragging the child to Pelopida. Epaminondas scolds him again. The little son will do the same thing to him. They leave. Pelopida's son hugs Epaminondas and goes with him.

Act III

Curcio

For the grain.

Zani

Sleepy, to have given it to him. They shout. Says Oracio is dead. He leaves. Zani stays.

---

[498] 'ciflo' is how this was transcribed maybe it was badly written 'ciglio', but this is an identifying gesture used latter, and 'wink' is a good possible choice for what it meant.

Magnifico

Tells him about the dream. Magnifico threatens him and he confesses; he tells him that Curcio had Oracio killed. Magnifico gives money to him to save Curcio.

Ortensia

She learns about Oracio's death, sorrowful enters. Magnifico says that he is not his son, and he has written to his father in Naples. At that:

Cassandro

Oracio's father introduces himself to Stefanelo, he gives him the news of his son's death. He laments, Magnifico puts him into his house.

Oracio

To have met someone who gave him the news that his father has come. Magnifico, thinking that he is a ghost, is frightened.

Curcio

Gets scared.

Zani

Gets scared.

Ortensia

Gets scared.

Trastulo

Gets scared. Oracio wonders. Magnifico recognizes that he is alive. He calls Cassandro.

Cassandro

Cassandro reveals to him that he is his father. Cassandro marries him to Ortensia. They pray for Curcio. Stands firm; Magnifico gives the couple his blessing; he forgives them.

The King Artaxesre - Literal

Play #3, RMB II-1586-0078.jpg, C-26 (History)

Act I

Artaxerse, Dulipo, King of Lidi

Asks him about his happiness. Dulipo praises him. King, that he would be happy if he could win the favor of Ariobarzane. Dulipo, that he should kill him. He gives him the figure of the falcon. King refuses. Dulipo accuses him that he gave him the ugliest sister. King calls Drusila, sister of Ariobarzane, who is pregnant.

*499

Confirms Daria, her sister, is more beautiful. King sends her to her house, and orders her to tell Ariobarzane to send to him the other one, and to Dulipo to take away Ariobarzane's Senechal's Staff. They enter. Drusila remains grieving and recounting how she became pregnant. At that:

Zani

Calls Daria.

Daria, Drusila

They understand the will of the King, they grieve, and they enter. Daria stays.

Ciro

Learns that the king wants to poison him. They leave.

Trastulo, Franceschina mute

They do a lazzo. Franceschina with Trastulo enters. Zani stays.

Magnifico, medical doctor

Leads him into the house to heal her.

Ariobarzane

Cheerful about his situation.

Dulipo

Asks for the staff. Ariobarzane willingly gives it to him and learns that the king sent Drusila home and how he desires Daria. He goes home.

Daria

She exits. She tells the brother that the sister is in bed about to to give birth and that it is necessary that she go to the King. She is sorry to be in love with Ciro. Ariobarzane consoles her and gives her the poison with which she can kill herself before she pleases the King. At that: she enters, he leaves.

Magnifico

Who has overheard of the poison and the King, thinks that they want to poison him. Because he wants to discover it, he leaves.

---

499 There is a break implying the entrance of Drusila.

Ganassa[500]

Cheerful because Franceschina speaks.

King, Dulipo, Ariobarzane

Reprimands about his pride, that he wants to be with him, that he does it to gain his grace. He that he would give him the most beautiful sister; he has her called.

Daria

Ariobarzane introduces her to him; he sends her to the palace. Ariobarzane gives him the letter, he leaves. King has Dulipo read it; he learns that Ciro is in love with Daria. He has him called. Dulipo gets upset.

Ciro

Finds the poison on his chest. He scolds him. He is afraid; He grants Daria to him. He calls her.

Ariobarzane

King embraces him, He gives to him his daughter with the kingdom of Lidi as a dowry, he refuses; he gives her his own fortune. Desperate Dulipo leaves and they enter.

Zani, Franceschina, Trastulo

Shouting, speaking, happy that Drusila has had a son. They do a lazzo of much talking.

Act II

Dulipo

Lamenting his misery.

Magnifico

He tells him about the poison that, by order of Ariobarzane, to give Daria to the King. He, happy, leaves. Magnifico, too.

Zani, Franceschina, Trastulo

Shouting that she wants to reveal the secret of the son who was born of Drusila. Reprimands her; speaks too much. They shout. Franceschina enters with Trastulo. Zani stays.

Magnifico

He asks him for a remedy. Magnifico, he will not hear her; he gives him a powder to make him deaf. He leaves. Zani enters.

King, Dulipo

He tells him about Ariobarzane's betrayal, that he will find the poison on Daria.

Daria

King finds the poison on her. Has Ariobarzane called and condemns him to the fire. They enter. Dulipo, also, rejoicing.

Zani

That he wants to go for the remedy. At that:

Magnifico

Gives it to him, and leaves. He pretends that he wants to be deaf. Calls Franceschina.

Franceschina, Trastulo

Zani slaps her with the back of her hand and beats her with a stick. She goes into anguish. They go for water, doesn't help. They play the prank of the fire and kindling.

---

[500] Ganasa (or Ganassa) is last name for Zani in this troupe.

Act III

Zani

He has calmed down Franceschina, cheers up.

Magnifico

Asks him for the reward. He pretends to be deaf; they argue and they leave.

Polione and Ciro

Mourning the death of Daria. Polione promises him to save his life and, also to his brother, on the condition that he confesses the truth. Ciro, yes. At that:

King and Dulipo

Polione asks the king for the life of Ciro as a gift, he promises it to him. Ciro confesses that he had wanted to poison him for the love of Daria. The King marvels. He offers himself to Polione. He asks him for a hearing for Ariobarzane. King makes him come.

Ariobarzane and Daria

Dressed for mourning. Ariobarzane tells the King that, if he had wanted to kill him, he would have agreed that Ciro would have given it to him, but that the poison he gave to Daria was because she wanted to poison herself, if his majesty wanted to take away her honor; and that Drusila, being pregnant, came up with the idea to give birth outside of the court, it being law that, if there is a firstborn son, all the others that will born are to be killed; and that she has saved the lives of him, Ciro, the infant, and conserved his glory by confessing the crime because he had been judged by an unjust judge. King rejoices, embraces her, confirms to him the daughter as wife and he takes Drusila. Daria, Ciro.

Zani, Franceschina

They bring the son of Drusila. King embraces him, enters to visit his wife.

Ramiro - Literal

Play #4, RMB II-1586-0084.jpg, C-27 (History)

Act I

King Don Sanchio, Garcia, his son

Says that, because Moors have risen up in Córdoba, it is necessary for him to go in person. To him, he leaves the kingdom that was going to Ramiro, who is lacking intellect; and the care of the infant Fernando and of the Queen; and that he should go to mark the field[501], because he wants to leave. At that:

Baylo, Ramiro

Making crazy antics with the King because he wants to go hunting. The King orders that they take him out to hunt and brings Fernando to obedience[502] that [...][503]. They enter.

Zani, Dorotea, his daughter

Preaching to her that she needs to be chaste and, because she wants to go to the woods, that she should bring a snack to him. He leaves. She enters.

Ermisenda, Trastulo

That she is in love with Don Garcia, gives him a letter to Garcia so that he can give it to him. They enter; He, to the road to look for him.

Garcia

Of his love for Dorotea, and that he was the cause of Ramiro's madness in order to inherit the kingdom. He goes.[504]

Dorotea

He reveals his love for her. He begs her. She modestly refuses. At that:

Trastulo

Gives the letter to him. He, without reading it, tears it up in front of Dorotea. Trastulo, upset, leaves. She, that does not want to give her honor to anyone except to her husband. She enters. Garcia leaves.

Zani

With stuff to eat, he goes for water.

Ramiro

From hunting, eats. Zani comes back, he also eats. At that:

Serpent

Zani wants to kill it; Ramiro defends him/it.[505] Snake speaks and leads Ramiro with him.

---

[501] This might be an idiom about going to battle.
[502] We aren't sure how you take an infant to obedience.
[503] About six words have been cut in the bottom line of this folio.
[504] He goes to Dorotea's house.
[505] The pronouns are ambiguous as to whether Ramiro defends Zani or Serpent.

Act II

Fada[506] and Ramiro, with his intellect

Predicts to him that must be next after twenty-two royal crowned kings of his kingdom, and she goes. He goes.

Zani

Frightened of the serpent.

Garcia

Resolved that he wants Teodora to be his wife, he asks for her of Zani, who is unrelenting at first and then is fine. Calls her.

Teodora[507]

Refuses, unless she goes on the horse, Saiano. He promises that to her. She enters. Garcia gives his signet ring to Zani, so that he can get as much money as he wants to put himself in order. He leaves. Cheerful Zani, too.

Queen, Domicio, majordomo

Doubts of an ambush and about the King's little boy. Majordomo comforts her; she goes into anguish[508] in the arms of the Majordomo. She gives the horse Saiano.[509] Trumpets & Drums, at that:

Garcia and Fernando

See[510] her; they are surprised. Garcia asks her for the horse Saiano. She grants it to him; the Majordomo reminds her that the King ordered that the horse not come out of the stable. She takes it back from him. Garcia is angry at the Majordomo and the Queen. Argues with him, she leaves. Garcia, Fernando, about wanting to accuse the mother of adultery. They enter.

Ramiro

Cheerful about his state. At that:

Teodora

Lamenting the new elevation[511], and that Zani is not coming. Ramiro sees her, falls in love, begs her. She teases him as if he is crazy. He withdraws. She enters.

Zani

Dressed as a gentleman. At that:

Trastulo

Leads him to Ermisenda.

Ermisenda

She makes him believe that Garcia is her relative, and that he wants to take honor and life of Teodora. She makes him put her in her place. [...][512]. He puts her there and stays. At that:

---

506 Fada is a fairy 'fata' or other spirit with mystical insight.
507 In act I and III Zani's daughter is Dorotea, in Act II for some reason she is Teodora.
508 faints
509 This seems to be erroneously added. The horse transaction is in the next scene.
510 This verb is plural so there is an implied 'they' as the subject.
511 Nova hauta is an idiom that we haven't resolved yet but have called 'new elevation' here.
512 There are a few missing words here cut from the bottom of the page during binding. Some ascenders give hints about what words might be there, but we haven't guessed.

Ramiro

He has heard all these arguments, begs Zani to introduce him, and that this is a trick of Ermisenda. He gives him gifts. He introduces him.

Act III

Ermisenda

With a ring on her finger, cheerful, thinking she was with Garcia. She enters. Trumpets.

King with Siriamamoli, Moorish king, captured in war

Grants him his life, sends him to lodge, and wonders how the prince did not come to meet him. At that:

Garcia, Fernando

They accuse the mother of adultery with the Majordomo and that Garcia will keep him in the field, and he leaves. King grieves. At that:

Ramiro

Talks to him about it. King wonders, then he knows that he is wise. He tells him about the accusation of the sons about the mother. He says that he wants to defend her. They call the Queen.

Queen

He, that he wants to enter the field for her. She wants to apologize to the King. He doesn't listen to her.

Garcia

Enters the field. Regina begs him to tell the truth. He confirms again that she is adulterous and threatens her. At that: drum.

Ramiro

In the field he challenges to disprove Garcia. The father makes them position with the Sun[513], they give to arms, they begin to fight. At that:

Fada with the shadow of Alfonso the First, king of Portugal badly wounded, and his mother

The mother cuts off his tongue. They disappear. Fada narrates to the King who they are. She scolds to Garcia that he tell the truth and tells Ramiro that she is the fada that freed him from death, and she leaves. Garcia exonerates the mother. The King wants to kill Garcia, Ramiro restrains him. He has his him taken away and he is captured. He begs Ramiro to ask the Queen's forgiveness for him. The queen embraces him, gives to Ramiro the kingdom of Aragon, which is her dowry. At that:

King, Siriamamoli, Zani, tied up.

Siriamamoli tells how he stole from him a little daughter. Zani says she is Dorotea, Daughter of the Moorish Prince, who will become a Christian if Garcia marries her. The King promises that; they call Garcia and Dorotea.

Garcia, Dorotea

And they want them to marry. At that:

Ermisenda

He is her husband. Ramiro reveals the deception [...][514].

---

[513] This is an old idiom meaning that neither combatant will start with the Sun in his eyes.
[514] This omission is a whole missing line.

Constant Love[515] - Literal

Play #5, RMB II-1586-0090.jpg, C-28 (Tragicomedy)

Act I

Magnifico, Zani

Waiting for the daughter from Naples, sends Zani to the door and enters.

Curcio and Oracio

Who have become friends while walking from Naples to Rome. One asks the other the reason for leaving his homeland. Oracio tells how he has escaped from Venice for having wounded his friend Decio, a Cypriot, and believes that he has killed him, and that was ten years ago because he fell into the water, and that his name is Sigismondo. Curcio, by another name Decio, realizes that Oracio is his enemy; he says angry words, the other one gets offended. He threatens to punch him. Oracio excuses himself [...] and he leaves. Curcio tells how he could have killed him and that he came secretly after his sister, who has come from Naples, and that he has to come to Rome to visit the father, and that he needs to learn where the house is. At that:

Zani

Curcio recognizes him, he pretends to be a necromancer. He learns of the house, tells him about the treasure. They agree to be called Pietro. Curcio leaves. Zani knocks at the door of the house.

Magnifico[516]

Gives the news as his daughter is coming. They go to knock for Cipriota.

Cipriota[517]

She shoos him away. He enters the house. Zani comes back to the door. She stays; she says that she is looking for revenge one day for one of her brothers who was treacherously killed. At that:

Oracio, Capitano

He guards his shoulders. He sees her, recognizes her as the one he has always loved. He greets her. She receives the greeting and thanks him for his offers. She says that she loves him, but that she can only marry the one who will give her the head of the enemy in her hands. Oracio offers himself. She says there will be time, bids goodbye, she enters. They part.

Zani, Isabella, Vechio, Trastulo

From Naples, they go to the house of Magnifico.

Magnifico

Outside, welcomes them. Everyone enters. Zani stays and Magnifico.

---

[515] The title in the manuscript is 'Constante'. In the play, long antipathy proves weak compared to love.
[516] The entrances for Magnifico and Cipriota in the next scene are difficult to read because they've been bound into the book, but enough can be seen to make an informed guess about who enters.
[517] Note that the names Isabella/Isabela, Cipriota/Cipriotta, Pietro/Pedro are inconsistently spelled in the manuscript, but here have unified spellings.

Curcio

Disguised as a porter, Zani pretends that he is his son; Magnifico receives him in the house. They all go into the house happily.

Act II

Pietro, Zani, Isabella

With the foam. Zani cheers. He tells her about the cup, she is taken by love, because he resembles her lover. She drinks from the cup.

Magnifico

Arrives; he sends her into the house; drives away Pietro. Zani, who is a necromancer, says that he will make him have his lover. Magnifico caresses[518] him, orders him to go and find him in the square. Zani with the foam. Magnifico enters the house.

Cipriota

He tells her about Pietro. She sends him away. He leaves.

Oracio, Capitano

Begs her to tell him the name of her enemy. She will give it to him in writing and he should send the Capitano for that, and make Stefanello get them out of the door, and enter. Oracio says that beatings be given to Magnifico. He leaves. Capitano stays.

Trastulo

He was kicked out and wants revenge. Capitano says that he must do the beating, he leaves. Trastulo remains.

Magnifico with Pedro

They do a lazzo of weak defense.[519] Trastulo beats him and ends the act.

Act III

Isabella

Says that she wants to reveal her love to Pietro.

Pietro

She reveals her love to him. Zani from the window that foams[520]. He gives her the promise to receive her as a wife. He leaves to get dressed. She enters.

Capitano

He goes to Cipriota for the note.

Cipriota

She gives it to him. At that:

Oracio

He believes he is the enemy; he complains, he resolves to present himself to her. At that:

Magnifico

Stands at the door, blustering, he reveals that he is Oracio's father, called Sigismondo; he promises Cipriota to him. Magnifico retires, calls her.

Cipriota

He presents himself to her as an enemy; Cipriota is uncertain whether to kill him.

---

[518] Caresses may mean something less physical such as 'flatters'.
[519] 'furtarelo' means little theft. 'fortarelo' might mean little defense or weak fighting, which makes more sense in context.
[520] This is an odd idiom, but in context seems to be an encouragement for her to drink.

Curcio

At that: that he wants to kill him, he reveals that he is alive and is her brother. He tells Oracio that he has married Isabella; he marries the Cipriota. Everything is revealed; Magnifico settles with the situation.

In Between - Literal

Play #6, RMB II-1586-0094.jpg, C-29 (Pastoral Comedy)

Act I

The Sorceress[521]

Complains about the love that Sireno does not return to her. Taking advantage of her art, and that, in spite of him, she wants him to want her, even though she knows that he is in love with Delia. She calls:

Argano, The Monster

She commands him to take all the women of Arcadia as prisoners. Zani yells from inside. The sorceress has him called.

Zani

He begs her for mercy. She will free him if he promises to beg Sireno to leave Delia and love her. He promises that to her. She leaves and Argano. Zani, happy to be free, he also leaves.

Sireno, Orfinio

One praising eating and the other love. At that:

Ganassa[522]

Enters as a judge: praises the food. They do a lazzo. They promise each other to help, and they leave.

Argano with the wife of Magnifico

Argano stole her from him.

Magnifico

Magnifico shouts at him. He takes her prisoner. Magnifico complains and leaves.

Delia

About the love of Sireno and that the sorceress disturbs her, still, Sireno loves her.

Sireno

They caress each other. At that:

Argano

Steals her from him. He, desperate, leaves.

Orfinio

With stuff to eat, eats.

Zani

Arrives. They do a lazzo.

---

[521] 'La Maga' is a female wizard.
[522] Ganassa is the other name for Zani.

Act II

Flori[523]

Cheerful, that Delia was taken and that Sireno, in spite of him, will love her. She enters to torment Delia.

Sireno

Complains about Delia's captivity. At that:

Zani

Promises him help and, with the food and wine, wants to make the savage fall asleep.

Argano

In the tower. Zani praises him. He lowers himself. They are convivial. He makes him fall asleep. He goes to take the chest where the book is. Sireno, stays guarding. He takes the chest out. They open it and find Zani's head in there. He despairs, there is a fire. [...][524]

Sireno

He despairs. At that:

Orfinio

Consoles him and tells him that this is the hour that the sorceress sleeps. He enters to take the book from her, then he exits and says that he has tied her up. Animal or lion or gelding unties the rope.

Flori

She laughs at them for having tricked them. Wakes up Argano and scolds him and kicks him into the house. Sireno begs her to give him Delia. She has her tormented; that she, if he gives her a kiss, that yes. He makes her swear on the Demogorgon god that yes.

Delia, Argano

Kisses her, while looking at Delia. Flori is indignant and transforms her into a tree and that she will not return unless it burns and enters. Orfinio tells him about a witch who can counteract her spells. He leaves. Sireno also leaves, after having hugged the tree.

Magnifico

Echoes. At that:

Orfinio, Sireno, Zani, the Witch

They bring tied-up Zani. The witch summons him. A spirit tells him to go to a nearby well, that he will find a shield, with which he will remove the strength of the sorceress and take away the book from her, with which he will destroy all of her power. Witch frees him: they make a frog disappear.[525] Zani, happy, leaves.

Act III

Argano, Flori

Asks for a dagger with which, giving a wound to Sireno, he will be forced to love her. Argano enters.

Zani

Tells her he has said right about her, and they enter. Zani stays.

---

[523] Flori is the sorceress who was unnamed in act 1.
[524] Entire line of missing text, perhaps Zani is turned into a frog here.
[525] There is a word 'sconicare' (Venetian dialect) that is an unknown verb to us. Also, note that the missing text in the scene of Argano's entrance above most likely says that Zani transforms into a frog (during the fire), so now it is the form of the frog that is removed from Zani.

Sireno

Goes to the well, they pull up the shield from the well.

Sorceress

With the dagger and the book. He asks her for Delia; she says she does not want to give her back to him. He reveals the shield. She is stunned. He takes the book from her, reads, finds out how one must burn the tree. He leaves.

Orfinio

Sees the stunned sorceress and the dagger. He takes it and is about to kill her. She comes to, and she falls in love with him, and she begs him. He runs away from her. She follows behind.

Sireno, Zani

With fires to burn the tree. They give prayers to Demogorgon.

Demogorgon with the Centaur, Flori tied up

Demogorgon takes the book from Sireno and tells him to burn the tree. They burn it, Delia comes out. Sireno marries her.

Orfinio, Flori

Demogorgon throws the book, the dagger, the shield into the well. He forbids Flori from using the magic art.

Argano

Demorgogon strikes him with lightning, the prisoners are free and come out.

Magnifico, daughter, his Wife

And the satire ends.

Jove & Io[526] - Literal

Play #7, RMB II-1586-0098.jpg, C-30 (Opera)

Act I

Inaco, Io
> That she does not depart from him. He leaves.

Jove
> Forcefully takes Io away with him. He hears Juno and he covers her with a cloud.

Juno[527]
> Asks him what is covered under the cloud. He says it is nothing. Eventually, the cloud disappears, and Io comes out as a cow. She asks Jove for her, and they leave.

Act II

Juno, Argo, Io
> Gives to him the cow to be guarded. She goes away and everyone else too.

Jove, Mercury
> Orders him to get the cow from Argo. He leaves. Mercury, in order to transform himself, leaves.

Inaco
> Lamenting the loss of the daughter.

Io, in a cow
> Moos, writes with the foot; Inaco recognizes her as daughter. He grieves. At that:

Argo
> Drives him away. He takes the cow and leaves. Inaco prays to Jove.

Jove
> From the sky, promises him the daughter.

Act III

Mercury, transformed, Argo
> Praising himself about the cow. Mercury praises him, sings, makes him fall asleep, cuts off his head. Mercury wants to take it/her.

Juno
> Screams from Heaven and sends a Fury in the cow. Everyone enters.

Jove, Inaco, The Cow
> The cloud disappears.

---

[526] This play was not named in the manuscript. Here we provide plausible names for identification purposes.
[527] Junone, Giunone spelled inconsistently in the manuscript, but unified as Juno here.

Juno

Jove requests her as a grace. Cloud covers her. Jove and Juno leave. Io comes out of the cow; the father embraces her. And it ends.

The Lion - Literal

Play #8, RMB II-1586-0100.jpg, C-31 (Comedy)

Act I

Magnifico, Zani and Francese

Puts them at the good guard[528]. He says he came to stay in the villa because he doesn't want to give Ortensia to Oracio. They, at the good guard. At that:

Oracio

Asks him for her to be his wife. He, that he doesn't want to give her to him. They argue. Magnifico, at the good guard. Francese, Zani, from the inside, they answer. Magnifico leaves. Oracio remains, complaining, including that he has only a little money.

Trastulo

Promises him a favor in order to make him speak to Ortensia. Goes to get cheese and wine. Oracio retires. At that:

Zani

At the guard.

Trastulo

With the cheese, makes him come out. Zani leaves.

Francese

On the guard. Trastulo, with the wine, makes him leave. They call Ortensia.

Ortensia

She promises him to be his wife. At that:

Zani

They flee. Ortensia, in the house. Zani, to have been played. He enters.

Francese

Drunk, the same.

Curcio, Capitano

Wants to leave Isabella because he is poor and is the enemy of everyone, and that he wants to take Ortensia, daughter of Stefanello[529], because she is rich. They call.

Isabella[530]

He tells her that and he drives her away. She, in pain, leaves. He sends the Capitano to Stefanello to ask him for Ortensia and leaves. Capitano stays.

Magnifico

Capitano asks him for Ortensia for his master. Magnifico does not believe him; at the end he calls Zani.

---

[528] 'bona guardia' is some specific idiom, but we don't know what it means. Are they in a guard house or other specific place? Are they just on especially careful watch?

[529] Stefanello is magnifico.

[530] Names are inconsistently spelled in the manuscript, Isabella/Isabela, Zani/Zanni/Ganassa, Leone/Lione. Here we have made them consistent.

*531

[...]532 Capitano, in his house, and tells Zani that [he] wants him to go as an ambassador. And they enter the house.

Oracio, Trastulo

Who has heard everything, being desperate, throws himself into the well. End of the first act: Trastulo, screaming "help", leaves.

Act II

Magnifico, Capitano, Zani

Gives him the ambassadorial message. Capitano, Zani leave. Magnifico remains. At that:

Trastulo with Porters

With ropes and porters, says that Oracio threw himself into the well out of desperation.

Oracio

Shouts from the well. They pull him out with a treasure chest. Magnifico regrets not having given him his daughter; he makes him offers, he, that now does not want her. Magnifico has given her in marriage to the Signore; he leaves. Oracio knocks for Ortensia.

Ortensia

They order that she run away, that he will wait for her at the Fonte Bella through the back door. Oracio, away. She, in the house. Trastulo remains; throws himself into the well for the treasure.

Curcio, Zani, Capitano

Gives the ambassadorial message. Curcio laughs and sends him to say that he will come in person to get her. They leave.

Isabella

Desperate, goes into the woods.

Ortensia

Flees with the veil to find Oracio.

Magnifico

Regretting not having given the daughter to Oracio. Trastulo screams from the well.

Trastulo

"Treasure!". Magnifico, cheerful. At that:

Ganassa533

He too. They pull it up with a pot. All three come to words; they throw hands at once; they get dirty; they shout at Trastulo. He runs away, they stay.

Curcio with Capitano

They came for the daughter. Wants to touch the hand of Magnifico; he, because he has it dirty, hides himself. Sends Zani to call Ortensia. Zani can't find her, now will come two or three times. Curcio, Capitano put hand at the swords. They flee. Capitano, that he will punish him. And they leave.

Ortensia

That she has gone to the Fonte Bella and that Oracio has never come. Zani, shouts from inside.

---

531 This appears to be an entrance for Zani.
532 One or two short missing words.
533 Ganassa is the other name of Zani.

Zani

Out, he scolds her and wants to bring her with him. At that:

Leone

Zani escapes. She also.

Act III

Oracio

How he came to the Fonte Bella and did not find Ortensia, he complains.

Zani

Says how a lion has come and that he thinks it devoured her. At that:

Leone

With the Ortensia's veil in its mouth. Oracio grieves. Lion flees; follows it. Ganassa remains, because the lion will kill him.

Ortensia

Complaining that she can't find Oracio. He tells her how the lion killed him. She, grieving, leaves. Zani, also.

Oracio, Isabella

Grieving that they want to die. Verses:
"Gentle spirit who, with such a clear trumpet,
    you left among the mortals the immortal cry
    of virtue and honor, here is your faithful
    husband sitting here today at your grave.
Come, oh soul as beautiful as a dove,
    to the murmuring of the bridegroom and leave the dear nest
    of Oblivion[534] while I pierce
    this dense air, which echoes in the sky.
Here you come; and stay with me, oh noble spirit,
    while I retell the pain of your death along with these shepherds.
Receive, dear wife, these flowers,
    sorrowful sign of this ominous fate,
    for they are made of cypress, poplar, and myrtle."

Leone

They beg him to kill them. It[535] makes fun of them and leaves. Desperate Isabella, leaves. Oracio remains.

Capitano and others

Oracio, who wants to kill those who come to him in order to be killed. They take him and leave.

Ortensia

Lamenting her misfortune [...][536]. Flee.

Oracio

Taken, he says he wants to die. The Signore gives him Ortensia.

---

[534] 'Lette' we translated as Oblivion.
[535] There is some unclear text in the manuscript, but this reading makes sense in context.
[536] The omission is an entire line of text.

Isabella and Magnifico

Who wanted to kill herself by fire. Signore calls her and tells her[537] of the inherited status. Signore marries her.

---

[537] The manuscript is a bit crowded here, but there is a scribble that probably means 'tells her'.

The Three Cuckolds[538] - Literal

Play #9, RMB II-1586-0222.jpg (line 13), C-201 (Comedy)

Act I

Magnifico, Wife

Talks about jealousy. She asks him for lemons to give to the nuns; He, that yes.

Cassandro, merchant of lemons

They ask for them from him. He gives them to them. Magnifico leaves. Cassandro and Ortensia stay. They talk about their love, and that he[539] is brought inside the box of lemons. He, on the road. She, in the house.

Curcio

About the love of Coralina, wife of Cassandro. Knocks. She gives him the order to go as a thug. He leaves.

Franceschina

About the pregnancy. She says she wants to do the laundry.

Zani

Sends him to get wood. He leaves. She stays.

Magnifico

Makes love with her, who takes money from his hands and makes him retire. She goes to the wife of Magnifico. He gets desperate.

Ortensia

She asks her[540] for laundry and a washtub. Ortensia gives them to her. Magnifico is happy. She makes him get into the washtub. At that:

Zani

Brings it to the house and stays. At that:

Ortensia

Calls for Zani and sends him to Cassandro for the box of lemons and reveals to him that Cassandro must stay inside the box. She enters. Zani leaves.

Curcio

Dressed as a thug, approaches Coralina's house. At that:

Zani

With the box, asks for help. He pretends to be mute. They do a lazzo. He leaves and Zani brings the box into Ortensia's house.

Curcio, Zani

He beats him; he talks.

---

538 There is no title for this play in the manuscript, but this play is very similar to a play in the Corsiniana collection,

539 This is not a gendered pronoun, could be anyone. Context says it is Cassandro.

540 This is a non-gendered pronoun. Context says it means 'her'.

Act II

Zani

Goes home.

Magnifico

Despairs.

Franceschina

Comes out and makes the lazzo of the quarta[541] to him. They enter. Magnifico stays praising his wife. Knocks at the home.

Ortensia

Of having dreamed of the eye that will be healthy[542]. They give it a try.

Cassandro

They enter. He stays; goes home.

Coralina

Does the lazzo of the mute to him. Cassandro gives a donation. They enter. Curcio stays.

Zani

Curcio tells him of the success, and they leave.

Magnifico

From the house, laughing about the quarta.

Cassandro

Laughing about the eye. Magnifico recounts about the quarta. Cassandro laughs. Magnifico leaves. Cassandro stays. At that:

Zani

Tells him about the trick. He tells him about the one of the quarta. First, he, of the mute. Cassandro leaves. Zani stays.

Magnifico

Happy, sees Zani; laughs at him. Zani tells him about the trick of the eye. Magnifico enters to kill his wife. Zani knocks at the house.

Franceschina

That he wants to leave. Franceschina pretends to cry. Zani, he also, who pretends to leave and hides. She laughs. At that:

Magnifico

Who couldn't kill his wife, enters with Franceschina. Zani sees; he goes to get wood and oakum[543] in order to burn down the house. At that:

Cassandro

Enters at Ortensia's. At that:

Curcio

Sees him. Enters at Coralina's. At that:

Zani

About to burn the house, calls his wife. He hears that they are giving each other caresses.

---

[541] This is not a known lazzo, but by context is probably that Franceschina positions herself to block a view.

[542] This is a lazzo. Most likely Ortensia asks Magnifico to look for some mote that makes her eye uncomfortable, and Cassandro escapes while Magnifico if focused on the eye.

[543] Flammable fibers.

Franceschina

Zani that he wants to kill her. She, that the laundry must be saved. She takes out Magnifico from the tub. Zani burns down the house. All exit.

Thefts - Literal

Play #10, RMB II-1586-0225.jpg (line 16), C-202 (Comedy)

Act I

Cassandro[544] and Oracio

That he robs the fabric warehouse[545] and that he doesn't keep Zani's friendship. They leave. Zani remains; that he promised Ortensia to Curcio, Isabella to Oracio. Knocks at Trastulo who is keeping Isabella.

Isabella

That he has promised her. Trastulo says no, because she is the daughter of dottore Alexandro degli Albertucci, who has come for her, and she is waiting for him. Trastulo enters.

Zani

Complains and leaves. At that:

Laura, Magnifico

Of the marriage with her daughter Ortensia. Magnifico is content; they call her.

Ortensia

Says no. She makes her touch his hand by force. Magnifico leaves. Ortensia enters with her mother.

Zani

Desperate. At that:

Ortensia

Calls him, tells him about the marriage pact and that he should[546] tell Curcio. Zani is desperate. Ortensia enters. He stays. At that:

Oracio

Caresses him. He tells him that he can't have Isabella. At that:

Curcio

He tells him that he can't have Ortensia. Everyone despairs and they tell them[547] to take care; they promise him something to eat.

Act II

Zani, dressed as Alexandro; Curcio, as a cook

Tells him how he wants to deceive Trastulo and pretend to be Alexandro, because he knows him, and he has dressed in his own clothes, making his beard similar to that of

---

[544] The manuscript is inconsistent about the spellings of some names which we have unified here: Casandro/Cassandro, Zani/Zanni, Trastullo/Trastulo, Magnifico/Stefanello

[545] Fondaco could have several meanings, but fabric store makes sense in this context.

[546] 'Should' is implied by use of the subjunctive.

[547] Indefinite pronoun, could be him or them. Both lovers are sad, so it probably means 'each other'.

Albertucci. Get the key from Curcio to his father's warehouse to steal a piece of damask. He goes to knock for Trastulo.

Trastulo

Pretends to be Albertucci; he gives him the piece of Damask. Trastulo enters crying.

Isabella

Also, crying for being apart from Oracio. Ganassa tricks her and shows who he is. They leave. Curcio knocks at Ortensia's house, with a fake beard.

Ortensia

Complains, thinking that he is a cook sent by Stefanello. Curcio shows who is. She cheers up. At that:

Laura

Curcio puts his beard back on. Pretends Ortensia to be cheerful[548]. They do that thing of turned bosoms[549].

Alexandro Albertucci

Who has come to pick up his daughter. Zani, who has heard him, gives him to believe Trastulo has gone to visit him. Alexandro leaves. Zani laughs and that he wants to entertain Stefanello.

Stefanello

He makes him believe that about the cure.[550] Puts him in the warehouse. He leaves.

Act III

Cassandro and Alexandro Albertucci

Having known each other from earlier, they exchange caresses. At that:

Trastulo

With the piece of damask, to sell it to Signor Cassandro, who recognizes it. He asks him who has given it to him, he replies Alexandro Albertucci. Cassandro complains about him, who is surprised about that and asks him for his daughter. He, would give her to him. Trastulo, to the justice. Cassandro, to the warehouse. They treat Stefanello as a thief. They go together to the justice.

Curcio, Ortensia

They flee.

Zani

That it is going badly for him, that he has seen Stefanelo outside the warehouse. At that:

Alexandro Albertucci

He recognizes him; he makes him believe that wants to sell his daughter and says be quiet because he will put him in his hands to bring him to justice.

[551]

He says similar things to Trastulo, and in such agreement they go to the Justice. Zani laughs and enters the warehouse.

Laura

Yelling and calling Ortensia. At that:

---

[548] We believe this might mean that Laura 'sees' that Ortenzia is cheerful, hence the lazzo of the torsos.
[549] There is a difficult to read word after 'torsi' which might be 'girato' (turned).
[550] The cure may be the cure for cheering up Ortensia who doesn't want to marry Stefanello/Magnifico.
[551] There is a scene boundary, and Trastulo must enter, but no entrance is marked.

Magnifico and Cassandro

That he will give to him prison[552] that is, because he is an honest man. Knocks for Laura.

Laura

That he is a traitor and that he has ruined a maiden. Cassandro to the warehouse to see what is missing. At that:

Zani

Confess everything. They all exit.

---

[552] This is a difficult to read word which we take to be 'prisonia', which is an old Italian word.

The Most Inane Lady[553] - Literal

Play #11, RMB II-1586-0229.jpg (line 9), C-203 (Comedy)

Act I

Magnifico, Tofano

Of wanting to marry his son, Curcio, with Isabela, daughter of Magnifico. They agree not to say anything. Tofano, away.

Isabella

Magnifico, that she should prepare to be a bride, and he does not tell her with whom. And he[554] leaves.

Curcio, Trastulo

Gives to him the letter for Isabela. They leave.

Zani

As a caterer[555] who has brought the banquet.

Laura

In love with Curcio, despairs for having learned that he is going to get married. She sees Zani, who tells that to her. She faints. Zani, thinking her dead, runs away. He returns and[556]. At that:

Trastulo

With the letter. Laura tears it up and enters. He, desperate, leaves.

Franceschina, servant to Laura, and Zani

At the window[557]. He tells her about Laura, that she is dead. She makes him get lower. Enters to see if it is true.

Trastulo

Crying.

Zani

Crying.

Franceschina

Does the lazzo of confetti[558] to them.

---

553 The name written in the manuscript is 'Ia Inans^ta'. 'Ia' is an abbreviation for 'prima', 'Inans^ta' is some word starting with inans, and having a longer familiar ending, but Italian dictionaries fail us on this. Latin gives us Inane or Inanity.

554 It says he leaves, but clearly, she also leaves.

555 Vignarolo could mean winemaker or grocer.

556 Reflexive verb missing, from the manuscript. No cut or inkblot, just never written down. In context it is probably 'parte' meaning Zani comes back and leaves again.

557 Zani is inside, and Franceschina is the one who enters (the house) at the end.

558 Confetti is candies with almonds inside which are given at weddings.

Act II

Magnifico

Cheerful about the new family ties.

Zani

That he brought nothing from the villa, makes him go back. Zani leaves. Magnifico stays.

Laura

She bad-mouths Isabela and Tofano. He leaves to undo the betrothal. At that:

Tofano

Laura bad-mouths Curcio and Magnifico. He leaves to undo the betrothal. At that:

Curcio

Seeing Laura, he imitates her[559]. At that:

Isabella

At the window. Laura insults her. Isabella enters. Curcio, in anger with Laura. He leaves.

Zani

Who forgot the cheese. He knocks.

Isabella

Sends him to look for Curcio. Zani leaves. She stays. Laura, who has heard everything. At that:

Laura

Pretends good words, saying that she is a relative of Curcio. They change houses.

Tofano, Magnifico

They argue, they undo the betrothal.

Act III

Zani

Who has not found Curcio. At that:

Curcio

Tells him about Isabella. Curcio caresses him.

Isabella

From Laura's window, calls him. Curcio, holding the key, enters. Zani stays to retain[560]. At that:

Magnifico

Zani keeps him. Finally, Magnifico goes into the house, finds the windows closed.

Laura

Runs away. He, behind with Zani. Laura, upset, goes home.

Curcio and Isabella

Receive her. At that:

Magnifico

Comes back home. Zani confesses. Everybody out. [...][561].

---

[559] La simula – it isn't clear what this means. Is it mocking by caricature? Somehow it provokes Isabella's anger.

[560] Zani starts keeping people from entering the house.

[561] The final line was cut off in the book binding process. Probably simply 'end of the comedy'.

Ambassadors - Literal

Play #12, RMB II-1586-0232.jpg, C-204 (Comedy)

Act I

The Signore, with servants

Narrates not wanting to get married because he has promised to one[562], going hunting in a forest with a wild boar's head, killed by him. At that time[563] he took away her honor and left her a ring as a sign of marriage. And for having promised a son of his first wife to be the husband of Bella Marina's daughter, and for not having been able to keep his word because he[564] died, and that the lord of Bella Marina, not believing him, wants to wage war, and awaits ambassadors of all his lands. He commands the Capitano to receive them inside.

Zani, Magnifico, Ambassadors from the Cyclades Islands

Tell[565] that it is the land of cowardice. They look for a tavern. At that:

Isabella[566], wife of the Capitano, Laura

Goes to her house coming from a childbirth. They greet her. Both of them fall in love with Isabella, who enters her house. Laura, staying, points them to the tavern.

Trastulo

Receives them. Magnifico enters and Laura with him. Zani stays and goes to talk to Isabella.

Isabella

Gives him the order of a woman.[567] Zani enters.

Ortensia, daughter of the Signore of Bella Marina, and Curcio

He reveals that he is not prince, but that, due to the resemblance he had with the lord of that place, she had been deceived. They tell about those who have robbed[568] them. She grieves. Curcio knocks.

Trastulo

Drives him away. At that:

Laura, his mother

Trastulo drives both of them away. Laura knocks at Isabella's house.

Capitano

Receives Curcio and Ortensia at home. Calls for:

---

562 The one is feminine.
563 Direct translation of 'Entro' is 'Within' or 'by', but we are using it to be 'At that time' or 'Then'.
564 Probably the son has died.
565 'Tell' in the plural so they both tell it.
566 Some names are spelled inconsistently in the manuscript, such as Isabela/Isabella, Signor/Signore. Here we have unified the spelling.
567 This order is to dress as a woman.
568 Either robbed, deceived, or stolen, not clear. In context it applies to con men and robbery.

Isabella

Receives them and she is glad about that. Everyone enters. Isabella stays. At that:

Magnifico

Speaks to her of his love. She gives him the order of a woman[569] and he leaves. She stays.

Curcio

She orders him to give beatings to the two who will come dressed as women. At that:

Zani

As a woman.

Magnifico

As a woman. He beats them.

Act II

Curcio, Ortensia

He comforts her by saying that it seems to them that he has seen those who robbed from them.

Laura

Laura gives him a piece of her jewelry, a ring, to go and sell it. Ortensia enters. At that:

Capitano

Leads him to the palace to sell the jewel. Laura stays.

Magnifico

Gives her a jewel to give to Isabella. She enters and accepts it. Magnifico remains.

Zani

Both of them[570] dressed as ambassadors. At that:

The Signore, Capitano

They deliver the ambassadorial message. The Signore takes them to eat with him. They all leave.

Ortensia, Laura

About the ring and whoever gave it to her. She tells her; Ortensia cheers up. At that:

Curcio

She shows him the ring; she says she wants the Signore to take it. He doesn't want to because he is guilty. At the end, both happy, enter. At that:

Magnifico, Capitano, Zani

Goes to introduces them in his house. Calls for Isabella.

Isabella, Ortensia

They recognize Ortensia. Magnifico refuses to enter. At the end, all enter.

Act III

Magnifico, Zani

About to run away.

The Signore, Capitano, Servants

Asks Capitano whoever gave him that ring. He, that it was Curcio. That Curcio must come into his presence. Capitano calls for him.

---

[569] Again, to dress as a woman.
[570] Both is Zani and Magnifico.

Curcio

Frightened, runs away, that they go and capture him.

Ortensia

Reveals to the prince that she is the daughter of the prince of Bella Marina, and asks Curcio to be pardoned and that the ambassadors be punished.

Zani, Magnifico

They flee. Signore has them taken and put in jail. The Signore calls Curcio, asks him who he is and who gave him the ring.

Trastulo

That he is the son of woman in this house, who took him away - for the love of God[571]. They call her.

Laura

Tells them what happened. The Signore recognizes him as a son. He marries Laura. He frees the prisoners.

---

[571] For God's sake is just an expletive.

The Inn - Literal

Play #13, RMB II-1586-0236.jpg, C-205 (Comedy)

Act I

Zani, Curcio, Magnifico

Fighting about the management[572] of the house, sends Curcio to the grocery. Talks about the pregnant wife. They call her.

Ortensia

That she wants red wine. Magnifico promises it to her and, because he[573] has to go to a banquet, he will send the wine to her through Zani. They leave, having asked Zani about who he is the son of and what is his name. He stays. At that:

Oracio

Of his love of Ortensia. He sees her. She gives him the order that Zani be called and that he[574] comes with a carafe of wine. And they enter.

The Innkeeper[575] and Franceschina

Shouting about the bad management he keeps, she sends him out to buy wine. She stays.

Curcio

Sees her. He enters with her.

Zani

With the wine. At that:

Oracio

As Zani, with the wine. They do the shadows[576]. They go to knock. Zani stays outside, Oracio beats him. Zani exits while crying.

Curcio, Franceschina

That she wants to leave for love of her husband. She, that wants to remove the Tavern sign; and they enter and take it off.

Ortensia, Oracio

He wants to go. They will put up the sign of the Tavern; they enter.

Magnifico

Half drunk, goes home.

Oracio

Beats him up. Magnifico laughs for having gone to the tavern. He goes knocking to the other house singing.

Franceschina

Goes out and beats him up. He leaves, in pain.

---

[572] Or maintenance ...
[573] Pronoun with ambiguous gender, but context says it is he.
[574] Zani
[575] Trastulo
[576] This is a lazzo. Probably of imitated mirror movement.

The Innkeeper

Does the same.

Act II

Ortensia, Oracio

They leave. They take off the sign of the Tavern.

Curcio, Franceschina

Put up the sign of the Tavern. They leave.

Magnifico, Zani, Trastulo

Crying[577] for being lost.

Ortensia

Lets Stefanello know that he is going around drunk. Everyone laughs. So do they about Zani[578].

Franceschina

Does the same with Trastulo, and enter Magnifico, Zani to the piazza to spend money. Ortensia remains.

Curcio

Reveals his love to her. She gives him sweet words. He wants to kiss her. At that:

Magnifico, Zani

Curcio retires. She tells them how Curcio wanted to force her. She sends them [...][579] to the house [...][580].

Act III

Curcio

Complains with Ortensia. He takes her into the house to enjoy one another. They enter.

Oracio

About to go back to Ortensia's place.

Magnifico, Zani

As women[581], they do a lazzo of a piece[582]. He beats them up and he leaves. They go to the mint[583].

Ortensia, Curcio

She orders him to beat up her husband. He goes to knock.

Magnifico, Zani

He beats them up. All outside.

---

577 Plural, all three are lost.
578 They mock Zani for being drunk.
579 There are four or five missing words here.
580 This is one word, with a double-t in the middle.
581 Zani is dressed as a woman.
582 We aren't sure what a lazzo of a piece is.
583 To get more money (coins).

The Tunnel - Literal

Play #14, RMB II-1586-0238.jpg (line 10), C-206 (Comedy)

Act I

Magnifico, Ortensia, Zani

Fighting because of jealousy. She enters. He, with Zani, stays discussing the love for Franceschina, woman of the Bravo[584]. They go to the piazza to see if she is there.

Curcio

Of the love for Ortensia. He knocks.

Ortensia

Makes the proof of the person[585]. In the end, she shoos him away. He leaves. She enters.

Franceschina, Bravo

Who wants to go to war. At that:

Magnifico, Zani

The Bravo brings Zani to war. Magnifico plans with Franceschina to go to dinner with her. At that:

Zani

Who has escaped from the Bravo, bumps into Magnifico. They go to the banquet.

Act II

Curcio

Complaining about Ortensia. At that:

Franceschina

Comforts him and that she will make him have her. She sends him home and she goes to Ortensia.

Ortensia

Deceives her by saying that Fabio[586], her lover, has come. She lets her in.

Magnifico, Zani

Who come from the banquet, leave drunk.

Ortensia

Cheerful.

Curcio

Laughing with Franceschina about the lazzo.[587]

---

[584] Bravo is a soldier or thug.
[585] Ortensia does something to find if Curcio is worthy, and he fails.
[586] It is ambiguous whose lover Fabio is.
[587] The lazzo was the imagined lover Fabio.

Franceschina[588]

Ortensia becomes upset. Tells her[589] about the tunnel, then they go to the fishmonger.

Magnifico, Zani

Who have slept, find her. They scream with Curcio. She passes through the cave and, having done so, does it one more time. Magnifico invites Curcio and his woman to the banquet. They enter. Magnifico and Zani go to Franceschina.

Franceschina

They make noises with playing around ('trastulo')[590].

Act III

Franceschina, Magnifico

That she goes to call Curcio and enters. Franceschina goes to Curcio, calls him and they go to the banquet with Ortensia. Magnifico receives them. Zani, with ceremonious pleasantries. They all go in.

Capitano[591]

From the war, they tease him[592]. Magnifico, that he wants to kill the wife. They appease him.[593]

---

[588] Note, Franceschina has a plot point in the previous scene.
[589] The gender of the object is ambiguous.
[590] Trastulo the character is not in this play, but his name means 'play around', which is probably what is happening here.
[591] Same person as Bravo above.
[592] Are they teasing Magnifico.
[593] Whose wife? Who wants to kill who? Most likely Magnifico is a cuckold and Ortenzia is his wife.

Fighting for Love[594] - Literal

Intermezzo: Adonis

Play #15, RMB II-1586-0240.jpg (line 8), C-207 (Pastoral/Opera)

First Intermezzo

Nurse[595]

Discusses Mira's love with the father, and that she joins them together by night, and that she is pregnant.

Mira

Begs the nurse to join her with her father again, before the delivery. She goes to the usual place.

Cinara

Wants to go and enjoy with someone[596] who he has never seen and who has brought the bait that is ignited with spit. The nurse guides him. She stays.

Messenger

He scolds the nurse for not guarding Mira. Leaves.

Mira

Within, upset[597] for having been discovered.

The Father[598]

Follows her. Converts to a tree. Cinara throws himself from a precipice[599]. Lucina[600] makes her give birth [...][601].

Act I

Sireno

Of being in love with Flori, sister of his friend Curcio[602], and that he cannot have her because the Prince separates her from him with enchantments. He goes to sleep.

Orfinio

Bragging about being the richest and strongest shepherd in Arcadia, sees Sireno, who reveals to him that he is in love with his sister. Orfinio that, if he wants her, has to come to battle with him. They go to the Prince to ask for her.

---

594 Neither the play nor the intermezzo was named in the manuscript. Here we provide plausible names for identification purposes.

595 Nurse for taking care of children (maybe a wet nurse or nanny).

596 Feminine, so it is a woman he wants to enjoy.

597 'asida' we are taking to be acida, meaning acidic, or unhappy.

598 The Father could be Cinara.

599 Idiom implies that he throws himself from a precipice, but also means rushing.

600 Lucina is another name for Juno.

601 The missing text is an entire line, perhaps eight words. Perhaps a shepherd takes the baby.

602 Note: for the rest of the play Curcio is called Orfinio.

Flori

Complaining that she loves and is loved in return but cannot have her love because of the enchantments.

Sireno

Sees her and asks her for a kiss. Fires rise. Sorrowful, they leave.

Magnifico, Zani

Of love and hunger. They want [...][603] Flori fall in love.

Flori

They sing. She makes the lazzo of a natural spring[604]. She leaves.

Young Shepherdess with the flour

Does a lazzo to them.

Second Intermezzo

The two Cypriots

Who do not know who they should elect as king of Cyprus and they want to pray to Venus.

Adonis

Says he is the son of Cinara. At that:

Venus

Tells them that they to take him as king. They leave. Venus tells him beware of the pig. They talk about their loves.

Mars

He threatens them [...][605].

Act II

Magnifico

He does an echo[606]. He goes.

Wizard, Orfinio, Sireno

They beg him. It is decided to fight. Everyone leaves. Sireno remains.

Flori

Who joins with the right[607] and wants to fight.

Serpent

Makes him run away. She stays.

Zani

She does to him a lazzo of tearing the eyes out. She leaves.

Magnifico

Takes him as Flori. Magnifico leaves. Zani, also.

Shephard

With things to eat, he places them at the tomb.

---

[603] Maybe one small word is missing from a burned page edge. We think it might be 'far' which means to make.

[604] Natural spring or possibly fountain, given Botarga's spelling consistency.

[605] A few words missing from the cut for the binding.

[606] "Fa l'eco" is a stage instruction that we don't know for certain what it means. It might be that he either repeats something from his last scene or echoing something Mars said.

[607] She holds his hand.

Magnifico

Eats. At that:

Zani

Also eats. They hear horns. They enter the tomb.

Wizard, Flori, Sireno, Orfinio, with many shepherds and instruments of war

Offer to the tomb. They fight. Sireno wins. Wizard, grieving.

Spirit

Takes Flori away. Wizard decrees that whoever gives him Sireno's head will have Flori. Sireno, desperate, leaves. They place Orfinio in the tomb; they find Zani and Magnifico. They take them. Zani does to them the lazzo of the scorpion. They leave.[608]

Third Intermezzo

Adonis

Bragging about the hunt.

Mars

From heaven restores life to the pig.

Pig

Kills him.

Venus

Is sorrowful. The land swallows him. A flower rises.

Act III

Sireno

Grieving.

Flori

From under the earth, screams. They make the climbs[609]. Sireno sets off intending to give his head to the Wizard to free Flori.

Zani

Echoes[610].

Spirit

Takes him underground.

Wizard

About to kill Sireno.

Sireno

Hands him his head.[611]

Shadow of Acrisius

That the decree is over, and that Flori is given to him, and that Orfinio is half dead. They open the tomb.

Orfinio

Alive. They rejoice. They make Flori and Zani come out[612]. They set the Magnifico free.

---

[608] Note: Magnifico must be left behind in the tomb.

[609] Fano le salite has a few possible meanings. Perhaps she tries to climb out of a pit.

[610] Another fa l'eco

[611] Perhaps merely offers. How is the head off his neck?

[612] From the underworld.

Two Crazy People - Literal

Play #16, RMB II-1586-0244.jpg, C-208 (Comedy)

Act I

Magnifico, Zani
> Talks about the lost son and that he wants to give Isabella as a wife to Tofano.

Tofano
> They do a lazzo. They call Isabella.

Isabella
> They make her touch the hand. She, in the house. They go to make a contract.

Oracio, Servant
> About the love for Isabella. They go for the help[613] of Franceschina.

Franceschina
> Promises them to talk to her. They leave. She knocks for Isabella.

Isabella
> They agree on introducing him. They enter.

Pazzo
> Narrates about his adventures.

Magnifico
> They do a lazzo. They all leave.

Oracio, Servant, Franceschina
> She lets them come into the house. She enters with them.

Pazza
> Talks about her adventures. At that:

Magnifico, Zani
> They do lazzo.

Pazzo
> Comes back. They all play Primero. Pazzo exits. They go into the house.

Spirits
> From the inside, they come out. They gesture to avoid bad luck and then they leave.[614]

---

[613] Literally the hand of Franceschina, which is an idiom meaning to help.
[614] This scene is not important to the story.

Act II

Magnifico[615]

Is suspicious. Zani interrogates her: She confesses that he[616] was her lover. Magnifico makes her go away. She pretends to drown herself. Magnifico and Zani are sad. Zani goes to get her. She, unseen, enters the house. Magnifico knocks.

Isabella

From the window shoos him away. He leaves.

Pazzo, Pazza

They know each other.

Act III

Zani, Oracio

They go to Isabella's; they want to escape. Zani with the luggage[617] of theirs. They leave.

Magnifico, Tofano

Zani tells him about his eloped daughter. They go to look for her.

Curcio

Not crazy anymore, asks about Stefanelo. Magnifico and Tofano recognize him as the missing son. He goes for Ortensia, the crazy woman.

Oracio, Isabella

Asks them for her to be his wife. They concede her to him.

Ortensia, Curcio

The same thing.

---

[615] Zani and Isabella are in the first plot points of this scene, so they must also enter.
[616] The 'he' in this case is not Magnifico or Zani, it is probably Orazio.
[617] In the manuscript, this word is obscured by an inkblot or otherwise not visible. We guessed it is luggage.

Jewels of Chastity[618] - Literal

Intermezzo: Perseus & Medusa

Play #17, RMB II-1586-0246.jpg, C-209 (Pastoral/Opera)

First Intermezzo

Neptune

In love with Medusa, he goes to transform into a horse to kidnap her.

Forco, her father, Medusa

That she shouldn't get far from him, because he has foreseen her damage through prophetic spirit. He leaves. She stays. At that:

Horse

She climbs onto the horse, it takes her away.

Minerva

That has violated her temple. She calls the fury.

Fury

Orders her to turn the head into snakes. Fury enters, then she goes up. They leave[619].

Forco

Grieving for his daughter.

Medusa

With a serpentine mane, furious.

Act I

Curcio[620], Sireno

Sireno praises "Love"[621], the other blames it. Both in love, Sireno with Delia, the other with Flori.

Pan, Cupid

They wrestle. Pan loses (falls). Sireno narrates about the strength of love.

Zani

Gets in the middle. Promises help to them, if they give freedom to Magnifico, Sireno goes to free him.

Magnifico

Promises them. They go to put themselves into order.

Flori

With jewels, looking for Delia, praising her chastity.

---

[618] Neither the play nor the intermezzo was named in the manuscript. Here we provide plausible names for identification purposes.

[619] 'sale' means to climb, go up, or in Spanish to go out. This is Minerva rising back to heaven.

[620] Curcio is in the manuscript, but almost certainly should have been written by Botarga as Orfinio.

[621] Love personified.

Delia

Flori gives her the jewel[622] on behalf of Diana.

Orfinio, Sireno

Beg them. They shoo them away. They leave. They[623] stay.

Magnifico, Zani

Fall in love with them, who do the lazzo of the burbe[624]. At that:

Wizard

With the book. Magnifico meets him. Asks him for help. He let him enter into his shack. He leaves Zani to him, to whom he gives the book, and he leaves, after having ordered him not to open it. Zani opens it. Evil spirits come. He makes them bring him macaroni. They beat him.

Second Intermezzo

Polidette, Servant

Of wanting to send Perseus to death.

Perseus

He sends him on the endeavor of the head of Medusa. Enters. Perseus stays. At that:

Mercury

Gives him the wings and the sword, and he leaves.

Minerva

Gives him the shield and that he goes to look for the helmet of Pluto.

Act II

Magnifico, Wizard

That the shepherds go to the Sphinx. Cannot find Zani nor the book, that it will cost him dearly. The Wizard leaves, he stays.

Sireno, Orfinio

Tells them about the sphinx, and about the riddles. They go to get in order.

Zani

With the book, of wanting to turn into a nymph with the nymphs. He leaves.

Magnifico, Orfinio, Sireno, Sphinx

<Italian> They propose the riddles and they solve them:

Tell me, wise spirit, in what season

The feather of the angel, that is so light,

Keeps the men of the Earth either with a sad face

Or a happy face?

I was by my enemies surrounded

From the left and from the right

My house went out of the windows

And I remained sad in prison.

---

[622] Note: in the manuscript is it jewels in the previous scene, and jewel (singular) in the second scene.

[623] They (feminine).

[624] Burbe: Possibly meaning being gruff or angry: see adjective burbero.

<Spanish>

I was surrounded by my enemies

From below and from above

My house went out through the windows

And I remained in jail, unfortunate.

When will that day be, wise spirit,

That the skin of an animal, hitting hard,

Will invite anybody to kill themselves,

Making with its sound a big commotion?

When, tell me, being warned,

He who is desperate, without mercy,

Let him suck the blood of those that have deceived him

And killed his father?

She gives to him the water of forgetfulness and enters. They leave in order to go find the nymphs.

Flori

That she has lost Delia. At that:

Delia

They cheer up.

Sireno, Orfinio

They throw water on them. They fall asleep. They take the jewels off of them. They leave.

Ganassa

Made nymph, sees the nymphs. He sits among them; he wants to kiss them.

Spirit

Takes the book from him. He, scared, leaves.

Nymphs

Wake up. They agree on their loves, they go to look for them.

[...]⁶²⁵

Third Intermezzo

Estenese and Euriale

They want to lend the eye.

Perseus

Takes it from them. He makes them promise the enchanted helmet. They give it to him. They enter. He puts it on. At that:

Medusa

Screaming. He cuts off her head.

Horse Pegasus

Rises up. He gets onto the horse. The spring of water rises up.

Polidette

From hunting, turns into stone.

---

625 There is a whole line missing which is likely a whole scene to end the act.

Act III

Sireno

Bragging about his flock.

Delia

Delia begs him. He shooshes her away. She behind.

Flori

The same:

Orfinio

Shooshes her away. He leaves. She behind.

Magnifico, Zani

Thinking him a nymph, falls in love. He reveals himself. They go to the priest or to the Wizard.

Nymphs, Shepherds

Return. They shoo them[626] away. They want to kill themselves. At that:

Priest of Diana

Takes away the jewels from the shepherds. They transform them[627], then he orders the sacrifice.

Magnifico, Zani

Magnifico, for the fire. They make the sacrifice.

Diana

Gives them license.

They end the comedy.

---

[626] Feminine them i.e. the nymphs.
[627] Feminine them i.e. the nymphs.

Prince Tireno[628] - Literal

Intermezzo: Choice of Paris

Play #18, RMB II-1586-0251.jpg, C-210 (line 6) (Tragedy/Opera)

First Intermezzo (The Choice of Paris)

Priam, Hecuba, Priest, Servant[629] with the child
They narrate the dream. They go to the Oracle, who replies to them: "He weeps, oh Priam, because your joy is extinct; there will be a flame that will burn down Troy." Hecuba enters grieving. Priam orders him that he be brought to death. He enters[630]. He abandons him in the woods. He leaves.

Shepherd
He finds him, takes him with him.

Act I (Prince Tireno)

King, Magnifico, Capitano
They talk about the infirmity of prince Tireno. Magnifico orders the banquet.

Contessa
Asks for an audience. She does that of the sword[631] and enters. Magnifico remains.

Zani
About the banquet.

Porter
Zani gives him a slap. The porter goes to tell the King. Magnifico, after him to appease him. Zani, too.

Oracio
Of his love for Ortensia and having heard that the prince is in love with her. He knocks.

Ortensia
She gives him the promise not to wrong him. They enter.

Tireno, Capitano
About the love of Ortensia. He knocks[632]. He begs her.

Ortensia
Out, refuses him. Sorrowful Prince leaves with the Capitano. She stays.

Magnifico
Tells her to go to the banquet. She refuses. At that:

---

[628] Neither the play nor the intermezzo was named in the manuscript. Here we provide plausible names for identification purposes.
[629] Servant is male, so is the child.
[630] Priam leaves.
[631] A threatening sword gesture.
[632] At Ortenzia's house

King, Capitano, Porter

Sentences Zani to death. Ortensia begs him that he be whipped. Enters for the banquet. Ortensia enters with the Magnifico.

Zani

Disguised[633] as a Doctor. The palace guards[634] find him out, they take him.

Second Intermezzo

Paris

Goes to sleep.

Mercury

Gives him the apple[635].

Juno, Pallas, Venus

Enters Ida's forest to give the judgement.

Act II

King, Magnifico, Capitano

Narrates that his daughter is the cause of the infirmity of Tireno. Capitano confirms that he wants her for his wife. The King accepts this. They enter.

Servant[636] of the Contessa

Who has heard everything, calls her.

Contessa

Says she wants to take revenge. They enter.

Magnifico, Ortensia

Arguing about the wedding. At that:

Zani

That he will advise her. Magnifico leaves.

Oracio

They order to flee. He, to a frigate. They, in the house.

Contessa

Who has heard everything, tells the Capitano, who wants to tell the Prince. He[637] leaves.

Oracio

Knocks for Ortensia, sad. They place themselves in order. At that:

Capitano

Capitano kills Oracio. Zani flees. Capitano, behind.

Ortensia

Ortensia weeps over Oracio. At that:

Capitano

Who has taken Zani, takes Ortensia by force to the palace and makes Zani carry Oracio[638].

---

[633] "da" in these plays usually means that it is a disguise.

[634] Note: Sbiri is Italian slang for police. They need an entrance.

[635] 'Pomo' is an old word. In context it is the golden apple according to legend.

[636] Bailo is a male servant (or bailiff).

[637] Singular pronoun, but both Contesa and Capitano have to leave the stage.

[638] This is merely giving the order. End of the act, so some porters will come drag the body away.

Third Intermezzo

Paris

Who wants to mislead Helen to take revenge on Ersiona[639]. At that:

Venus

Encourages him, leaves. Noises from offstage. They[640] steal Helen.

Act III

Magnifico

Who has heard about Oracio's death.

King, Tireno

Complaining to him about his unworthy love. Tireno, that Ortensia does not want him. The King threatens Magnifico with death. Tireno enters for Ortensia.

Ortensia

Pretends to accept, asks for three favors: to give the funeral for her husband in her own way and for Zani to remain in her service; they make him cupbearer. She commands that she be obeyed. The King and Tireno, at the temple. She has the coffin taken out. She cries.

King, Tireno, and Priest

About to perform the wedding. They make her get up. She drinks and makes Tireno drink. They exchange sweet words. They fall dead. King, in order to kill all the women, enters the palace.

Magnifico

Finds his daughter dead. He wants to kill himself.

A Hermit

Stops him. He goes with him and Zani.

King

Wounded, falls to the ground.

Justice

Covered, she reveals herself, scolds him. He, desperate, dies threatening her.

---

[639] Probably Enona, a nymph that Paris formerly loved.
[640] Who is they? Helen isn't on stage, so this is all implied.

The Deadly Sword - Literal

Play #19, RMB II-1586-0255.jpg (line 8), C-211 (Tragicomedy)

Act I

Philosopher, Curcio

Scolds him about his love, and that he is not his father. He gives him the jewel. He leaves. He, grieving, also leaves.

Prince, Magnifico, Capitano

Tells of the sword that haunts him; that he has been to the oracle; of the son of death. He sends Capitano to give the announcements, and tells Magnifico of the death of his sister; and about the secret. They leave.

Ortensia, Franceschina

About the love of Capitano. She sends her to find him.

Ganassa as a haberdasher and His wife

Screaming. Then, they agree. She enters. At that:

Franceschina

They make love. He puts her in the shop and leaves for breakfast.

The Wife

Who has heard everything, kicks her out [...][641] in the shop.

Curcio

In order to speak to Ortensia.

Zani

He begs him and leaves. Zani knocks.

Ortensia

He gives her the fleeces. She enters.

Magnifico

Asks him for good clothes[642]. He, in order not to be unhappy[643], puts him in the shop.

Trastulo

The same thing.

Magnifico

Who would like to see her[644]. So that he doesn't get bored.

The Wife

Comes out. They do a trick[645] to her.

---

[641] Missing text from manuscript, but this is required from later in the play. From context, we think it means "and takes her place".

[642] 'roba' might mean 'stuff' in Italian or 'clothing' if this is a Spanishism.

[643] 'scorozzarse' is a lost word but seems to be related to being unhappy or offended from a bad choice.

[644] It is ambiguous whether Magnifico would like to see the merchandise or the woman, which can be done onstage using pronouns. If left ambiguous, this adds to Zani's surprise in the next scene.

[645] 'burlano' is a verb meaning trick or joke. 'burla' is a noun which we've mostly used to mean 'lazzo'.

Act II

Curcio

To talk to Ortensia. At that:

Zani

Sees him; knocks for her.

Ortensia

He asks her for a kiss. She gives it to him and makes him stay one year without talking, and that he cannot defend himself and talk to himself. And enters.

Trastulo

Seeing him mute, he takes the jewel. Zani, the clothes.

Franceschina

Grieves, calls Ortensia.

Ortensia

Screams at him and threatens him. To him [...][646]

Capitano

Ortensia begs him. He, that she should[647] love Curcio. She, desperate, enters. He, to kill himself.[648]

Magician

He prevents him and tells him not to speak, until he sees him again. At that:

Zani

For the box, he knocks.

Magnifico

Calls Ortensia so that she gives it[649] to him. He leaves.

Ortensia

She does a lazzo to him.

Act III

Prince

That no one appears who can free him from the sword. In this:

Curcio

Frees him.[650] He orders the prison of the castle and to cut off the head. He leaves. Magnifico remains. Knocks for Ortensia.

Ortensia

That she will make him speak. She enters.

Prince with Curcio

At that:

Zani

To make him speak, he is taken.

---

[646] Missing text.

[647] 'Should' is implied by use of the subjunctive.

[648] 'precipitarsi.' has many meanings, but we wants to kill himself makes the most sense in context, but could also be to plunge, fall, crash, etc.

[649] Feminine "it" probably the above mentioned box.

[650] Missing here is that Magnifico has the box that proves that Curcio is the nephew, or that the Prince recognizes Curcio from his dreams.

Trastulo

The same.

Ortensia

The same. They call the Justice.

Philosopher

He makes him known as the nephew[651] of the Prince.

---

[651] Nephew or grandson.

Emperor Maumet - Literal

Play #20, RMB II-1391-0206.jpg (line 6) (History/Morality)

Because this is the first published transcription of this play, we are including both the transcription and the translation here in a somewhat different form than in the other nineteen plays.

Transcription and Literal Translation

Page 1 (Image 206)		
Line	**Transcription**	**Translation**
1	Imp. Maumet acusa friati suo bassa	Emperor Maumet accuses his brother
2	Guiacet - secretario & Imperatore condire (conduce?)	Guiacet – Secretary & Emperor embellishes (speaks with)
3	cose gli cerca la sua distruzione Imperatore	That he looks for his destruction. Emperor
4	ordina sia posto priggione. In questo:	orders that he will be put in prison. At that:
5	Gaiacet Io pongono priggione. In questo:	Gaiacet they put him in prison, At that:
6	Diogene prega a lui Inq. Lo vol condannare	Diogene begs him, At that: who wants to condemn
7	alla morte egli da termine un' hora finale.	him to death, begs him to give the date of his final hour.
8	Intramedio	intermission
9+10	Imp. Insidia Judicanta sententia alla	Emperor: The trap judgement sentence to
11	[...]652 Guiacet Inq. 8653	[...] Guiacet. At that:
12	[...] ano Inq.	[...] year At that:
13	[...] un lunie Inq. Si ride lo ch..(?)	[...] he laughs At that: lo ch...

---

652 On lines 11-14 there is more than an inch torn out of the bottom left corner of the page leaving one to three words of text to make informed guesses about.

653 This symbol looking like an 8 is on the manuscript, but so far we haven't guessed if it means something germane to the play.

14	[…] passan	[…] They pass.

Page 2 (Image 207)		
1	uomo con zechie d'asino et tiene loro	Man with ears of donkey and holds them
2	Calumnia incognita a mano	Pretending not to know about them in his hand
3	Ignoranza sospiticione	**Ignorance** is suspicious
4	Calumnia sabrosa con un torchio in	**Slander** delicious with a press in
5	mano stratinando un giovine il quale	hand beating a youth who
6	ulcia le mani ab ciello et invoca dio.	raised his hands to the sky and invokes God.
7	La Invidia con ochio acuto equali ila	The sharp-eyed **Envy**
8	la calumnia e' In mezo	The **Slander** is is in the middle
9	Penitezia di nesi e la cosati pani vestita	**Penitence** of nexus and the thing dressed
10	Tutta Dioniginte	all Dionysin
11	Verita de lei compagnatta , e flumiti	Truth By her accompanied and
12	mente guarditta / laquale mon(n)a la	The lady who lies has
13	bugia con la lingua sua In mano /	her tongue in his hand

The Prologues

Here we give translations of the eight prologues in the main collection. We note that there is one full one, and one fractional prologue in manuscript RMB-II-1391 which do not appear in this book.

Of the eight, one is in the form of a Latin sermon, two are in Spanish, and the other five are in Italian. A few of them seem to be written for other actors to perform, but about half of them were probably delivered by Zan Ganassa (AKA Alberto Naseli) who played Zani.

These prologues are not specific to a particular show. Depending on the prologue they take between six and fifteen minutes to perform, and in this modern day, will tax the patience of any audience. That said, we include them here because they do have some beautiful and clever passages. They do tell us something about the audience to whom they were playing. They, in most cases, tell us things about the life of the troupe members and the world in which they lived. One in particular claims to tell us how Commedia dell'Arte was performed.

We haven't found reliable information on this, but after some discussion, we suspect that these were delivered while the audience was finding seats. If this is the case, you might imagine some soft string instrument playing in the background to augment the mood.

The structure of the prologues

Each of these eight prologues are about 90 lines of text long and take about ten minutes to present by a single person. Experience indicates that this is too long for a modern audience, unless the speaker is amazing, or the audience is otherwise distracted, like perhaps getting to their seats, or buying things to eat or drink.

The prologues are funny, sad, beautiful, insightful, and at times tedious as they use the rhetorical method of making lists from history that seem to support the argument of the prologue. The tedious parts feel like reading excerpts from "The Natural History of Pliny the Elder", which are fascinating if you like lists and history, but can at times seem repetitive.

In the overall structure, most of them begin with some self-deprecating rhetorical question about why this speaker is talking to you. Then the speaker weaves in the main topic of the prologue and makes the case that no one would be better to present this idea. In most of the prologues, the speaker talks about those with the contrary opinion and shows that they are self-serving liars or are otherwise not as noble as they may seem. Then the speaker expands the idea and gives historic support for various aspects of it, frequently decrying strawman nay-sayers, again citing numerous historical examples. In the end it gets tied up nicely.

The tedious lists may serve the purpose mentioned in the first prologue as evidence that the actors read a lot in preparation for their performances and are full of arcane knowledge. If you have an interest in knowing every reference in these lists, the internet often helps, but once again, we recommend the notes and footnotes in Calvo-2007. She didn't find them all, but she got nearly all, and cites historic books that the reference most likely came from in most cases.

What they tell us

The reason for this chapter, is not to teach you how to present or write a simulacrum of an authentic 16th Century prologue, but rather because within these eight bodies of prose are some things expressed about how Commedia dell'Arte (not always comedy) was performed at the time. The fact is that we have few sources that tell us details about this, and this, never-before-translated into English, is one of those rare sources. Granted we have to see this source through the filter of knowing that it was things being said to an audience by the performer, and so may be exaggerated to support an impression they want to give. Let's go through them, one-by-one.

Latin Sermon on Old Age

This prologue starts off saying that the speaker is an old man, and wouldn't it be better for some energetic person with all their wits to give the prologue? The speaker states that the performers have all done the reading in preparation for the show, and now the speaker wants to talk about old age. The rest is a beautiful look at the end of life, and the sweetness of fully ripe apples. It borrows from Cicero's "On Old Age".

On Old Age

Prologue #1, RMB II-1586-0007.jpg, C-008

For I wonder that I myself, a most illustrious man, already worn out with too much old age, dared to lay so much of the burden on my own shoulders and since the office of reciting at length seems to belong more to the young than to the old, and having entered this senility, I neither have the talent nor the constitution of the body, to have this office conferred upon me[654] and moreover, in the presence of so many men and so many who have been possessed by the purifying alum[655] of almost divine genius, and who were preceded by so many divine and human sciences. Was it not enough that Cicero, Demosthenes, and Aristotle had given their abundant eloquence to this? Nor Plautus, Terentius, and Menander, who composed it and recited it together? But still, having exhausted your kindness and clemency, we have done the reading[656] for the comedy that we want to give you, and before I come to the end of my prologue, let them say a few words of praise about old age, since it really concerns me. It is, however, first of all to praise old age, since all dream of reaching the end of their age as the safest port from the sea of[657] dangers; those seen to have been established in this final degree of aging[658] have escaped from all the hostility[659] of the world. For we have seen that by old age I will be liberated, unfettered, and freed from all the dangers of lust; that unbridled love of Venus does not return to my breast, even if she can cast a thin and enervated spell, for I have other work[660] and my mind is fixed like a bow, and as that excellent poet, Horace says: (*Epistles book 2, poem 2, lines 205-213*)

> You're not greedy; go away. What? Have the other vices fled with that one? Does your heart lack empty ambition? Do you lack dread and wrath? Do you laugh at dreams, magical terrors, witches, ghosts in the night, and Thessalian portents? Do you count birthdays gratefully? Forgive friends? Are you kinder and better as you approach old age? What does it help you, having removed one thorn of many? If you don't know how to live properly, yield to those with experience.

---

[654] We have cleaned this up to make an easily spoken statement.

[655] Alum "alumine" is an alchemical metaphor related to purification and spirit. We added the word purifying here to convey something a modern audience wouldn't pick up.

[656] "recitavimus" literally we have recited, but also can mean read out in preparation.

[657] Periculorum doesn't include the "sea of" metaphor so directly, but it is implied.

[658] "Of aging" is our addition to add clarity.

[659] The manuscript reads 'virelis', but 'viralis' makes more sense.

[660] "I have other work" is not in the original but seems implied by context. Note also, in the original this final clause was all in third person, but the previous part of the sentence was in first. For clarity when spoke, we converted it to first person.

Indeed, songs are worthy of memory. What did I not desire?[661] While there will be nothing certainly to benefit from old age, one uses easy manners. Our old age is gentle, humane, honest, modest, temperate, and being accustomed to religious matters, one restrains oneself from the public, it does not brag about other people's affairs except its own, and in the middle of the state of the state, it is held as the governor of the whole ship: no praise, no glory, nothing finally the premium of honor which is not due to old age. Oh, admirable old age, that in that golden age, when the Roman Republic flourished most in morals and laws, you were worshiped as the greatest god. From the thirteenth satire, I will illustrate this custom with the excellent poems of Juvenal (*SATVRA XIII – End of the 2ⁿᵈ paragraph*):

> Dishonesty was admirable in those days; men deemed it a heinous sin, worthy of death, if a youth did not rise before his elders, or a boy before any bearded man, though he himself might see more strawberries, and bigger heaps of acorns, in his own home. So worshipful was it to be older by four years, so equal to reverend age was the first down of manhood!

And Ovid also says, if I remember well:

> Great was the respect formerly paid to the hoary head and great the honor to the wrinkles of age.

And further on, who would dare say words worthy of blushing in the presence of an old man? Long old age gave censure. Let the youths depart and be silent[662] in the presence of the old, for if they take up iron weapons for their defense, the weapons of old age are indeed the most apt and most noble; certainly, the arts and lifelong practices[663] of the virtues, bring forth wonderful fruits[664]. And when I embrace these with my heart, I see the teacher Leontinus Romanus[665] who lived to the age of one hundred and seven years, as if saying "I blame nothing on old age[666]," since he did not cease his long study and work of renown. To be sure, imprudent old men contribute their vices and their faults to old age, but clearly Ennius did not do this, nor Plato, who died writing in the eighty-first year, nor even Isocrates, who spent his ninety-fourth year writing and is said to have lived five years afterwards. Oh elderly! To all old men, honor and complete praise! And if you wish to read[667], in the works of the Lacedaemonians, those who held the most extensive and honorable office were called elders. Who indeed, except the old, held up the state, which was undermined by the young? For whom is left to restore the laws violated by the young except the old? For whom, except the old, have extinguished the wretched adulteries and murders committed by the young, with the maximum punishment? This is to be praised if you are prepared[668]. On the other hand, you can say that the old are to be lamented, for

---

[661] Is "Quid ne avebam" a familiar line of a popular song?

[662] Mutescare and emutescare are indistinguishable in meaning.

[663] Note: Exercise is the direct translation, but we want to emphasize a little more the military sense of the word in latin.

[664] The original of this is a clumsy sentence, and we are applying a little freedom in the translation.

[665] This is a reference to Cicero's "On Old Age" and citing someone from the 4th Century BCE in Sicily.

[666] This is another somewhat free translation of a fake quote.

[667] This is the direct translation, but it could be reworded to if you like to read, or something even more provoking to those who don't read.

[668] Ready is the direct translation, but begs the question, ready for what? Simply to praise the elderly's efforts?

gradually, without realizing it, they are already approaching death; to this I answer with Cicero: "but all things, which are according to nature, are to be considered good things". But what could be more natural than old men dying? Young people also die, but with hostility and in a violent manner. And so - says Cicero himself – To my mind it seems that young people die in a way like when the flame is overwhelmed by a flood of water, but the old pass on like an old fire that is extinguished of its own accord, without the use of any force; and like an apple from the trees, if they are unripe they must be plucked, but if they fall ripe they are sweet and in their time."[669] And that emperor Caesar thoroughly praised the old man of Egypt[670], saying, "I understand that the gods, as one, love you, since the path of your life has been such a long one." Is there anything in the course of this life that is so immutable [671]? Is it so strong that the pursuit for time is never satisfied?[672] And there is no pain so bitter that it is not gradually diminished, not by spasm[673], not by force, but by an onion. Did not ancient Babylon perish? Were not the strongest walls of Corinth overcome[674]? Have not the proud buildings of Troy been destroyed? Was not rich and opulent Carthage ruined? Are those tombs built of marble still standing? By no means! And if all these, which were built of the strongest stones of the living earth, perished slowly, and were gradually diminished, why wonder that the human body, when it is made of the strength of rich mud[675] and ashes, is diminished by the length of time.

---

[669] This was freely translated to give the sense of what Cato said within Ganassa's prologue.

[670] Removed short redundant phrase "lived a long time".

[671] Estabile may a mild Spanishism for the Latin Stabile. Here we have chosen to translate it as Immutable.

[672] This sentence needs a free translation. It is possible that consumo in the manuscript actually means consummo. The context drove some of our choices.

[673] The original text was a bit enigmatic, and we suspect that there may be some transposed letters or b-d substitutions, but Medieval Latin Wordlist by Baxter and Johnson gives "gutta cadiva" as meaning epilepsy. The sense of the whole passage is that bitter pain of loss does not dimmish by quick actions, but by the natural passing of time.

[674] Menia is Italian for bull manure, but context says it is talking about moenia, i.e. town walls or fortifications. Note that General Mummia who destroyed Corinth in 146BCE.

[675] Terra means "Earth" in a dirt sense. Here we used rich mud to make the statement a bit more visceral.

Italian Prologue on the Way of Acting Commedia

This one is fascinating to Commedia performers interested in how it was performed in the past, but it is still rife with numerous lists of examples to support the ideas. The short form is this: Commedia dell'Arte is improvised and performing it emphasizes body movement, expression, vocalizing with a focus on conveying emotion rather than, as in Commedia Erudita, the beauty of the words in the poetry. Commedia dell'Arte permits expressions using the idioms and customs familiar to the locale of the audience.

This prologue seems likely to have always been recited by Zan Ganassa.

On the Way of Acting Commedia

Prologue #2, RMB II-1586-0013.jpg, C-009

O what great strength envy holds, illustrious spectators, but not, to the detriment of the envied, but to the good of those who envy! With such a quick bite it makes their wound itch[676], of what subtle flame she burns them, with what sweet bitterness she holds them! Such pleasant poison makes them thirst for, such a delectable disease makes them enamored with, such a playful torment she brings them to, and in what a beautiful way she leads them to a flattering death! She invades the envious person, oh spectators!, just like he was the only[677] one who holds a viper in his hands, intending to throw it at his enemy, so that it will bite him and kill him, but he feels first wounded by her and, dead, falls to the feet of the one whom he wanted to see dead.[678] So, it will happen to certain envious people, who allow some things to come out of their mouths, which they are good at supporting with reason, and all against us, howling like furious imitators, they get inflamed, blaming the way and the means by which we try to show the world how we must act comedies, which are, just like salt, a condiment for our life, they are the imitation of ourselves, the destruction of the hateful, entertaining the wise, moderating and restraining the dissolute and idiots, who, when they come here, while we are acting and they are listening, do not think, do not see, do not operate anything that causes them infamy and damage to others. These angry dogs[679] of envy blame us because we do not perform in verse and because we do not dress the young actor as an old man, as if the robe makes the monk, wanting to imply that the statues, mute and dressed in gold, speak. And this I believe: that they do not do it for any other purpose, if not to stop us from those studies that are a cause, gentlemen, for your entertainment, and for us of discipline[680] and sustenance of food and clothing, with that little and low reward that you so happily offer us every eight days. And please know, gentlemen, that the bad-mouthing of these slanderers does not matter to us, because we are neither the first nor the last who have sustained the venomous strikes of lies and envy. To show that this is true, Plato is found to have been accused of untidiness; Aristotle, because of to his writing's obscurity, is nicknamed cuttlefish; Empendocles, Anaxagora, Democritus and Leucipo were taxed by the arrogance of Aristotle; Virgil was called a thief of others' work; Marco Tulio says that it seems to him that Homer often sleeps, nor is he very satisfied with Demosthenes; the same Tulio is also

---

[676] Gratta might mean to more simply to be aware rather than sting or itch.
[677] Sole would mean Sun, but Botarga's inconsistent spelling and the sense of this suggest that it means only.
[678] We are translating this a bit freely to capture the sense of the whole prologue.
[679] Allani? Alani is Great Dane.
[680] Dotrina means doctrine, or possible discipline or duty.

accused of being redundant, slow in his principles, lazy in his digressions, late in the advice, and not very warm in his conclusions; Xenophonte was reputed to be a sleepwalker[681]; Livio in his divine orations could not avoid being condemned by Trago Pompeio. What can Plautus do if Horatio does not like him and if he is considered incomplete by Lucilo? What can we do against these biting tongues, if Pliny was still bitten as too quick in writing, of not having digested well what he wrote, and resembling a turbid river, was Ovid, the light of Sulmona, condemned? Salustio could not keep Asinius Polione's tongue from accusing him of affectations; Terence was forced to pervert the orders of his prologues because of the tongues of his slanderers; Seneca could not avoid that his compositions were compared as an arena without mortar; Tulio was thought envious and hateful, because of the many orators who lived in his time, he does name only two; Pompilius kept his silence about all the writers of his age. And if this is true that envy blinds the taste of all mortals, how should we, weak virtuosos, fear it? And if there is a common problem, how can we avoid it? Therefore, let the envious say what they want about us. Let them gossip, saying that we do not want to represent our comedies except in prose and we want to dress her naturally and not artificially, according to height, girth, shortness, age, and the quality of each character; and we want to defend the comedy with reason, so that it is not obscured, convoluted, forced, and interrupted by the verse, but we want it to appear in free, clear, current, pleasant, and coherent prose, both beneficial and delectable, and not like the books of Heraclitus, about whom Socrates said that it would have been necessary for him to have been like Apolline, a very famous swimmer at that time, in order not to drown in the depth and obscurity of his own compositions. And, if the comedy is a beautiful and very subtle arrangement of our actions, we want to be both poets and representatives of our comic poetry and talking painting. What does it give us that the stork of ignorance hates the falcon of our eager intent? In spite of that, we want to understand these bad things about the nature of prose that we are easily persuaded to declare, because here the closed things are opened, here the tangles develop and dissolve, here the rare stories are amplified, the occult fables are manifested, and the secret doctrines of the most wandering intellects are imitated and demonstrated. We want to accompany the height of the sublime concepts with the sweetness and using the most common words and with the harmony of the most used words, showing in our hearts how we live, and just like painters, with the variety of rhetorical colors teach it to you, all this the verse cannot do, because it goes begging for weaving, chains, declinations, terms and inexplicable and dense concepts in which the ignorant get lost, the learned studying them remain doubtful, the actors become confused and the listeners get annoyed. Therefore, leave aside the verse, not to blame it, but because, in comedies the verse is not convenient, and moreover because we know that we must give in to the audience, because we already know that the majority of those who come to comedies come for pleasure, the ignorant, by nature, and the learned, in order to escape idle hours, because of this we must conclude that, because we cannot always give pleasure with ridiculousness, we must give pleasure with the easiness of comprehensible words and with the familiar speaking more adapted to the use of our natural practice. Most people come to laugh, and others criticize the character for their pronunciation and gesture. The performer will be criticized for the difficult pronunciation of the verse which, not well understood, is pronounced badly and, if it is pronounced well, is not accompanied by the gesture and, if it is intended, pronounced, and gestured, one cannot quite hear the endings but do hear the sound of that lyrically worthy cantata rather than the meaning in vulgarly pronounced and spoken prose, and moreover it being necessary now to be angry and now

---

[681] snombolatto -sleepwalker? Weak from overwork?- we are guessing at the meaning.

saddened, neither can anger be versified and by versifying making those words and gestures that anger generates; that is, to stammer, tremble all over, speak in a high pitch, being arrogant, hoarse, and interrupted, grit your teeth, bite your lips, stiffen up, to blush, to withdraw, press forward, bring your hand to the sword, wound and parry, offend the enemy now with words and now with the actions, and all this is obligated to the endings of the verse, spoken to the position of the fellow actor and remembering what he has to answer to the actor, because, while doing this, he leaves aside the interior emotions that are born from anger and converts his fury into calm and skill into disgrace, cooling the meaning that he has to say, but the prose does not cause these problems as it is closer to to us, in all respects and accidents. The prose moves the intrinsic and the extrinsic, according to the moment, of love, fear, hate, hope, despair, sorrow, contentment, fraud, liberality, misery, wealth, sadness, joy, wisdom, ignorance, anger, meekness, magnanimity, pusillanimity, hubris, and humility, and, in short, everything that can happen in the world. With the beauty and ease of words, prose gives light to the order of all the theatrical occasions and the gentle order gives the actor splendor and honor and, to the audience, delight and contentment, with the arrogance inflating the pride and, with sweetness, diminishing humility, both in the gesture and in the pronunciation. Moreover, what happens to these people who try to compose comedies in verse is, much like Timante the painter, who covered many things that he could not well paint with a veil, leaving them to the imaginations of others rather than trying to create them with his brush and colors. So they, not being able to find part of an ending nor easy words to express their concepts, veil them with an astonishing slip, with an obscure heroic act, with a bitter hexameter and an accidental unseen pentameter, and thus they leave the very obscure concept and take from the actor the grace to well interpret it, and gives the spectator nauseated for not being able to understand it. So, gentlemen, enjoy these comedies of ours in prose and not in verse, because I believe that I have proved enough that this is the way that we must act them. Being images of the truth and of our common humanity, take them from us as an example, because here we show you evil to help you escape it and the good to help you embrace it, here we show that the punishment for the vice is suitable, and the reward is given that virtue deserves. Everything begins and ends with graceful manners and clear freedom, where the character is depicted according to the custom, the place, the nature, and the time, and rest assured that we regret not having the treasure of Crassus and Midas.

Venetian Prologue in praise of Order

This is the shortest of the prologues, about half the length of the others. In it the speaker claims to be an unusual person to be speaking, and that the others are angry that he's out here doing it, implying some kind of ensemble, rather than dictatorial, internal structure of the troupe. The rest of the prologue is about the natural order of things, spoken, perhaps by the character Trastulo, who is driven by rules. It has elements of being in a different dialect, perhaps Venetian. It is mostly Tuscan. The speaker addresses his audience as though they are nobility. Is that hyperbole? We don't know, but he tells them that the natural order dictates that they do not speak while the actors are talking.

In praise of Order

Prologue #3, RMB II-1586-0062.jpg, C-022

Here, in front of you, if you don't mind, I want to be the first one to talk. Ladies and gentlemen, you will forgive me if, today, in this Spanish colony of Valladolid – because I don't dare, and it doesn't seem convenient to call it a town – You will see me for the first time going out angry against my company, because I am moved by a great furor. Them not wanting me to go out, they would alter[682] the order, and I, knowing that order is the life of everything, I don't want the order perverted.[683] It is certain that, I am new to your presences, to you as an audience, someone else was supposed to come to delight you all and, with this delight, attract your attention to our comedy. Even if this had happened, he wouldn't have given you the pleasure that we would give to you, he would ruin the order's support of everything visible and invisible. If, in order for this to be, true,[684] we want to first see in the sky with its fixed and errant stars, its houses, and conjunctions, we want to see the Arctic and Antarctic poles, with its continuous and most ordinated movement, we discover the clarity of the Sun, its warmth, its rays, with its rising in the East and setting in the West, it illuminates us, and at the antipodes, the Moon with its waxing and waning, in its crescents, fullness, and eclipses; all things are in order by the obedience that keeps them at the prime mover, below which, orderly is the element of fire, to which obeys the air, that stays over the water that sustains the Earth. Among the planets, the most noble is Saturn; Among the elements the fire; Among the animals, men; Among the birds, the eagle is queen; Among the beasts, the lion; Among the fish, the dolphin; that eat only air, the chameleon.[685] The order has its most sublime place in men. In him, as if it were a microcosm, resides all four elements, composed by body and soul, keeping in the souls, three powers; in the body, five feelings; in the intellect, faith; in the memory, gratitude; in the will, charity; in the heart, anger; in the liver, desire; in the throat, abstinence; in the middle of men, the heart; in the middle of the heart, life; in the middle of life, the soul; in the middle of the soul, immortality; An element of the body that contributes to beauty, the eyes; the most necessary one, the heart; the thinnest one, the blood; the heaviest one, the flesh; the most delicate one, the ears and the tip of

---

[682] Here this is not quite the literal translation, but a few antecedents were added to make it have a consistent meaning.

[683] This is a difficult bit to translate with some Venetianisms mixed in with the Italian. The self-deprecating beginning, and the dedication to rules suggest it was the Trastulo character.

[684] This is another loose translation to make a consistent message.

[685] We think the chameleon bit is a punchline, but modern people don't get the joke. Pliny the Elder VIII, page 51, says that chameleons eat only air.

the nose; the most unsettled one, the lung; the least healthy one, the stomach; the most dangerous one, the tongue. In order to sustain the machine of the lineage of Adam, it is necessary to nurture it with order, to procure the food with industry; the hands put it in the mouth, the teeth chew it, the throat swallows it, the palate tastes it, the stomach receives it, drinking makes it soft, the natural heat digests it and transforms it, one part into blood, one part into urine, one part into semen. Spoiling this beautiful order, if the hands wanted perform the office of the feet, or the mouth replaced the natural heat, look how fast this machine will be reduced to nothing, and, just like that, in the republics, in the laws, in the judiciary, in the families, this scrambled order happens; to pervert the order, all the foolish people want to steal these positions from one another. Here it is certain – I hope – that order must be conserved in our comedy, when, however, it will be free to speak, you, your lordships will be quiet, *in another way, every rule is introductory, compositional, and explanatory*, will stay imposed.

Spanish Prologue In Praise of Women

What is remarkable about this prologue is that it is spoken by a woman (probably Barbara Flaminia who played Ortenzia and was married to Zan Ganassa). In the beginning of this she indicates that people didn't want her in her girlish gender to speak to all the dignified men in the audience. Some of the clues she gives about the perception of female actors gives help make clear the status issues at play in that place and time. In the bulk of this prologue, she gives examples of famous women who had a big impact on the world.

In Praise of Women

Prologue #4, RMB II-1586-0130.jpg, C-129

Illustrious audience, great is the strength of those who oppress the weak, not because of the fact of Nature, but because of the ambition and tyranny of those who want to oppose the strong and bring them down, and because of the enmity they have against those who could quickly take away the strength of their empire. Do not be amazed at my antique way of speaking, because these, my companions, have moved me to this. They did not want me, being a woman, to suddenly go out and speak in this theater, just as they usually do, saying that girlish gender is of less value than yours. It is more certain that, if I did not know that envy made them talk and that arrogance made them incite against women, that I had no way out to defend the part and the whole. The part, because I am a woman; the whole, to declare how much the feminine sex can not only equal the masculine virility but surpass it by far, both in weapons and in letters and in all kinds of virtues, both active and speculative. And, in this and for this, I offer myself here later with authentic reasons to prove that all the good of men had a beginning from the wisdom and value of women; and that this is the truth. It is already known that Minerva created the olive grove; Ceres, agriculture; Carmenta, the letters; Phemone, the hexameter meter; Sapho, the saphic; Clio, the histories; Melpomene, the tragedies; Erato, the music of flutes; Erratto invented geometry; Eurania, astrology; Polynya, rhetoric; Calliope, the Greek letters; Gulfila, the Gothic lands; Nicostrara, the Latin characters; Argentina, wife of Lucan, wrote the books on the wars of Caesar and Pompeo, the books on the burnings of Rome and Troy, and the unfortunate adversities of Priam.

Who surpassed Claudia's doctrine? Who overcame Corina, Theban, who wrote five books of epigrams and won for poetry five times Pindaro, prince of lyric poets? Queen Telinda had the cunning to write against Theophrastus and Strina, queen of the Scythians, learned the Greek letters from her. Lastemia Amantina, Axiotea Pilasia dressed in a man's habit to go to hear the philosophy of Plato. We come to arms: we do not have a Pantasilea, who invented the axe, Camila, Hipolita, Semiramis, who designed the long ship, Zenobia, Ipsicratea, Valasca, Artemisia, Tomiri, Artita, Tiburna, Teuca, Lesbia, and Amalanthea, and the Amazons, with so many others who were signaled in arms and cavalieres? Do you want to know more about prophetic spirit? Wasn't there a Cassandra, an Artitia, a Carmenta, a Manto, Ysimachia, Cambiro, Phemonea, Sosipatra, Amaltea, Marta and the Sibyls? Constant and strong in misfortune: Vuno, Simphorosia, Sophia, Phelicia and Agata, Liga, Emilia, wife of Scipion, Femela from Amatricina, Lucia the Syracusana, Cornelia and Rutilia. Liberals and magnanimous: Pudenciana, Paxeda, Tomiri, Clelia and Telesi. Faithful to their husbands: Penelope, Evadne, Thisbe, Portia, Ipsicratea, Gunilmunda, Alceste, Julia, Artemisia and Pantea.

Of devotion? Keep quiet here men and see if you can match the devotion of any man to that of Pola, Eudosia, Mirta, Cornelia, Aspasia, Telesila, Hiparchia, Manto, Amaltea, Delbora, Demofila, of Claudia, of Aglache, of Mito, of Exiotea and of Musca and of those who were and who are today; which, due to their dignity, must be set apart in this place with the honor and respect that suits them. Men complain about women saying that we are by nature cruel stepmothers, limiting the cruelty of Phedra against Hipolito and Martina against Constancio Eraclito, wanting that the small quality of these alone obscure the great quantity of all and give him so many other pious and loving ones, which are: Ypodamia, Ino, Gasperia, Stratonica, Julia, Cidica, Giunone, Opea, Anbra and Alfriala. Let these biting hounds cease from the envy of howling so bravely against us, because we have been the cause of so much good to the world, and look at Dominga, a woman from Vallente, emperor, who made her go back and pacify the Goths who were going to destroy Constantinople; Placidia, wife of Ataulpho the Goth removed the sack from Rome; Augusta was the cause that Hermogilo, made the king of the Goths, converted to our Christian law. Let's look more: Plauntia, Elena, mother of Constantino, and Moniga of Augustino. In cleanliness, beauty, and bodily disposition, what man could be equal to Rosana, Laodomia, Elena, Cenis, Aegina, Deyopeya, Deianira, who enamored even the gods of Heaven? Say Diana, Leda, Clori, Siringa, Europa and Semele. But let's set it aside. Shall we now speak of those who were chaste and modest? Sulpicia, Marcia, Eugenia, Sophronia, Etelfrida, Arias, Rodolguna, Daphne, Bibli, Zenobia and Beltraca, who, even though she was extremely poor, did not want to accept the mountains of gold that Otton offered her as a reward for her honesty, and many others. But men say that, because we are shallow in understanding, the Romans ordered that we should not drink wine. And they did not do this for any other reason but because they knew that we were stronger and more courageous than them in all things. Out of envy they took away our wine, which modestly consumed sustains the bodily strength and enlivens those of the spirit. Shut up, shut the nauseating mouths of men from always saying bad things about women. They know that they could not be without them, for no other reason, at least because nature, a friend of all good things, in the world makes more women be born than men. If this is not enough for them, let them give in to us because we are more in number than they are, if they do not want us, animated by the abundant reasons that we have, to make us kill Orpheus. Hey! since I see you all too pleased with your lot to consent to reason, I beg you all to be happy to hear the women, give to them, hold them in esteem, and hug them because the man separating himself from woman, separates the power from wisdom. Be silent, you are worthy.

Italian Prologue on the Ingenuity of Man

Toward the end of this litany of the inventions of mankind is a bit about how shepherds invented the pastoral comedies, and then gives some plausible history of how they were improved, and how God has given people the intellect to weave stories from history with their own words mixed in with phrases from great works.

On the Ingenuity of Man

Prologue #5, RMB II-1586-0150.jpg, C-169

While I, with the eye of my mind, contemplate and with my physical eye, I am seeing flowers and fruits, with the marvelous riches that human ingenuity is full of, I am amazed. Why should I marvel and be stupefied if there is nothing that is difficult for men? The stingy and miserable nature happened to create this massive body, whatever we want to call it, needy and naked, deprived of clothes, weapons, and lodging, and food, to which for many animals, she has been generous. Nothing less. Oh, grand love!

The supreme god liked to give men ingenuity as compensation. Ingenuity with which we can dress, arm, feed, cover, and defend ourselves from the insidiousness, from the strength, the nails, the teeth, the scales, the horns, the bites, and the poisons of infinite animals, and furthermore, with the same judgement, to stop them and lead them to obey us, and finally, kill them. Men, with their judgement, can make birds speak, oxen to plow, bears to dance, doves to carry letters, we can train eagles to come eat from the lap[686] of virgins, and trained elephants to write Greek letters. A man, to his pleasure, can walk the ground, sail the waves, dare to climb into the air, and to his comfort, he can enjoy the fire, not only for light, for food, and for heat, but he can make sure to regulate it, moderate it, and measure it, so that it can burn more and less to the time and place to his desire. Go to the blacksmith's, to the forges, to the alchemists, ask, if after having invented the arquebus, the bombards, wheels that imitate lightning, and shining sparks, and the earthquake, and yet they have invented cold fire. In the air, I will not talk about Dedalus, and the pains of Icarus, but I will say about Nembriotte's tower, which rose so high that it caused God and the angels to come down from the sky and ruin it; about the dove by Archita of Tarantino that flew thanks to counterweights being made of wood; about the copper sky made by Archimedes of Syracuse that made thunder and lightning just like our sky; without mentioning the other towers, strongholds and fortresses that also have been built by human ingenuity. These are in the air. In water, how many rivers, how many lakes have they made to innovate? How many such machines of galleys, big things and ships to do naval battles with so much variety of the thinnest wood to run postal mail both by water and by land? And how many ways to make live fountains almost to spite nature? And finally, by Earth, after having adorned it with delicious valleys, beautiful gardens, green plains, fruitful mountains, and flowery hills, men have built on them buildings so superb, theaters so rich, arches so wonderful, temples so venerated, towers so tall, castles so strong, and cities so grand! Oh, truly admirable, the ingenuity of man! After that, inside the viscera of this earth, ingenuity has found metals so rich and so beautiful, and those metals through speculation are applied to the the Moon, to Venus, to Mars, to the Sun, to Jupiter, and to Saturn. Great thing is, Oh spectators, human ingenuity. Don't you see, the subtle and exquisite computation of numbers that this ingenuity

---

[686] Lap, bosom, breasts, unclear what it means, but we picked lap to be less provocative.

has discovered and diligent and curious description of figures, the minute observations of celestial mounts, the new ways of every kind of music, the grace and wit or poetry, the abundance and fertility of oratory art, the inconceivable stratagems and and astuteness in warfare, and the marvelous crafts in writing and printing, the unusual simplicity, worthy of many praises, in medicine? Men have wanted to know how the sky turns, how the stars shine, what is the body of the Sun, how the Moon becomes full and empty, what the fire does above the air, what the waters do beneath the skies, how the Earth shakes, from where the tides are born, what is the wind, and how it blows with such strength, how the arch of clouds is made, and how in the sea that is salted, we can find sweet fountains (springs, sources), how the most majestic tall mountains were created, how the Earth stays immobile when it rests on the fluid water, from where comes such a variety of seasons, so many differences in the faces of men, why do stones have so many virtues, that makes them so precious, how the words that enchant snakes can have such strength and take out their poison, and finally, they have had such courage to go so high with speculation that they have wanted to know about the rotation of the world, of the prescience of the speculation, the declaration, and the justification[687]. Never does the human intellect stop, Oh spectators, similar to a clock that always moves, every day invents new things, and in all of them it wants to be a winner.

The inventor of grammar was Teano, others say Moise; Coracie and Chtensia of Rhetoric; Zenone distilled logic to a method and order, Teuf the Caldean, arithmetic and geometry, Ptolemy, astrology, Orfeus music, Carmenta invented the letters [...][688] and so on; Cosmo seven Greek characters; Bello invented war, Nino, added archery; Bacco gave them military gifts; Bellerfonte was the first one to domesticate horses. Archimedoro the first one to measure the Earth; the people from Nibia were the first who taught sailing, Zoroastro first invented the art of magic; Talette was among the first who preached about the Solar Eclipse [...]; Eudimione was the first to know the nature of the Moon; The daughter if Debude found the design; the same Debude made sculpture; Tesephone the architecture; and Catto [...] the first to write the site of the world; Illesocho, the first to write the nature of "pechie"[689]; Socrates, the first to teach about the active life; and Poicho, the first to find the torments; and many and many more invertors of arts and sciences which in order for me to not be too prolix and boring, I will stop enumerating.

Shepherds were the inventors of comedy, Vene Crattino and made it beautiful, after Pluatus, Terrence, Menandro, who obligated it to the verse, to the prose, and to the dressing. In sum, we modern people came, we take ourselves away from the influences and the obligations with which they represented (played) comedies, because just like they played them decorated and memorized, we on the other hand, only taking the pure subject on then we expand them, and while doing that we show the agility of that intellect that the nature and the God have given to me. We want that intellect to be like that, in particular, like my intellect so that I can carry on the great memory of Locullo and Ortenzio, of Locullo in practical things, and of Ortenzio in the words. But I doubt that the one and the other, and the same Terrence and Plautus, together with Roscio et Cicerone or Demosthene or others even wiser and more eloquent, if they were in the presence of such highly ingenious men, not only would they pale in their face, but who knows, they would sweat from the head to the forehead, just like I do.

---

[687] Not sure about the middle one here. This is part of oratory & rhetoric.
[688] There are three small single words that we can't decipher in this paragraph.
[689] This is a mystery to us. Many of the examples in the list required a look-up, but we didn't find 'pechie'.

Italian Prologue on the Uncleanness of the World

This prologue depends on the audience getting that in Italian there is one word that means both 'clean' and 'the world'. It is a long collection of bits of evidence the the world is corrupt. It ends with the interesting premise that our comedies are needed to mirror our lives and step on the world as the world has stepped on us. What we want to point out here was that the troupe needed to defend, showing unseemly things in their plays.

On the Uncleanness of the World

Prologue #6, RMB II-1586-0159.jpg, C-170

Truly, I do not know with what reasoning the name "the world"[690] was given to this visible machine, being it is lurid and filthy just like we can see that it is full and overflowing with trash and vices, such as: robberies, envies, usuries and betrayals, hatreds, hidden scams[691], injustices, adulteries, cruelties, fake praise, hubris[692], arrogances, disdain, despising of men and gods, and so many others, vices, and mean things, that the eloquence of Demosthenes, Ischinae, Isocrate, and Cicero, neither the memory of king Mitridate, Mestocle, Cinea, Julius Caesar, and Cirro, not even the memories of these men would be enough to remember them all. Whereas it seems to me that rather than use the word "mondo" for the world which means "clean", we should call it inmondo, which means "dirty";[693] unless we want to say that it is swept clean[694] of every goodness, courtesy, fidelity, love, and, in some, from the entire group of virtues. You would ask me perhaps what it is, world/clean. I will tell you that it is a cesspool of vices, a tyrant to virtue, a scourge of the good people, and a concentration of bad people, an enemy of peace, a friend of war, a deceiver of its followers, a defender of lies, a persecutor of the truth, an arouser of the ignorant, a sea of betrayals, in Charybdis where hearts are in danger, and Scylla where our desires are drawn. This, oh spectators, is what the world is, and what it was in the past, because even though the past ages were called the golden era, and of silver, they were also of iron, just as being stained by every kind of vice. Do you want to fall into the abhorrence of the gods. You should remember about Glauco and Venus, of Ligurgo with Bacchus, (remember) about Pirro, son of Achilles, who killed the older Priam before the alter of Jove Erceo, about Cleope (Pharaoh of Egypt), who as Heroditus narrates, locked all the temples of Egypt so that no sacrifices to the gods could be made. Remember about: Flegia; Demonacie; Erissitone; who ate his own limbs for having had little respect for the woods of Ceres. Of avarice can attest: Midas, Crassus, Polinestore, Calligula, Pigmaleon, Sergio Galba, Aulo Posumio, Nemesso and many others who venerated avarice. Strange examples of cruelty are given by: Silla, Mario, Masencio, Nerone, Cambise, Dionisio, Atilla, Falari, Diricie, Medea, Tulia sister of Tarquino, and others who reached the hardness of a diamond, after that (diamond) as we usually say, it is broken if it is stained by vile blood and these (people) stained by human blood, not only they were not broken or softened, but on the contrary, they get harder. You will also find adulteries if you remember Paris and Hellen, Egiso and Clitenestra, of Alcibiade et Irnea, wife of Angide, of Zoe (of

---

[690] Note: Mondo means both "The World", and "clean". It is a big pun-type joke.
[691] Insidie might mean insidiousnesses (plural).
[692] The word is plural. In English the singular can apply to many instances of hubris.
[693] The original listeners to this spoke Italian or Spanish and did not need this explanation of the pun mondo being both world and clean.
[694] Swept clean is a loose translation.

Byzantium), empress, who killed her husband Argirophilo to enjoy a certain Michael of Paflagonia. If you ask me about flatterers, I will tell you about Topiro to Dario, of Aristipo Cirneo to Dionisio, of Apolofane to Antigono, of Andromaco Carneo to Craso. Of the arrogant, the hubris, and the vainglorious, and usurpers of ranks and titles I will not elaborate, because you know better than I do that Nabudonosor (of Babylon) gave himself the title 'king of kings', Sapiore king of Persians, not only called himself king of kings, but also part of the stars, and son of the Sun and Moon. Alexander the Great, king of the World, Demetrio, conqueror of cities, Caesar Dux of Rome, Matridatte, restorer of the world, Attila the punishment from God; Dionisio the enemy of men; and Cirro, vindicator of the gods. About eaters and drinkers, they have been so numerous, it would be marvelous to recount about them, but I will only tell you of Combe, king of Lydia ate his own wife, of Adebunto who ate and drank so much one night at a banquet that he died; Teagene ate a bull for fun; Luscio Galba, emperor, Ginosipo; Pitero and many others who died either for too much drinking or too much avid eating. I will only tell you about those not fully at fault but who were ungrateful to their benefactors, who were: Deciobalo against Trajan, Jason against Medea, Crasso to Cirro, Dario to Artaxerse, and Hercules to his teacher Lino. Of those stained by envy, Ajax, Cato, Aristotle, Zoilo, Caligola, Homer, and infinite others. Do you perhaps want tyrants? Bring to your memory Gatoche of Syracuse, Falario in Agrigento, Busiride in Egypt, Procopio in Constantinople, Meloni in Pisa, Melano in Ephesus, and Cipselo in Corinth. I won't talk about fathers and mothers who killed their own children, and sons and brothers, sisters and mothers, husbands, and wives and mistresses. I am ignoring examples of deceptions, betrayals, injustices, and an infinity of vices, in which mortals have been immersed. In order to narrate them, we should have more tongues than the sky has stars, but if thousands and thousands were vices of the past, there are many more for vices in the present; vices that you can attest your ongoing experience with them every day. And if you want that I give you my reason of the fact that the world is doing worse today compared to the past, we can see that now there are more laws than in the past, clear sign of the infirmity of our souls, of which (infirmity) the world is full. Asia contaminated Rome, and Rome the entire world, for having filled Asia with infinite treasures, which in order not to be seen ungrateful has sent as a gift, to eat in public banquets; to dress princes royal red opposite to the ancient custom; [...] in secret gardens; to eat twice a day as Diogenes the Tyrant used to do; to have a wife and a concubine; those of Tyre; in the theater to mask your faces; Priests of Janus; to say blasphemies that were never heard in the empire; to dress women as men; to oil men as women do in the baths; now senators bring come to the senate wearing perfumes. Now, being the head like so, it was natural that the arms and legs would follow. Since this secular world is so sad, do you think a man should desire to live 300 years like Nestore, or 400 like Richard, the 304 years like Heroino or the 140 of Galen? Certainly not, because the world only pays his followers with vain hopes. And knowing that our nature is corruption of our senses; and our senses are the judges our soul; our soul is the mother of our desires, our desires are executioners of our youth, our youth is the revenge to our old age, our old age indicates our death; and our death is the end and the harbor where our life ends; and this comedy being the mirror of our lives, who is going to be the one who wouldn't desire to reflect in the comedies in order to be able to step over this world as it deserves, just as the world is stepped upon by us in different ways; like the one that like Seneca represents all the stratagems that are used in the world? Goodbye.

Spanish Prologue by Botarga

As noted above, most of the prologues were given by Zan Ganassa, until his participation stopped. In the early 1580s, Ganassa was gone, and Botarga took over the troupe (briefly). This prologue is by Botarga saying that things will be different without Ganassa, but after a few shows, you'll get used to the new situation, like a widow marrying a new husband. One other thing that maybe of interest is that he is directing this prologue to monarchs of Spain.

Botarga's Prologue

Prologue #7, RMB II-1586-0167.jpg & II-1586-0203.jpg, C-172

Oh, what a laugh! Oh, how wonderful! I was scared of myself, <Latin> *illustrious men, that I dare to put the burden on my shoulders* </Latin>to be bold - of having formed such a great and serious weight on my shoulders - , <Latin> *because - because - your greatness is so great, therefore you are deserving,* </Latin> that I get confused, I lose the thread, the subject, the talk, the speech to pacify the spirit of your graces in listening to me such that, finding myself in a rotten pot of confusion, I lay mute and deaf. Deaf to hear the opinions of many who say: "How is this possible? Botarga without Ganassa? It will be Vinegar." Others: "How do you cook these sweet wafers?[695] How dare he? How will they perceive each other?" The other says: "Come on, everything will be joyful uproar. It would be better if he didn't get down to it; It will be bad for him in this move". And also left speechless because I couldn't answer him with words but, not knowing how my plays will happen to me with the works, knowing how <Latin> *there is no determinate truth about contingent futures*</Latin>, I am waiting for the occasion, neither knowing nor being certain of what is to come, and I have waited until now to answer those who say that I did wrong to put on new work and that I was wrong to leave my own nature and conversation for someone else's. And I say that everyone who marvels at this novelty is right, but I also answer that *omnia nova placet* (I like everything new). And in this I want to become like a Roman matron did, who was left a widow and fell in love with another and, because there was a law among the Romans that the woman who became a widow herself would not have to take another husband under penalty of being called adulterous and dishonest, and this one, wishing to succeed with her attempt and break this law, imagined taking the most beautiful horse she had in the stable and skinning it. And this I did, so much so that the horse could be alive, I ordered two servants to take him through the city, one to go in front and the other behind to listen to what the people were saying, and return home in the afternoon, and tell her. The first time the whole town was scared: "What is this? What is this?". And they asked whose horse it was. This was done two or three times. The second day, the clamor ceased, and they stopped trying to stop it. She did this, summoned all her relatives and told them that she did this to show the Roman people that she wanted to get married again and, giving the reasons that this was convenient for the benefit and honor of the Republic, they broke the law, and they were happy. So I, although it is a natural law to love the country, because it is often said to fight for the country, I wanted to show that it was convenient for me to separate myself from it, not with hatred but with some respect of mine, to ruin the most beautiful horse of my stable that It is my free will and I will take it to Valladolid for two of my servants; the one thing that guides him is the will and what goes behind him is the patience to hear what they will say. And I know that

---

[695] Wafers of pumpkin seeds, peppermint, and other sweets.

this first day they will say a lot; the second, they will loosen; and the third, all the admirers and gossips will remain silent, so that the will and patience will return to my house with their free will without anyone looking at it. In this way, I shall be free, I will explain how this corruption was, responding with Aristotle that the corruption of one thing is the cause of the generation of another. And may truth, be the wheat; first it generates, is corrupted and more, that after harvesting it is of benefit, because, if the tallyers have it locked up to sell it more expensive, if there is so much to rot, then they take it out to sell and lower the price so that the poor can eat. I nodded to the seed of the man first becomes corrupted and forms that embryo that has no form, neither more nor less eats bear that, when it is born, is born without form and the mother gives it shape by licking it with her tongue. The bee that is for so much benefit to man, both in example and in fruit, is born from the corruption of a fruit's skin; the worm, which makes silk, first becomes corrupted and then removes the silk; the phoenix, dying is renewed. More: from the corruption of chaos came the union of the elements with elements; between doctors, lawyers, and theologians, first there is dispute and contention before the truth is brought out clean. Your Graces will tell me that all this is true, but that this thing, in its nature, gives rise to these effects. To these I reply that for man every quality of man is common, and that the world is a city for all men, and that moving from one city to another and, from another province and nation to another nation and province is like moving gives one house to another, because there is a sky, a world, a sun and a moon. And I will tell you more, that many things taken from their nature and inserted with others are more perfect. What if the truth, leaving aside the sacred scriptures and others, if there is a sour apple tree grafting it with the very sweet one, does that not make some more temperate composite of fruits? More: the peach had its origin in Persia and whoever ate it there ate venom and died; bringing it here, the fruit became so soft and pleasant. More: the viper does not bear fruit in the moray eel that is not poisonous: it is the treasury (whistle?) on the edge of the sea and joins with her, from where other moray eels of so much taste and shadow flavor come out of this conjunction?[696] And the snake itself puts itself in the remedy that is an antivenom! Allow me to tell your highnesses that I will be more agreeable among mine. I say that I am not accepted in the country, not because I am not loved by my countrymen, but because I know that there are few of them who love me and I try to give in to the multitude like the balance, which leans where there is more weight. And, like the tree that, loaded with branches of many fruits, bows them to the root because it wants to thank you for the abundance that is born because of it, so I, balance loaded with the great affection that your graces have for me and tree that I know to be, because in this way I enjoy as good a land as this, here I lean and here I want to stay because *ubi bonum, ibi patria*. That is: where there is good, there is the country!

---

[696] Not clear what is meant but the implication is that some eels you can eat, and some are delicious.

Italian Prologue on Solitude

This ends after praising getting some alone time by saying: *See that I am solitary and free, and that talking with me, I come to know what you (audience) desire, and that the comedy that you are about to hear is beautiful, vague, wise and brief, ornate with sentences, with mottos, with intrigues, and finally finished with suave and agreeably unbound, closed by the method, tied to the obligations of Plautus and Terrance ...*

Prologue on Solitude

Prologue #8, RMB II-1586-0169.jpg, C-174

Oh, blessed solitude! Oh, wondering without shipwrecks! Oh, road without dangers! Oh, rest without worries! You are blessed because we cannot find anyone more blessed than the one who knows how to be on his own; no one can know himself without the tranquility of the spirit, which you cannot find unless it is in the quietness of a solitary life, which we can have away from the business of men. This is quiet because is placates the spirit, just like a pond that is not moved by the fury of the winds or by some act of man, because even in the center of it, we can see the splendid quietness. So, the one who lives in solitude is calm; to be in peace clarifies the spirit and judgement which humanity has within themselves, in ourselves we can clearly know and watch the reflections of ourselves. Solitude allows us to live away from the accidents of the sea, from the [...], by the envy of your imitators, from the ambitions of the nobles, from the hubris and tyranny of Princes, and finally, away from the desire of having honors, status, grandiosity, and riches. All of these things we acquire with sweat, are possessed with fear, and are left behind with desperation. I, therefore, Oh! By me beloved solitude, in you I want to live accompanied by Cicero, who, in you (in solitude), composed along with the book "About Work we Must Do" many other volumes very useful to all men. With you I want to live accompanied by Scipio, who, left behind his military affairs, in you, reflected, saying that he never felt idle when he did nothing, and never felt alone when he was in solitude. In the company of Manio Curio, I want to enjoy you. Who after winning over the Sabines, the Samnii, Pyrrhus – king of Epirus -, appreciated you more than the celebration of proud Rome: while he was with you in front of the fire, ambassadors came to offer a lot of Gold to him, which he refused, replying that if the enemies could not win over him in war, he did not want to be won over by Gold in peace. I want to share in your glory Cincinnatus, who left behind the plow, to become a dictator, afterwards being done with the office, he went back to the plow to have you (the solitude). I want to get closer to Cecilio Metelo, who turned down the consulate and the dictatorship he wanted to have peace everything he'd earned in war. I want to be the servant of Canton Censorino, who prefect, captain, then orator, senator, military tribune, praetor, censor and council, after all this, he stayed in one of his villas to end his days plowing and seeding the fields. But how can I leave behind Anaxarco, the philosopher that for you, - oh solitude! – refused to be Prince of the Athenians, saying that he wanted to be sooner the servant of the good people, rather than [...] sad? Empendoncle Agripino for you (solitude) renounced his reign; Zenon the merchant cheered up after he lost all his possessions in the sea, that loss made him solitary, and that solitude made him such a great philosopher, saying that he never sailed with better wind than when he lost his ship. Antistine the Cynic was saying that he too had gathered his life around solitude simply because he would go with himself, resting. Anaxagora, in order to dedicate himself to philosophy, exiled himself from his own land, and then returning to it, found that he had lost all of his possessions, and he said that he could not be safe if those were not lost. I have glory, therefore with all of these people, and with many more, embracing you, oh solitude! And, with the poverty of Tibulo together with Pericles of Athens, I would dare to say like him, he who was wise in science, perfect in practice, sage in counseling, suave in conversation, strong against dangers, humane in prosperity, patient in adversity, I will dare say writing <Latin>'I came to the port, goodbye to hope and fortune' </Latin>.

Don't be surprised, oh spectators, if you hear me, that I am called 'the prologue', saying today things so fantastic and not used in parts used in tragedy, because I live in solitude, far from the story of the tragedy, which is in charge of making you (spectators) capable of what you need to reason about or excuse the poet for the uncomfortability of the places, importune of the wise, the loquacity of garrulous, the insidious, and the ignorant. See that I am solitary and free, and that talking with me, I come to know what you (audience) desire, and that the comedy that you are about to hear is beautiful, vague, wise and brief, ornate with sentences, with mottos, with intrigues, and finally finished with suave and agreeably unbound, closed by the method, tied to the obligations of Plautus and Terrance, obligations that you should not expect me to say, because I live alone, separated from her (the comedy), from her story, from her [...] and from her blames, all of these things she will acquire for what my solitude demonstrates, if the author of it will not be able to excuse himself with the story that is coming next. Goodbye, because I'm returning to my solitude.

Monologues

Botarga included in these folios not simply the play outlines (scenarios) and the prologues, but numerous monologues, and longer expository speeches to be given under the right circumstances. As a Commedia actor, it is helpful to have handy some memorized bits that you can use or modify and draw from. Typically, these are from older sources, and he took liberties with them, pulling them out of context and dropping a few words here and there so as to make it mean something different or be more universal.

Rather than simply post them in the order in which they appear in the manuscript, we've split them loosely into categories:

- Speeches for Pastorals
- Speeches for Olympian Operas
- Speeches To or By Royalty
- Advice for Conmen
- Insults and Condemnation
- About Characters
- Jokes
- Wisdom About the Human Condition

Speeches for Pastorals

Caliroe and her Father

This is a lengthy bit of dialog, of Pastoral or Olympian Opera about a man whose daughter refused to marry a priest of Dionysus, leading the god to make everyone crazy. This is part of a lost tragedy. Note that this piece has parts written into a few blank areas later in the manuscript.

Monologues #2, RMB II-1586-0026.jpg, etc. locations embedded in the text, C-013

- Tell me, daughter, who is the one who saved your life, so that I can thank him and reward him for the good he has done.

- Here, father, is the one who eliminated my death with his. Here is the one who had to sentence and kill me and, to save my life, then with his own hands, he executed himself. This is the one, if you could restore his life, it would be too little to give him your kingdom. Here is the example and image of faithful love.

- Daughter, since he cannot return to life, let's try to honor him with an appropriate ceremonial funeral that is worth his virtue.

- If it pleases you, my father, that his death be honored, as it rightly suits the death of a man of constancy triumphant, leave it to me to care and honor him. Oh holy priest! Oh loyal lover! What theaters, colossuses, or amphitheaters, what pyramids, arches, and what trophies can you raise to your fame? No, no, none of these things will reach even the thousandth part of your merits and your worth. I well know that no other tomb will be pleasing to your spirits than that of the woman who kept you buried in the lively flames of love when you lived. Therefore, I attempt to honor you and your life[697], contentment, merit, and love, but I fear[698] so lofty effort that I can never give enough[699]. **[II_1586_045, line 14]** Receive, beautiful soul, this spirit that we give to you as a sacrifice to the gods for you. And you, father, if you want to celebrate my life, do not disturb such a piteous duty.

– **[II_1586_202, line 7]** Certainly, whoever contemplates and looks at our royal status, as low and weak as its foundation, will know this handling of scepters, commanding the populous, and dominating many, is nothing more than a miserable trafficking with which we vainly try to fill the eyes of the people's ignorance to claim this high name of the King. All these things I know and look at them with pity, I see openly the sweetness of this ambition in a most unfortunate tragedy returned with the end of the lives of many of my kingdom, of my good priest, and my daughter. If this is not enough, oh wise men, I am at your mercy.

Here exits Bacchus[700].

Smitten with a Nymph (Italian)

The pastorals are about a beautiful magical world with shepherds, nymphs, satyrs, gods, demons, spirits, etc. The opportunity for actors to wax poetic and paint images with their words made this type of play very popular. This monologue is for a young shepherd, who has recently fallen in (perhaps one-sided) love. Note the assumption that the audience knew more about the sky and the constellations and the related mythology than we should count on today.

Monologue #14, RMB II-1586-0143.jpg, C-134

When, Oh my dear Tirsi, I fell in love with my beautiful Flori, it was in the beautiful and delightful season when the scenic hills are covered with many sweet herbs; Euro, sweetly blowing, moved the soft new twigs of the trees, and the darting Orion, with tears, ceased chasing the bull whose shoulder is decorated by the seven sisters with the fastest course towards our

---

[697] Missing text. Possibly means 'life' which is part of a string of words.
[698] Missing text We chose the word 'fear' from context.
[699] This is a difficult phrase to translate.
[700] It is a little odd to be telling a story about Dionysus, but end with the Roman name for the god.

East; Piroo and Oo, horses of Helios and Eos, hide them with the paint of her vermillion chariot, and solicit Lachesi who has let her age stretch eight by fifty years.[701]

Inviting a Nymph to a Place (Italian)

This has more word play mixed in with the fabulous description of Arcadia and Olympus. What does it take for a young shepherd or satyr to lure a Nymph, who has vowed chastity, to go somewhere with you? These descriptions sound idyllic.

Note that there is an inserted paragraph that mentions the 'five' Fs, some of which are not Fs in English, and so we supply the Italian word with English in parentheses. Also, note that the five Fs is classical, and the writer Botarga is borrowing from included several more, some of which are not desirable. As footnoted, it seems likely that the five F's paragraph is a stray thought written while composing this piece.

Monologue #15, RMB II-1586-0144.jpg (line 6), C-143

Come with me, oh beautiful nymph!, let's go here, to this near and beautiful and flourishing hill, through which runs a sweet brook, which with its babbling invites every pilgrim wanderer to its banks to rest, so, if you could you see the beauty of that place where I want to take you, you will be surprised because you will be able to stay in the shade of leafy myrtles on which harmonious little birds are singing filling the air and the meadows with sweet songs. You will then at the end of the hill see crystalline and flowing water: You thirsted for gold, now drink the gold drink says Midas.

The imagination never stopped its judgement, but it moves in the nature of coincidence.

A little further ahead, you will find a verdant and wide meadow looked upon from the East and from the West by two high and steep mountains which abundantly resemble Mount Olympus.

It has a perfect profit. Five 'F' creations that mean: felicitas (happiness), fatum (fate), facultas (facility), fames (hunger), [?], favor (good luck), [adding in Italian]: fame (hunger), fredo (cold), fetor (rotting smell), fatica (fatigue) and fumo (smoke).[702]

There you will see the green meadows wet by the fresh tears of the daughter of Hypersion[703]; and it was, in the season that Phoebus was running with a fast pace before the serene forehead of Leucotea[704] came out of the ocean waves and the delicate flowers feared nothing from the heat of the Sun.

---

[701] We don't really know who is being solicited, or why. It looks like it is one of the fates Attripo or Lachesi, but who has stretched her life 400 years? Is it Flori? Is it Eos? It is a singular female. Also, Botarga may have mixed up which of the Fates does what?

[702] The five F's sentence seems to be an odd paraphrasing from an obscure proverb. This paragraph seems likely to be a separate thought unrelated to the other four paragraphs.

[703] Aurora weeps for the death of her Son.

[704] Leucotea was the goddess of mist and fog.

I've Made a Garland (Italian)

This is another description of idyllic Arcadia.

Monologue #16, RMB II-1586-0147.jpg (line 6 - middle), C-143

For have I made for you a garland of burgundy violets, sky blue yarrow, pure white lilies, sweet clover, coffee flowers, cardamon leaves, crocus leaves, and climbing cyclamen, and white and yellow jasmine. You will see lascivious and goat-like satyrs, two-horned fauns, rampant goats, shy rabbits, jumping deer, graceful ladies, swift hares. Here you will hear chirping little birds, the voices of lonely sparrows, naughty parrots, pitiful lavinee[705], spotted blackbirds, shrill cuckoo, lascivious partridges, scratching birds of Palamedes. This forest is full of firs, pines, beeches, larches, cypresses, myrtles, lahore and tedi with fruitful branches, vitric palms, fragrant cedars, lemons, oranges, rowan, pistachios, pomegranates, quinces, live myrtles, medlar, dogwood and mountain ash.

---

[705] 'lavinee' and later 'tedi' are things in these lists that we are unfamiliar with.

Speeches for Olympian Operas

Aeolus, Lord of the Winds

This is a statement by one of the gods about how important he is, and why he should be respected and feared.

Monologue #1, RMB II-1586-0025.jpg, C-013

I well know that you do not need flat winds, more soft, beautiful, and loving winds, but contrary, discordant, thundering, blowing, and stormy winds; because of this, go away gladly, oh graceful goddess, to whom I promise to serve you as you desire. Or, how I rejoice when I see that Jove and the other gods urge me to delay Spring, because with my gusts I undress her and her tender flowers, and in the Summer the fruits and fodder, and I disturb and unsettle the kingdom of Neptune, and with heavy breaths, down in the lower domain, I make Pluto and his kingdom tremble! Now, in order to satisfy Diana's desire, I want to summon my servants to call right now, and I want to start a war among them. I will call Euro[706], who will be the first to enter the field, behind him, Notto rises who will obscure the sky with dark and heavy clouds, then will come from the cold Scythia, Boria, angry and taken up in a chariot by Zeus' hand of lightning will flatten and break the trees of oaks and elms[707], and tall towers so that everyone knows my power and my strength.

Gift From Prometheus

How pathetic would man be had not Prometheus given us, at enormous sacrifice to himself, the gift that gives us dominion over the Earth.

Monologue #17, RMB II-1586-0166.jpg, C-171

Plato, still under the disguise of fables, as he usually does, with great mystery none-the-less, teaches us, through Prometheus[708], how nature is the deadly enemy of leisure. And this was when Prometheus gave all the gifts that mortals deserved. To each animal he distributed the gifts that matched their worth right away. To one, speed, to another strength, to this one the hardness of scales, to the other the sharpness of teeth, and to one a kind of food, and to another a different food.[709] Dispensing so much, free and wide, having already distributed everything that he had, coming to man and having nothing to give him, it was a fact that he left man disarmed and needing everything, which Prometheus seeing this, moved to pity that the most noble animal that was in the world would stay so unhappy and, seeing all the mortal qualities were already distributed to the others consumed, he thought to take the divine ones, and taken from Vulcan and from Minerva the art and wisdom, those wrapped in the fleece of reason and

---

[706] Euro is a Southewase wind.
[707] The actual word was "elce" which means Holm Oak, or Live Oak, but for poetic balance, I put in Elm here.
[708] The first half of this story is actually partly about Prometheus' brother Epimetheus. Did Botarga/Ganassa make this error on purpose for humor, or were they simply quick and sloppy in their paraphrasing mythology? We don't know.
[709] This a different food is implied but not explicitly stated.

gifted to man, and right away made man more noble than other animals, advanced as much as celestial, immortal, and eternal things, and mortal forever. With this gift, with this splendor stolen from the middle of the heavens, man was adorned, thanks to which, from naked, weak, and unarmed, he clothed himself, armed himself, and made himself strong.

The Erifile Priest (Italian)

This is a story about how Pluto and Proserpina decide to send the shadow Seline back to the living to get revenge on her husband for killing her, and to protect her daughter Orbecche. This would have been for a play based on the story 'Orbecche' by Giovanni Battista Girardi (1541)[710].

Monologue #21, RMB II-1586-0191.jpg (line 9), C-195

ERIFILE
- Venus, to your power bows the sea, the earth, the sky, and the blind hell, and whatever is hidden in peace and in war; goddess, from your true value and knowledge all mortal things take peace and strength, nor can anyone ever find peace in heaven or on earth, nor in any element, without your power, being[711] the one who sustains and loves how much the sun glorifies the sky, hear my prayers today and fulfill your priest. Show me your favor and your strength, and you, who quieted the quarrel of chaos by bringing together the warmth and the frost into loving climates, deliver the defeat today of that the haughty priest of Diana, who despises your power and your son's bow. This plea is because of the death of my son, who was your loyal servant.[712] Now I pray to you. See how I pray you well of all the celestial spheres, light of the sun and of the moon, firmament of the fixed stars, motion of the wanderers, movement of every circle, flowers, branches, fragile fruits, and trunks of trees, tranquility of the sea, serenity of the sky, abundance of the earth, clarity and warmth of the fire, purity of the air. Clear, purify, warm, move, and make serene the mind of your priest by giving me that remedy that you promised in a dream.

PLUTO
- Gentle Proserpina, dear niece and wife, your grace and beauty, but more than all these, the just and steadfast love that you bring me, make you worth every grace you desire. Give your command, but the longer she (Selina) has been here the more difficulty she carries with her, the more I will work to help her and you will see it as a test, just to show you how much I love you.[713]
      She asks him for the quiet of the souls. Pluto replies.
- Your prayer is so just that I do not intend to deny you anything, even if I break my eternal obligation. But I command and I want, in order to satisfy your light desire, that today, all the pains of all the sad souls of my kingdom will be lifted. Therefore, right now, that sharp wheel that tears the limbs of poor Ixion will stop; and you, Sisiphus, will possess the stone without pain; and the daughters of Danae shall not take water from the river to the basin. Quiet the vulture who gnaws the renewing heart of Ticius, and only for today Tantalus may taste the sweet fruits; Cerberus the dog shall quiet his black and deadly mouth; and my faithful servants, Tesifone, Megera with Alletto (the furies), will make their snakes not taste their poison for

---

[710] In the manuscript there are several bits of poems and verse, one of which starts on image 28. This 440 lines of verse are an incomplete copying of Girardi's work. Botarga apparently tried to translate it into Spanish and never finished the effort. This monolgue is in Italian.

[711] There is a masculine pronoun here that we have removed. It might be referring to 'power'.

[712] This sentence is loosely translated to more clearly convey the meaning.

[713] This is a loose translation.

today, so that all of my kingdom will feel peace today to satisfy my delicate Proserpina. Here you are, now happy.

Here the soul of Selina cries out. Pluto summons her before him; He asks her who he is:
- Tell me how your husband killed you, unfortunate soul, that by the waters of Stiggie I promise you to avenge these wounds that you have, if I believe that he has killed you wrongly.

She tells how he killed her. She asks for revenge.
- Selina, your request is just and it seems to me that such a evil tyrant will not remain without the his faults being punished and, even though it is up to Jove to punish his wrong-doings, he will not therefore deny, and will want what I want, because I am his brother. In the meantime, you celebrate with the other souls, because soon you will see your enemy here in the flames, if I will be the Pluto that I usually am. Let Selina be brought to her own place, free from all pain, just like the others. And you spirits, by my desire, if there is anyone among you who wants to avenge her, that I promise to leave him free for a hundred and a hundred years, as well as receiving a gift from the beautiful and white hand of my Proserpina, a crown of infernal poplar, if he returns triumphant in this enterprise.

Speeches To or By Royalty

The Innocent Boy (Italian)

This is a passage from a lost play in the 1580 season. It is a long dialog telling a prince that he must be dead to his own desires to make just laws.

Monologue #20, RMB II-1586-0178.jpg (line 18), C-189

- Oh, how I rejoice in seeing you brought down by this misfortune, which to a greater extent cannot be made less bad. Therefore, it is a greater sign of being unfortunate, when someone like you with no practice suffering must face it.[714] Oh impatient prince, brother-in-law, also, most vile man and my enemy, here is how you will come to know what I foresaw for you to be true. You will also know that vice is its own punishment and of those who possess it, and virtue is its own glory and of those who use it. You see, unhappy man, that at this point you are not the master of yourself, but everything transformed into wrath and hubris so that you have become a monster of nature and almost infernal fury. So, get away from me, for not only do I not want to help you, but I also don't want to suffer your frightful presence.

- And it is true that you are outside of yourself because anyone is very much outside of himself who, because of impatience, departs from himself, as you did and do with these angry words of yours. But tell me where are your knights now, your guards, your harpies, your flatterers? Because to those truths[715], you see that, in spite of yourself and your displeasure, you are forced to bow to virtue, as finally all the vicious are forced to do, where I, who, find myself completely obliged to virtue, must abandon you completely and rejoice in your damage. Therefore, it shouldn't be less glorious for virtue to see you punished as a tyrant, just as it would be to reward you if you were a just and good prince, so that you should not hope from me anything but the joy of your sorrow.

- I wanted to reduce it to this level of despair, so that there is more strength, and we may receive some benefit. It would have been very easy for me to run away, but I wanted to do it like that valiant surgeon who, having found an infected wound, so that it does not infect and rot the whole body, cuts with a knife and burns with fire removing with the sick member a little of the good, so that the cure will be perfect.

- My brother-in-law, now I embrace you as my lord and family member, because you have come to know yourself and take off the veil of the fat ignorance that you had over your eyes, and you know that now it is necessary that you be dead to yourself in order to live for the benefit of your subjects, by governing them with just laws, to which you must be the first to submit, because the law can be said to be mooted by one who does not observe it but wants it to be observed by others.

Intermezzi of the Arrows (Italian)

Sciluro, King of the Scythians (according to Plutarch), was on his death bed. He had a bundle of arrows, and gathered his 30 sons, and said whoever could break the arrows would succeed him.

---

[714] This sentence is loosely translated to better capture the meaning.
[715] 'truths' is our best guess for a word lost from the manuscript.

None could do it. Sciluro then took the bundle and broke each arrow individually, and told his sons that if they ruled together, no one could break them.

Monologue #22, RMB II-1586-0195.jpg (bottom half), C-196

- My dearest sons, because for us nothing is more certain than death, and because this life, while we are living, cannot be called perfectly life, but rather a prolonged death sentence that cannot be appealed; since, because of what we work on while running and rushing, we keep giving up to the limit of our end, my sons, I want to have you here in my presence and of these outside witnesses made to come before you all, already feeling tired of living, I want to teach you as a loving father what life you must lead until you walk to your end. And I do this because I know that the years go by, the days pass away, the hours flee, and the moments disappear. And as well thought things don't give fear of being in vain to the one who puts them into action, I wanted to bring these examples to you, which are perfect keys to open the door of the senses, to see, understand or know, and embrace my loving and fatherly advice. And, for this reason, take you, oh my eldest son, this bunch of arrows and see if you can break it with your strength.

Here he tests the arrows with his son, then he takes his hands off, and says:
- Stop now, son, trying to break these arrows. Since none of you who are my eldest seven sons, has found the way to give me the material with which I would show you the path for which you have to walk in order to preserve the kingdom with power and knowledge, I tell you that I thank the highest of the gods, since, by means of the weakest and my young son, I am given the matter with which I can open the way for you to walk at very quick steps, in order to feel strong and peaceful in the kingdom, because we cannot call really strong the one who does not give peace, strength being the blood sister of peace. Therefore, you will understand that this bunch of arrows so strong and tight means nothing but union, which is invincible in war, this union is reason for the good people and advice for the strongest. With this I win every war.[716] And, finally, it is an impregnable mountaintop fortress of every living and inanimate thing, which I command you with my paternal power, that you hold and embrace (the idea of union). And, from her (union), like from your mother, take the milk, which will make you strong against every resistance and every power, because while you are united and in agreement no force will be able to win over you, but, if you are in disarray, every little force, just like that of my youngest son, you will be able to subject you and bring you to submission.
- And, in order to maintain this union of yours you need many things, I will briefly teach you a virtue, through which you will embrace all the things good for love and your preservation; this virtue is justice. I therefore embrace this, my dear sons, in order to preserve yourselves, because justice means nothing else and is nothing more than a habit that makes our will constant in determining to give what is due to whoever deserves it, in his time and place. However, accept justice as the steward of the ranks, statuses, profits, and happiness for all, if you want to live in peace. With this virtue you will be victorious over this old man (time) whom you see coming. You look at his face. He is lame and slow for those who do well, and very quick and on wings for those who live badly. He is the bookkeeper of ancient things, the inventor of new things, the fabricator and devourer of all things and of himself; we call him Time. That wheel that we see with him is that goddess who is called Fortune, Fate, or Destiny, by fools, you see how he turns it, loaded with crowns and scepters. Soon you will see the ones that are at the top will be put at the lowest bottom and placed at the top are the ones found at the bottom, not only caused by

---

[716] There is about six words of of missing text here which we filled in as "With this", which seems very plausible to the message.

Fortune, but mainly through the fault of the one who does not know how to govern and support himself with virtue, acting with justice in his every action. Therefore, my sons, do not become arrogant and say that you are kings who dominate scepters, crowns, and the most powerful ones, because you could not overcome this devourer of your works and the turner of this wheel if not with the good reputation that you will acquire by acting well, which good fame is the goddess of perpetuity and conquers time. And because the greatest sign of our misery is our arrogance, I wanted to compare this transparent and shiny crystal vase, which is truly like our lives.

This is beautiful, resplendent, and fragile; so is life, beautiful, resplendent and fragile and at every little encounter with infirmity or trouble it tears and breaks; and just as this vase is not durable in form and fragile in matter and we are not durable in matter and fragile in form, which is composed of soul and body, the latter short-lived and putrid and the former immortal and incorruptible. This vase takes on the color and smell of whatever is placed inside it, this flesh receives and makes visible on the outside all the good and bad actions that man does while he lives. If this vase breaks, every tiny sliver retains upon itself the odor it received from the liquor placed inside it. As this flesh of men decomposes, it retains within itself in every small part the odor of the good and bad reputation that man acquired by living, if it is good, it lasts eternally, in spite of time and death, and, if it's bad, it dies with the dead man, operator of vice and destroyer of virtue.

Advice for Conmen

Short Speech (Spanish)

Here is a way to get money from a philanthropist.

Monologue #4, RMB II-1586-0111.jpg, C-033

Have your mother, your sister, your daughter and your Moors ask you-know-who, who gives away a lot of money and, when they ask for it, say: "Oh shameless people, It is not necessary to ask him for money for I want nothing but his love."

Insults and Condemnation

Short Speech (Spanish)

The speaker wants little to do with whom they are talking to going forward.

Monologue #5, RMB II-1586-0111.jpg, C-039

I pray to God that you suffer perpetual exile; and when you want to eat, may you have broken teeth, may you always be thirsty and have everlasting pain.

Short Speech (Spanish)

The speaker thinks little that is complimentary about the other woman.

Monologue #7, RMB II-1586-0118.jpg, C-042

The envelope that my lady wrote says: "To the most (plural) [...][717], infamous, vile, detestable, horrendous and abominable, lowly, dirty and disgusting, astute, sagacious, cunning, deceitful, fraudulent, deceptive, disloyal, witch, unholy scoundrel, enchanting Circe, fortune-teller, traitor, appalling, treacherous[718], exorcist, surrogate matchmaker, sea of vices, frightening hell, cursed malice, God-fearing monster, is more of a gold-digger than a tavern wench."[719]

---

[717] Two words are unreadable, clipped off during the bookbinding process.
[718] 'Engannadora' appears twice in this list. We translated it differently each time.
[719] There are some nice internal rhymes in the original, that we didn't reproduce.

About Characters

Toned Lady (Spanish)

This is a paraphrasing of "A Una Dama Entonada" by Mendoza in the mid-1500s. It seems to be a satire by a nephew serving his aunt who is a now a sex-worker During it he seems to be addressing the aunt, and later her clientele.

Monologue #6, RMB II-1586-0112.jpg, C-040

Why should I greet thee, if no medicine could repair thine attitude? I do not want to talk, madam, because you have a haughty air. Shut up[720] old monkeyface, you spectacled barn-owl, Madam Melisendra. She's[721] all dressed in taffeta, and also the finest fleece of Castile. She is a woman who wears an old plush demi-cloak, and she is also a woman who carries a fan in the winter and in the summer. Shut up, now. You are a woman who wears a complexion-mask by night, and with hands slathered with unguents and gloved. She keeps quiet to give gravitas and moves her neck with taught sinews. She is a woman known for breaking more spats[722] than anyone because she pulls them all the way up to her ears.

I offer the Devil the jewel she keeps at home, *saying it has owners.* If you saw her get up at noon, unshaven, you would be horrified, for when she says her lower back hurts, spitting as much as the ocean, with a headband on her forehead, saying she has long hair, she looks like Melissa invoking Ruggero. Have you seen her sick-monkey, pregnant-lady face? She's the kind of woman who makes love to herself in front of the mirror, saying, "Oh, what pretty eyes! Oh, what a sharp face!" And, in reality, they are like the droppings of ugly women. Comfort yourself with that! I have a lady who goes about dressed in ancient taffeta. Her jeweled bonnet[723] is more than one-hundred summers-old. My lady is *so* beautiful, her forehead is narrower than an ape's and her cheeks are long and sunken-in, like a glory of Venus[724]. One cannot talk with my lady, for she is (*often*) busy with a toothpick in her mouth. Consider who my lady is, and how elegant she is, when once, in the company of guests, wanting to show her importance, told me: "Come here, boy. Take this key and take out my chain. And for lunch, slaughter me a bird." And since I actually knew what she meant and knew there was actually neither chain nor bird—except for the hound's chain and a little bit of garlic—I replied saying that the chain was at the silversmiths, so he could straighten it, and that the bird was laying eggs.

I had a very honorable aunt; the doctors say that she died of fantasies[725]. She is a very well-trained and disciplined woman, who never leaves her house without having given her cheeks luster; and she is quite the gourmet, for she always keeps various sauces in the house. She is such a noble woman, that she always wears a headdress and, under her gloves, has a cord wrapped around her fingers, to show she is wearing rings. My lady is rather Ciceronian and she chirps with a fine beak. Furthermore, she is quite delicate, too, for she always sashays while

---

[720] Here, the tone shifts from overly formal to rudely informal.
[721] In cascading levels of rudeness, the speaker is now using the third person addressing this woman.
[722] The shoe covering.
[723] "escufión" is a head-covering decorated with blackwork and jewels.
[724] The glory refers to an intimate part of Venus' body.
[725] Most likely the honorable aunt is still alive, but her honor was killed by the fantasies she weaves to lure in men.

walking. My lady is also a tailor and can trim any dirty trick. If you try to trick her, she'll come right at you, clear as day, like a falconer. My goodness! My lady is as careful with her gold as others are with their copper. Yes, tomorrow you *will all take pleasure with her*, and I promise you, she sells her fruits well. Whoever may come to my house, my lady has a fixed price, just like a bushel of wheat. Get out of there; she can skin every escudo from the closest of friends without giving them a chance, like a hound from all angles, like a rental donkey, tested out by old and young men alike. She is someone who has all the opportunities of fortune-tellers, who can predict the rain; she's got more ointments than a witches' chemist. If she uses a needle, she wants to use a whole skein. My lady is a good woman, convent-like, she is quite brave and would fight one hundred people. She knows how to trick anyone and is skillful at games. And she would rather pull out a tooth than redo an important task. She is quite friendly with all new postures, and therefore there is no tailor who hasn't been to her house, for she pays everyone with a thrill.

Leave her, already. She sighs for one man, while keeping another at the door. She is truthful to the rich, but full of lies with the poor. She's always half-lying and she professes – listen carefully – to whomever is the bravest and shows the most adoration. Watch out for her, because in less than an hour, she is capable of dispatching thirty or forty gallants. Let anyone just go up to her, for she is like the counter of a market stall. She does get her touchés, like any brave fencer, and she loves no one, but tells everyone she loves them. She gets angry and tired of dealing with anyone who understands her. She sells all kinds of worn-out fantasies, of making and ruffling beds. She is arrogant with important men, and no official could ever love her; her closest relatives are the Goths[726]. Hush now, for she is blushing. Because she has good taste, your talk might inflame her pelvic area. My lady is restrained, not like some nun's nocturnal dinner during Advent. My lady understands much; she has and sends more papers than a Council secretary and has memorized *La Celestina* and all its drawings; she is quite wise, but has lowly, fleeting thoughts. No one creates a bigger crowd than she does, when walking down the street. She has more suitors than the chancellery has litigants.

Jokes

Joke (Italian)

This joke is about caring about the least among us.

Monologue #8, RMB II-1586-0120.jpg, C-056

Once there was a friar who, going to Milan to comfort someone who was about to be hung, said to his donkey, "Ari!" and asked a doctor where [...] asked what he must do to unload his conscience. He said that as many times as he says "ari", he should say "xo, xo".[727]

---

[726] Gothic ancestry in Spain at that time was essentially a claim to being royalty.

[727] Ari was a common word used to spur donkeys into action. "xo, xo" is to stop the animal.

Joke (Italian)

This joke might be insulting the French, or some other group of outsiders that might show up in an Italian church service.

Monologue #9, RMB II-1586-0121.jpg, C-057

In Spain it is customary to give peace during mass: while one was standing with a very greasy beret, he touched the peace and wanted to kiss the beret to another and he, seeing it so greasy, said: "Forgive me, I don't want to kiss it because I don't eat fat".[728]

Joke (Italian)

This joke is about why you shouldn't expect priests to pay back debts.

Monologue #10, RMB II-1586-0121.jpg, C-058

One man going to collect money from a priest, the priest took him to a cemetery that was full of grass and said, "How do you expect me to pay you if it's been more than three years that I don't get any income from this land?"

Short Speech (Italian)

This is a language-specific joke for the Dottore. Love, "Amore" means "without mores". It cites a Greek philosopher Acephalous.

Monologue #11, RMB II-1586-0128.jpg, C-121

"Amore", many think that when you follow it you go to your death, and I say that it means 'without death', because this letter "A" in Greek, means without, just like "Acefelo" in Greek means 'headless', and in Latin "amens" means mindless, therefore "amore" means 'without death'. Instead, since "more" in Latin means morals or decency, it means that the one one who follows it is without morals.

---

[728] We are missing a few local customs that might explain this.

Wisdom About the Human Condition

Short Speech (Spanish)

This appears to be a eulogy from a son or daughter that believes their father is dead.

Monologue #3, RMB II-1586-0054.jpg, [Not in Calvo-2007]

Picking up the lost strength, and from the face calling the heart, I answered the grief as best I could. My beloved and sweet father, whose love which until now I have never been without, I cannot remember any time when I have not been loved by thee.[729]

Short Speech (Italian)

This is about not thinking about the people and things you don't see anymore.

Monologue #12, RMB II-1586-0128.jpg, C-122

It happens to important people, to children, and to most people, who, when they play, while the game lasts, are on your mind, but when the game is over, they are dropped to the ground, and it is done.

Short Speech (Italian)

This is about not being able to hold on to money. This could be in either the Joke or Wisdom category, but we placed it here.

Monologue #13, RMB II-1586-0128.jpg, C-123

The one who doesn't have money, has to work, and still has no money; yet it is better to have work with money than without money. The one who has money has a pot to piss in because we say "din ari". Like the chamber pot[730], money is round because it cannot stay with nobody[731] and always is rolling away. Ancient people used to spend square iron coins, because they weighed a lot and when they fell on the ground they wouldn't move.

---

[729] Note that the writing in the manuscript was especially rushed and cramped for this piece, and there can be some doubt as to the original Spanish, and therefore with this English.

[730] We aren't certain of the translation of "arino".

[731] This double negative is in the original but is taken as a single negative for this to make sense.

The Importance of Friendship (Italian)

This may be a rebuttal by a man whose romantic bid to a woman has been rejected.

Monologue #18, RMB II-1586-0168.jpg, C-173

Friendship, Aristotle says, is more necessary than justice, so much so that, where we find friendship, there is no need for justice. The philosopher Archite states that if one could reach the sky and become intertwined with the beauty of the stars and the purity of all celestial bodies, it would be bittersweet if he had no friend to tell about them. Therefore, despise and destroy the precepts of nature oh Erifile, denying me to join you with the embrace of love and with[732] the bonds of friendship and family, that this bond is almost supernatural and overwhelms the ties of every other friendship. You say that I despise you; you know that you are the cause of it because you violate the first point, because love is the cause of the perfect line of friendship, because you cannot be honored by me, if you are not loved by me first, because you cannot honor him who does not you love.

Commentary on a Sonnet (Spanish)

There is a lovely sonnet which we have not translated, but included with the sonnet is this speech given by a gentleman to a lady that he is drawn to, but he cannot read her level of interest in him.

Monologue #23, RMB II-1586-0213.jpg, C-198

My Lady, in this sonnet, which my affection has composed, I speak with my heart and with love, which if my affection isn't tricking me, I understand in the actions and words that your ladyship will display to me, whenever you will abandon your fear, which is the enemy of whoever wants to know whether he is loved or mocked. May your mercy relinquish the fear that is the cause of my torment, and with your discretion don't make a liar of that heart that surrenders to you, already obliged, I won't say as a captive, but rather as a servant, because a captive never has faith in his lord. May that door covered in oriental lacquered pearls open and allow yourself to know my desire, the desire is placed on a high peak, where the only thing that must fall is my guile.

---

[732] There are several missing words from the manuscript which we are filling with good guesses. 'Erifile' is [...] file in the manuscript. It is possible it is a Greek or Spanish female first name. Nothing Italian seems to fit. Here we used a name from another fragment.

One-Liners

Interspersed, where space permitted, Botarga wrote a number of single sentences in Italian, Spanish, Latin, and maybe Venetian (his spelling, and the short samples make distinguishing language sometimes difficult).

Some of these were intended as jokes to be delivered on stage. Some are poignant things to say on stage. Some are just sentences to think about before going on stage. Sometimes he notes the type of situation these lines would be good for, but mostly he doesn't. Some of these are still good after almost half a millennium of cultural change, most are not, but are still interesting to someone with an interest in Sixteenth Century Southern European people and culture.

As with the Monologues, we have put these into categories, rather than preserve the order they appear in the manuscript. The topics are:

- Unknown Meaning
- Riddles
- Justice and Injustice
- Favoring Diligence and Hard Work
- Sixteenth Century Medicine and Health Tips
- Commentary on Sex-Workers and Gold-diggers
- Commentary on Men's Vices
- Assertive Statements
- Commentary on Scholars, the Church, and its People
- Commentary on the Human Condition
- Romantic and Marital Advice for Men
- Romantic and Marital Advice for Women
- Insults
- Commentary on the Greedy and Wealthy
- Short Lists to Memorize

Unknown Meaning

One-liner #2, RMB II-1586-006.jpg (Italian), C-003

The beard, the man eats for piuels[733] the grain of the guinea hen.

One-liner #11, RMB II-1586-062.jpg (Spanish with Venetian spellings), C-020

When we made the law that you should not steal 'muy^{ti}'.[734]

One-liner #36, RMB II-1586-121.jpg (Italian), C-061

My house is like the sound of a trombone [...] one wants.[735]

One-liner #44, RMB II-1586-122.jpg (Italian), C-069

How much smoke of a beloved one of wood, the recipe of soup from greyhound.

One-liner #48, RMB II-1586-122.jpg (Italian with Spanishisms), C-073

To play primero, to pull the figures by the feet, to sleep together.[736]

One-liner #116, RMB II-1586-145.jpg (Corsican, Italian, & Latin), C-151

<Corsican> Be persistent, don't be afraid</Corsican> as we say, *he sleeps without that (fear) which is good for man.*[737]

One-liner #120, RMB II-1586-146.jpg (Italian & Latin), C-155

Sadness is *like absinthe*[738] *put in the food of God.*

One-liner #121, RMB II-1586-146.jpg (Latin), C-156

From the spirit because in this state, the body sinks.[739]

One-liner #149, RMB II-1586-181.jpg (Latin), C-193

However, the passion of the head elates the mind.[740]

---

[733] 'piuels' is our best guess for transcription. We haven't found a word close to this with any known meaning.

[734] 'muy^{ti}' – we don't know what this is an abbreviation for.

[735] This is missing a few words from the binding cut, but the sense seems to be that the house is adaptable to situations like the slide of a sackbut.

[736] Note: "Jugar a primera" is also an erotic idiom. The overall sense of this sentence is unclear so far, but it is likely romantic advice.

[737] It is possible/likely that the Corsican parts are some other dialect.

[738] Absinthe, or abstaining. It isn't clear how abstaining could be put into the food of God, but avoiding such food could be a reason for sadness. Similarly, putting bitter wormwood into the food could also be sadness.

[739] Exanimo or Ex animo, the former means exhaust, the latter means from the spirit.

[740] This is another one we don't completely have the context for.

Riddles

One-liner #1, RMB II-1586-006.jpg (Italian), C-002

A thing that exits and we cannot see it, if we could see it, we could not have it.[741]

One-liner #45, RMB II-1586-122.jpg (Italian, answer in Spanish), C-070

My bag doesn't hold food: los genitivos.

Justice and Injustice

One-liner #3, RMB II-1586-006.jpg (Italian), C-004

The spider web holds the little ones and lets the big ones pass.

One-liner #24, RMB II-1586-118.jpg (Italian), C-046

I am your (plural) treasurer and teller for they can whip me as a vagabond, I will not leave from this 'sunrise' unless 'sunset' of what you owe me comes,[742] I am your block and chain.

One-liner #50, RMB II-1586-123.jpg (Italian), C-075

When the law was made, I was not there. I didn't consent to it, so I'm not obligated to serve it.

One-liner #51, RMB II-1586-123.jpg (Italian), C-076

The staff has been stolen so many times that we cannot find the true owner.

One-liner #72, RMB II-1586-124.jpg (Italian), C-097

The lazy man is like gold, and the hardworking man is like lead.

One-liner #102, RMB II-1586-143.jpg (Latin & Italian), C-136

God's will is to give freely and to deprive: To some he gives, to some he takes away.

---

[741] No answer is given. We suspect it is one of the following: love, the throne, earthquake, a caress.
[742] There is some clever word and idiom meaning here that hasn't been translated. East and West are also sunrise and sunset, and also the winds from East or West, but here he's saying you can't get rid of him until you pay him what you owe him.

Favoring Diligence and Hard Work

One-liner #9, RMB II-1586-055.jpg (Spanish), C-017

There is no shortcut without work.

One-liner #109, RMB II-1586-145.jpg (Latin), C-144

Labor nourished noble minds. If you refuse labor, you can do little. Don't be afraid to sweat.

One-liner #110, RMB II-1586-145.jpg (Latin), C-145

Nothing will not give up to stubborn work and concentrated and careful attention.[743]

One-liner #111, RMB II-1586-145.jpg (Latin), C-146

The rude rustic has strong and muscular sinews.

One-liner #112, RMB II-1586-145.jpg (Italian & Latin), C-147

A man who sleeps a lot lives *just as the dead live.*

One-liner #113, RMB II-1586-145.jpg (Italian & Latin), C-148

The idle man *is just like a target to an arrow.*

One-liner #114, RMB II-1586-145.jpg (Italian & Latin), C-149

Brother, do it now while you have time because *he who postpones today, tomorrow will be less apt.*

One-liner #118, RMB II-1586-145.jpg (Italian & Latin), C-153

Note: the 'for a small man' refers to someone not wealthy or otherwise important, and in this line, it is referring to who this line would be said about.

It is as much a virtue to seek and find, as to protect what has been won or earned: for a small man.[744]

One-liner #119, RMB II-1586-146.jpg (Italian & Latin), C-154

Lazy people always say: *A rested boxer is better than one with injured hands.*

One-liner #122, RMB II-1586-146.jpg (Latin), C-157

Idleness must be avoided. It is the mother of trifles and the stepmother of virtue.[745]

---

[743] Note: the manuscript has a poor transcription of one of Seneca's Moral letters to Lucilius. The translation here is from Seneca.

[744] Similar to Ovid "Ars Amatoria" Book II, part one, line 13. There is no less virtue in keeping than in finding. Note, that the final thing in Italian is a direction for who to say this to.

[745] Ociositas could mean swiftness, but this could be a letter transposition of Otiositas which means idleness. We're not clear what is meant. The fact that the next one is about idleness strengthens the idea of idleness.

One-liner #124, RMB II-1586-146.jpg (Italian & Latin), C-159

Acumen does not grow without vigilance; if one is not vigilant, one must continue studying. - Casiodoro

One-liner #148, RMB II-1586-181.jpg (Latin), C-192

That which is earned by labor is owned with merit.

Sixteenth Century Medicine and Health Tips

One-liner #5, RMB II-1586-006.jpg (Italian), C-006

Two syrups and a medicine, or sangria (leech), I am only asking, madam.

One-liner #23, RMB II-1586-118.jpg (Italian), C-046

If there weren't any (medical) doctors, we would not fit in the world, or the world would be small for many ...[746]

One-liner #70, RMB II-1586-124.jpg (Italian), C-095

Love is like a pill that you take silver[747] and easily, and then makes your insides hurt.

One-liner #79, RMB II-1586-125.jpg (Italian), C-104

The elements of the various foods and drinks that contrast each other in the body, will putrefy and fill the body with bad humors[748].

One-liner #89, RMB II-1586-126.jpg (Italian), C-114

A pitiable doctor makes a wound wormy.

One-liner #146, RMB II-1586-181.jpg (Italian & Latin), C-190

To a stingy man with a weak liver: *debility of the liver, debility of love.*

---

[746] This suggests that doctors are killing us off, and that keeps the population under control. Note that there are about seven illegible words after 'mundo', so we are guessing about the meaning here.
[747] This is an idiom about something smooth and perfect.
[748] This about Gout and uses medieval understanding of the four humors and the qualities of foods.

Commentary on Sex-Workers, Gold-diggers, and Bad Wives

One-liner #6, RMB II-1586-006.jpg (Spanish), C-007

The woman who is vulgar all the way to her innards and a phlebotomy for the purse.

One-liner #10, RMB II-1586-062.jpg (Spanish with Venetian Spellings), C-019

The woman, just like a vine, every year wants to change the pole.

One-liner #13, RMB II-1586-078.jpg (Italian), C-025

Three servants: one, a diamond piece, the other a ring with a lace, and the other with a necklace: servants of the courtesan.

One-liner #18, RMB II-1586-111.jpg (Italian), C-038

Women always[749] know a bit more than the devil.

One-liner #31, RMB II-1586-120.jpg (Spanish), C-054

To clean the stall[750] and shave her beard, three reales[751].

One-liner #47, RMB II-1586-122.jpg (Italian), C-072

The woman is made by the rotten rib of the man.[752]

One-liner #58, RMB II-1586-123.jpg (Spanish), C-084

Would you know how to make a delantera[753] out of a bed?

One-liner #59, RMB II-1586-123.jpg (Spanish), C-085

Women are like fava beans, whoever leaves them in the house for a long time, a worm will come and make a hole in them, and later when they are old, they are good for the pigs; it is necessary to put the worm on them.

One-liner #64, RMB II-1586-124.jpg (Italian), C-089

The woman who skins, ex-courtesan, spirit of queen, spirit of thief.[754]

One-liner #65, RMB II-1586-124.jpg (Italian & Spanish), C-090

The genitalia of the naughty woman is the door for the one who brings a gift.[755]

---

[749] 'Always' is not in the text but is implied.
[750] This appears to be a price for some metaphorically described services.
[751] Reales are a modest-sized unit of currency.
[752] The 'rib' may be a euphemism.
[753] 'delantera' is an old-fashioned article of clothing that is a highly decorated cloth-covered card that conceals a woman's cleavage. It is possible that this one-liner is a pick-up line.
[754] This is clever wordplay in Italian, but all that is lost translating into English.
[755] This is a joke that works for people who know both Italian and Spanish (or Venetian), because the same sounding word is used for female genitalia, doors, bringing, and gifts.

One-liner #66, RMB II-1586-124.jpg (Italian), C-091

What you gave me is forgotten, if you have no coin, go with God.

One-liner #71, RMB II-1586-124.jpg (Italian), C-096

Unlucky the one who says he's loved by the whore.

One-liner #76, RMB II-1586-125.jpg (Italian), C-101

The woman who puts makeup on is like the house that we want to sell or rent.

One-liner #87, RMB II-1586-126.jpg (Italian), C-112

A palace, What a palace? Hello dead magpie.[756]

One-liner #90, RMB II-1586-126.jpg (Italian), C-115

A go-between (pimp) is like horseradish that helps digest other foods but is itself hard to digest.

One-liner #91, RMB II-1586-127.jpg (Italian), C-116

Like a tavern sign that tells who may enter, but the sign stays outside.[757]

One-liner #140, RMB II-1586-178.jpg (Spanish), C-116

The coin that runs all over the world and soils everything.

One-liner #144, RMB II-1586-178.jpg (Italian), C-187

Leave her alone because she provokes the souls in hell. Lookout because neither children nor servants can escape her. She keeps a rosary and keeps a cellar of children's blood.[758]

One-liner #145, RMB II-1586-178.jpg (Spanish), C-188

She is a woman who will[759] admit many people and will give them the balding venereal mange. She should hug Midas and let go of Apollo and his nine drunken daughters at the fountains of Parnassus.

---

[756] There is some wordplay here. The magpie may be referring to a chatty woman or a matchmaker. In the original he uses 'palazo' and 'pallazzo'.
[757] Like 115 above, this may also be talking about pimps.
[758] Professor Calvo suggests that this is about a go-between (pimp) who look like a fake saint, while stealing souls.
[759] Instead of 'will' the original says she 'knows how to'

Commentary on Mens' Vices

One-liner #4, RMB II-1586-006.jpg (Italian), C-005

The gambler/sportsman who earns money is like green ivy that stays on a wall, and adorns it, but then with its roots eats up the mortar and takes down the entire building.

One-liner #25, RMB II-1586-119.jpg (Spanish), C-048

The secret should be confided to a liar, for he never tells the truth.

One-liner #35, RMB II-1586-121.jpg (Italian), C-060

Many times, I have offered money to the devil, and he never wanted to take it, and once I promised it to you, and you have taken it.

One-liner #52, RMB II-1586-123.jpg (Spanish), C-077

The game is like ivy.[760]

One-liner #80, RMB II-1586-126.jpg (Italian with Spanishisms), C-105

The one who when he drinks, lasts a long time is a good swimmer.[761]

One-liner #95, RMB II-1586-127.jpg (Italian), C-120

When I want to go hunting for a wild boar; the old one, because it is blind, attaches to the tail of the young one; waiting and cutting off the tail, and bringing the boar home with the tail in the mouth.

One-liner #117, RMB II-1586-145.jpg (Italian, Spanish, & Latin), C-152

A man consumed by vices is *a sleeper in the middle of the sea.*

One-liner #142, RMB II-1586-178.jpg (Italian), C-185

Throw in there that you hold a falerno[762] liqueur in your head.

---

[760] This is a shorter version of #4 above.
[761] We aren't sure what this means, but it seems to be a joke about drunkenness.
[762] Bottle of a specific wine

Assertive Statements

One-liner #7, RMB II-1586-055.jpg (Spanish), C-015

Signor, you/they have not left me against/on the wall.[763]

One-liner #21, RMB II-1586-118.jpg (Spanish), C-044

I believe that you have mistaken me for a mean fool[764].

One-liner #57, RMB II-1586-123.jpg (Spanish), C-082

If you want to kill me, know that I am like moray eels which have their souls in their tails; bite[765] the soul of my tail.

One-liner #92, RMB II-1586-127.jpg (Italian), C-117

The gallows has to do with me like a leopard to a rabbit that takes three jumps to get its prey. If it has taken two toward me, I don't want it to take the third jump."

---

[763] The slashed choices are from words translatable in multiple ways.
[764] 'birote' had many meanings but it could be a local mob-member who is supportive of his community.
[765] Bite in the sense of sting.

Wisdom & Commentary on Scholars, the Church

One-liner #8, RMB II-1586-055.jpg (Spanish), C-016

There is something under the habit[766].

One-liner #98, RMB II-1586-130.jpg (Italian), C-127

Astrologers are beasts because they put beasts into the sky.

One-liner #125, RMB II-1586-146.jpg (Latin), C-160

Time leads art to the light of truth.

One-liner #126, RMB II-1586-146.jpg (Italian), C-161

Time unveils the truth and leads all things to an end.

One-liner #130, RMB II-1586-147.jpg (Latin), C-165

Nature is the teacher of charity.

One-liner #131, RMB II-1586-147.jpg (Latin), C-166

Nature makes everything according to order.

One-liner #132, RMB II-1586-147.jpg (Latin), C-167

Nature makes nothing in vain. Nature is neither deficient in what is needful, nor overflowing in superfluities.

---

[766] Habit in the sense of monks/nuns clothing.

Commentary on the Human Condition

One-liner #17, RMB II-1586-111.jpg (Spanish), C-037

Some women give a needle and want an iron fence in return.

One-liner #20, RMB II-1586-118.jpg (Spanish), C-043

It flies more than the thought of a vain man.

One-liner #22, RMB II-1586-118.jpg (Spanish), C-045

For an ox that has walked much: I never thought that the world was so big.

One-liner #28, RMB II-1586-120.jpg (Spanish), C-051

To someone who is called a gentleman, I say that you are a gentle man.

One-liner #37, RMB II-1586-122.jpg (Italian), C-062

I don't fall because I am afraid, but I am afraid because I do fall.

One-liner #40, RMB II-1586-122.jpg (Spanish), C-065

Men of arms in the field, the bishop in the pulpit, woman in a gondola seat[767], thief on the gallows.

One-liner #41, RMB II-1586-122.jpg (Spanish with Venetian spellings), C-066

The beautiful woman has a letter of recommendation.[768]

One-liner #42, RMB II-1586-122.jpg (Italian), C-067

We should get advice from the dead, because (they are) without love and fear they tell the truth.

One-liner #43, RMB II-1586-122.jpg (Italian), C-068

Who are they anymore, the dead or the living?[769]

One-liner #49, RMB II-1586-122.jpg (Italian), C-073

She is like the skin of the cow that we pull in all directions, and like the spiderweb that keeps a small weight.[770]

---

[767] This could be translated, as 'trash', or some other idiom. The whole item appears to be that everyone has a place, and that there is some joke about the woman's place, or some statement about it being polite to let the women have the gondola seats.

[768] Her beauty recommends her.

[769] It is possible that this is a barb said by young people about older people with less interest in festivities.

[770] This seems to imply that she is under stress and can't handle big new tasks.

One-liner #63, RMB II-1586-124.jpg (Italian), C-088

Who doesn't steal and rob doesn't last.[771]

One-liner #77, RMB II-1586-125.jpg (Italian), C-102

The woman shouldn't stay at the window, if she doesn't want to be seen, but she should do like the one who doesn't want to be bothered by flies and close the window.

One-liner #78, RMB II-1586-125.jpg (Italian), C-103

Women are like buttons; they always want to stick their heads out the window.

One-liner #82, RMB II-1586-126.jpg (Italian), C-107

There is no better sign of being stupid than thinking yourself wise; to the one who wants to be wise, stay away from stupid people.

One-liner #97, RMB II-1586-129.jpg (Italian), C-125

The eyes are against love and getting drunk; without Ceres and Bacchus, Venus gets cold.

One-liner #99, RMB II-1586-130.jpg (Italian), C-128

Life is better known in a man who strongly feels his senses, just as loves gives signs of a better life to one who follows it (love).

One-liner #115, RMB II-1586-145.jpg (Latin), C-150

You have come late: the merchant has dashed off to farthest India.

---

[771] We have some doubt about 'ge dura'.

Romantic and Marital Advice for Men

One-liner #12, RMB II-1586-062.jpg (Spanish with Venetian spellings), C-021

The woman is just like death, who runs away from the one who goes after her and goes after the one who runs away.

One-liner #19, RMB II-1586-118.jpg (Spanish), C-041

True love should be flat, it shouldn't have an illustrious title, because that was lost in your first love, for here the magnificent has no part; it is not a good idea to mix majesty with morning prayers[772].

One-liner #34, RMB II-1586-121.jpg (Spanish with Venetian spellings), C-059

Why not [meorirn?][773], the woman must stay below the husband, and the husband should kneel before her.

One-liner #46, RMB II-1586-122.jpg (Spanish), C-071

The husband who lets his wife order him around eats with his feet and walks with his hands.

One-liner #53, RMB II-1586-123.jpg (Italian), C-078

Lusty love enters through the eyes, to the mouth, it comes out from the behind. From the eyes to the mouth there are no more than four fingers.

One-liner #53, RMB II-1586-123.jpg (Spanish with Venetian spellings), C-078

With women, whoever wants to remove their poison, it is necessary to do as one does with the unicorn; that is, often wet the horn in the fountain.

One-liner #61, RMB II-1586-124.jpg (Spanish with Venetian spellings), C-086

Mezetious who used to unite the living with the dead, the old man with the young woman.

One-liner #62, RMB II-1586-124.jpg (Spanish with Venetian spellings), C-087

Love is like scabies because it sticks to everyone.

One-liner #67, RMB II-1586-124.jpg (Spanish with Venetian spellings), C-092

Loving[774] a woman is like mustard, it enters smoothly, then you have to sneeze.

One-liner #68, RMB II-1586-124.jpg (Italian), C-093

(It is) For getting married, and not for sneezing, that we must say 'God help us!'

---

[772] Mixing majesty and morning prayers is an idiom about being untimely or inappropriate.
[773] These letters are difficult to make out. We suspect it is a word about morning prayers in a double entendre.
[774] More literally 'The love of' but this phrasing removes ambiguity.

One-liner #69, RMB II-1586-124.jpg (Spanish with Venetian spellings), C-094

It happens to those that love a mean and beautiful woman, just as it happens to a little goat that gets into a bramble[775] of thorns to eat it, but then leaves its wool in the thorns.

One-liner #73, RMB II-1586-124.jpg (Spanish with Venetian spellings), C-098

Love is like the bite of a dog, that cannot be cured except by the hair of the same dog.

One-liner #74, RMB II-1586-124.jpg (Italian), C-099

To the one who keeps a beautiful woman it happens just like the one who carries a lighted torch at night. While the torch burns, he will find many who follow him, then when it is out, one goes one way and the other another.

One-liner #83, RMB II-1586-126.jpg (Italian), C-108

Just like the Sun stays above the Moon, the man has to stay above the woman.

One-liner #93, RMB II-1586-127.jpg (Spanish), C-118

Give to the wife and the girlfriend the same as they give to you.

One-liner #94, RMB II-1586-127.jpg (Italian), C-119

Love has the opposite effect on me as it does on the viper that kills its mother on the way out. For me, the more I keep it hidden, the more it hurts me.[776]

One-liner #96, RMB II-1586-129.jpg (Italian), C-124

She is made of the element of Earth, and I of Fire, one stays up above and the other stays underneath.

One-liner #98, RMB II-1586-129.jpg (Italian), C-126

Three things we have to agree upon about women: The sword, when you go to argue; to take whenever she invites you to eat, and in the bed also[777]. It is needed to keep the little fountain clean, so that the rivers don't get to the brain, so that desires are relaxed,[778] and not that the rivers will make them go to the head making the horns.[779]

---

[775] 'Ciesa' translates to church, but it may be a misspelling of a word meaning 'bush'.
[776] This is an odd statement, which seems to be an allegory about abstaining from sex or perhaps not telling your feelings to a would-be lover.
[777] This word's abbreviation is difficult to read, we inserted 'also' based on context.
[778] There are about three words missing from the cut for binding. It is probably a phrase meaning 'desires are relaxed'.
[779] Need more work. There are some implied words that we need to understand. The corni (horns) may be an implication about avoiding being cuckolded.

One-liner #100, RMB II-1586-139.jpg (Spanish), C-131

Note: This has a lot of double entendre that works in Spanish but not English. It would probably be an on-stage pick-up line.

Oh! my love, boat of my oar, wealth of my hacienda, lady of my merchandise, syrup for my stomach, fountain of my tears, hen of my rooster, honor[780] of my lineage, and door of my Introductory Rites (of mass).

One-liner #141, RMB II-1586-178.jpg (Spanish), C-184

There is no woman who doesn't love frivolity, money, wine, and the bed while inebriated.

Romantic and Marital Advice for Women

One-liner #14, RMB II-1586-111.jpg (Spanish), C-034

If love cools down, find a competitor, for if your partner sees gifts coming from others your partner will give even better ones.

One-liner #15, RMB II-1586-111.jpg (Spanish), C-035

If they keep their purse closed, slam your door on them.

One-liner #16, RMB II-1586-111.jpg (Spanish), C-036

Ask to borrow something from him, and pay him a thousand sweet nothings, and then he'll let you keep it.

One-liner #26, RMB II-1586-119.jpg (Spanish), C-049

The young (male) lover is like the painted lead ball which soon loses its paint.

One-liner #27, RMB II-1586-119.jpg (Spanish), C-050

The woman regrets having loved without thinking, just like a man who got the French disease.[781]

One-liner #38, RMB II-1586-122.jpg (Spanish with Venetian spellings), C-063

The tail of the sheep is like a drape that covers the services.

One-liner #54, RMB II-1586-123.jpg (Italian), C-079

The pouch of the lover is tied with the leaf of a leek.[782]

One-liner #55, RMB II-1586-123.jpg (Italian), C-080

Madam, if you want (it), give (it).

---

[780] 'hondra' is possibly an old spelling of honra (honor).
[781] We aren't 100% sure about this translation.
[782] The Leek is a phallic image, but it also fragile.

One-liner #75, RMB II-1586-125.jpg (Italian), C-100

The curtsy[783] that a woman does forward is like offering a table set for the one who wants to eat; the curtsy needs to be straight so that it is not considered too shy, nor too blatant.

One-liner #84, RMB II-1586-126.jpg (Italian), C-109

I am not Mira who fell in love with her father; Phedra with her brother, Biblis with her son.[784]

One-liner #85, RMB II-1586-126.jpg (Italian), C-110

It happens to the one who marries princes just like it happens to a lemon; the prince takes the juice, and tosses the rinds, then the flies poop it out.[785]

One-liner #134, RMB II-1586-177.jpg (Spanish), C-177

Women do not want small money nor coats of arms from ancestors, rather they want coins, and let them be golden with two faces.

One-liner #135, RMB II-1586-177.jpg (Spanish), C-178

When you begin to cast the net, pay no attention to the price, do not allow any of them to escape you, and to all those who love you, tell them that you are theirs, but you haven't been caught yet.[786]

One-liner #136, RMB II-1586-177.jpg (Spanish), C-179

If you don't like them, or you recognize that they just haven't got it, pretend that you have no time, or you are freshly from confession.

One-liner #137, RMB II-1586-177.jpg (Spanish), C-180

Shut your door to whoever is loudly begging to come in, but to whoever is quiet and spends money, open it quickly.

One-liner #138, RMB II-1586-178.jpg (Spanish), C-181

Arguments are good, but don't linger in them, don't be afraid of swearing, for whatever a lover does to justify himself is not perjury, because the goddess Venus has plugged the ears of the other gods, so they do not hear the lies of lovers.

One-liner #139, RMB II-1586-178.jpg (Spanish), C-182

When someone angers you, or asks what's wrong with you, tell them you have rheumatism or melancholy, because that is appropriate for ladies.

---

[783] 'reverencia' is like a curtsy in Sixteenth Century Italian dance.
[784] This line would be spoken by a female character.
[785] We are not sure about the 'creatti', unless it is part of an idiom about garbage or compost.
[786] The actual words translate to "you're not in the bucket", which we take to be the bucket that the fisherman empties his net into.

Insults

One-liner #29, RMB II-1586-120.jpg (Spanish), C-051

(Spoken by a woman, insulting another woman)

If I were so fat, frivolous, and very bad off as you are, I would still be worth more than you are worth.

One-liner #33, RMB II-1586-120.jpg (Italian), C-055

The Spanish go to Rome like monkeys, and in Spain they take off tails like foxes.[787]

One-liner #39, RMB II-1586-122.jpg (Spanish), C-064

With your stretched out neck you look like a wounded donkey with a wicker basket[788] over the neck, as if they are taking him out to shame[789].

One-liner #88, RMB II-1586-126.jpg (Italian), C-113

If you dress up a donkey (an ass), it will look like a (female) mule.

One-liner #101, RMB II-1586-143.jpg (Latin), C-135

The font of unquenched human thirst.

One-liner #143, RMB II-1586-178.jpg (Italian), C-186

Not if he goes with that woman because he is flying her at night among the night shadows: she is a witch.

---

[787] We don't know what this means. It seems to be about comparative fashions and how people dress when traveling.

[788] 'Cesto' is a cone-of-shame for donkeys, mules, and horses to prevent biting themselves.

[789] Shame in this case is a public shaming, such as being in the stocks.

Commentary on the Greedy and Wealthy

One-liner #30, RMB II-1586-120.jpg (Spanish), C-030

Count them, it seems to me that you don't feel like paying with them.

One-liner #56, RMB II-1586-123.jpg (Italian), C-081

A man eats for pleasure, and I am pooping more than you are eating.[790]

One-liner #81, RMB II-1586-126.jpg (Italian), C-106

The poor man eats when he has (food or money), the rich eats when he wants.

One-liner #86, RMB II-1586-126.jpg (Italian), C-111

What to do with this money, horses, servants? Are you making fun of me? Gnaf gnaf.

One-liner #103, RMB II-1586-143.jpg (Latin & Italian), C-137

Like the man who goes *toward the dark light*, wealth.

One-liner #104, RMB II-1586-143.jpg (Latin), C-138

The end approves the act.[791]

One-liner #105, RMB II-1586-143.jpg (Italian), C-139

A closed fist to show avarice.[792]

One-liner #129, RMB II-1586-147.jpg (Italian), C-164

The asinine king Midas was the oracle of the greedy and the ignorant.

One-liner #133, RMB II-1586-177.jpg (Spanish with Venetian spellings), C-176

Whoever has money is an even greater poet than Homer, and he who has more is the first to enjoy, and whoever does not have it will be left for the fools.

One-liner #147, RMB II-1586-181.jpg (Latin), C-191

He who savors too much trims insufficiently.[793]

---

[790] We aren't sure why this is funny. It may be saying that the speaker gets to eat more than the listener.
[791] A minor nuance away from 'The ends justify the means'.
[792] This is a reminder to actors how to show the audience that they are greedy.
[793] We aren't really sure what this means. We guess it has something to do with a glutton not trimming the fat before eating.

Short Lists to Memorize

One-liner #106, RMB II-1586-143.jpg (Italian), C-140

Architects: Apolodoro, Nicone, Demorate, Esisfone

One-liner #107, RMB II-1586-143.jpg (Italian), C-141

Ajax, Alexandro, Hiparco, Clodio, Quinto Flaminio, Palemone, Fillipo of Macedonia, Chieldrico King of France, Ugutio fiorentino.

One-liner #108, RMB II-1586-143.jpg (Italian), C-142

Rich was Pifio Bitinio, Scila, Narciso, Marco Crasso.

One-liner #123, RMB II-1586-146.jpg (Italian), C-158

The idling ones: Atalo, brother of Eumano (king of Pergamo)

One-liner #127, RMB II-1586-146.jpg (Italian), C-162

Nerieds and Oceanatides are sea nymphs, the Naiades are nymphs of rivers, the Nape, are nymphs of springs, the Amadriades are nymphs of the trees.

One-liner #128, RMB II-1586-146.jpg (Italian), C-163

Vergil praised Amarila; Ovid, Atlanta; Catullo, Ariadne; Propertio, Antiope; Stacio, Argia; Marciale, Fabula; Horacio, Glicera.

Accounting Sheets

These accounting sheets from the end of the manuscript are all from the Spring of 1580 and show a number of things about the troupe's expenses but are also interesting for showing that they performed quite a number of different plays, including many that are not in this collection.

Please note that it isn't clear what all the numbers represent. Some are credits, some are debits, usually the numbers don't seem to add up. Julio seems to have been the troupe's money-guy.

Sheet 1

On the day of May 6th, 1580
Julio is left to give me:

	208.8
	35.21
	————
	172.21
	72.13
	35.21
	————
	108.

Sheet 2

I owe to the Capitano in the tragedy[794]	12.1/2
The second, he pulled the part	————
Al Cavalero ingratto[795], also	————
Al inocente fanciulo[796], he pulled the part	————
Al Bravo falito[797]	18.4
	5.-
	————
	35.21

Sheet 3

Today, Friday, at night, on April 15th, balanced	
The accounts with Julio. He owes me, Reals	146.7
For a part of the wine	5.
For the expenses until Wednesday night April 20th	14
For leggings/hosery	12

---

[794] This may be referring to "Prince Tireno" which is a tragedy with a Capitano.
[795] *Al Cavalero ingratto* "The Ungrateful Cavalier" is a play with no know extant scenario.
[796] *Al inocente fanciulo* "The Innocent Boy" is a play with no known extant scenario
[797] *Al Bravo falito* "The failed Soldier (or Braggart)" is another lost play.

For the loans	4.
For the expenses until Thursday May 5th	18.8

	199.15
	107.21

I am accounting until May 5th, he owes me, Reals	91.28
Moreover, he owes me one real	1.28
He owes me the accounting done until Friday the 6th, Reals	16.14

	108.8

Sheet 4

I owe the Capitano on the day of April 5th of the comedy	23
	188.46
Of the patina	11.
	70
Then he lent me	1.32
The comedy of *Cavallier Constante*[798]	22.29
The comedy of *Intronati*[799]	20.
The comedy of *Don Ramiro*	26.
La Persiana[800]	....24.

				94.29
199	11	200.15	.29	
			71	
		97 11	9	
		111.28		

Pazzo Amante[801]	11.1/2
Tarquino	....14.
Formenti[802]	8.21
Leone[803]	27.17
Furti Novi[804]	21.
Pastoral	25.

	107.21

---

[798] *Cavallier Constante*, "The Constant Cavalier" may or may not be the play we've labelled "Constant Love". The Capitano in that play is not the constant one.

[799] *Intronati*, is a famous play from 1531 and beyond with a daughter who dresses as a man to avoid getting a geriatric husband. That play is not in this collection.

[800] *La Persiana*, "The Persian Woman" is not in this collection.

[801] *Pazzo Amante*, "The Crazy Lover" is not in this collection, though it might be similar to "Two Crazy People".

[802] *Formenti*, "The Wheat" in this collection.

[803] *Leone*, "The Lion" in this collection.

[804] *Furti Novi*, "The New Thefts" is probably "Thefts" in this collection. 'Novi' may indicate it is an updated version of a previous play of the same name.

For the pastoral 14.17
11.25

———

26.28

Sheet 5[805]

Julio lent me one Real in Madrid

———

Julio owes me:
Of the expenses from Madrid 9.22
Given to the landlady 10.
For the leftover loan .10
For the carriage 15.
For money given for charity .6
For eating at the court in Valladolit 23.
For a long loose men's coat (baladran) 150.
For expenses until April 5th
Saturday Morning 23.9
For given to Cencio for food on Thursday 2.11
For accounts made until Wednesday evening April 14th 3.3
For accounts made 4.9

———

241.2
94.29

———

146.7
94.29

———

[805] There is another sheet between 4 & 5 which is just Abagaro playing around with the Greek alphabet and spelling his name using Greek letters.